Art History Revision Notes for Leaving Certificate

Áine Ní Chárthaigh

Gill & Macmillan

Gill & Macmillan Ltd
Hume Avenue
Park West
Dublin 12
with associated companies throughout the world
www.gillmacmillan.ie

0 7171 3029 0
Print origination in Ireland by
Carrigboy Typesetting Services, Co. Cork

The paper used in this book is made from the wood pulp of managed forests. For every tree felled, at least one tree is planted, thereby renewing natural resources.

CONTENTS

Exam Hints

Planning Your Revision

- Read over past papers.
- Pick the sections of the course that you can answer best.
- Learn several periods fully to give yourself a choice of questions.
- Look at art works and learn to describe them in your own words.
- Learn to compare works of art by other artists of the same time, earlier and later.
- Practise your illustrations.
- Questions may be very specific so make sure you know your selected periods thoroughly. For example, in a wide area such as the Renaissance make sure you know all areas of the period:

  Painting – Florence and Rome, Early and High Renaissance;
  Sculpture – Florence and Rome, Early and High Renaissance;
  Architecture – Florence and Rome, Early and High Renaissance;
  The Renaissance in Venice;
  The Northern Renaissance.

  Remember also the question may be concerned with a particular **aspect** of the Renaissance – such as perspective, portraits, or the human figure. Be sure you can contrast the various artists' approaches to these. Know as much as possible about the artists, their backgrounds and their work, so that you can answer in considerable detail and contrast their work if necessary.
- Approach the study of other selected areas in a similar manner.

Planning an Art History Essay

- Study the wording of the question carefully and select the facts needed for its particular emphasis.
- Plan a brief introduction, giving general background information and mentioning some of the points you will develop throughout your essay. Refer **if appropriate** to art of a previous era or, in the case of Irish art, refer briefly to comparable developments in Europe.
- Develop your points giving each its own paragraph.
- Plan these points to follow each other in a logical manner.
- Make sure your points are factual and historically correct.

Answering an Art History Question

- Take time to read the paper carefully and make sure you understand exactly what is required from you in each question you attempt.
- **Always** introduce your answer by giving general information concerning the period or artist. Never go straight to your first point.

- Assume that you are writing something about which your reader has no knowledge and give as much relevant information as you can. Vague information is **not** enough.
- Only give information relevant to your chosen question. Irrelevant, off-the-point information is of no benefit.
- Give as much detailed relevant information as you know and time will allow.
- Display your knowledge of facts where possible.
- Pace your answering and plan your time carefully.
- Do not try to write too much as you may run out of time before you have given enough facts.
- Answer in a clear, sequential manner.
- Lay out your answer in an attractive, easy-to-read manner.
- Be extremely careful to avoid repetition and vague meaningless padding – this will gain no extra marks whatsoever.
- Describe examples in your own words and compare works from other artists or eras in appropriate cases.
- Include relevant background facts if they help to make your points stronger.
- Illustrate your answers.
- Remember a short, well-planned essay which is to the point and factually correct is far better than a long, irrelevant, padded-out one.

Sample Plans

Below are two questions on the same topic that require a very different emphasis in answering and should be planned accordingly.

Question 2 (1992 Higher Level)
Give an account of the development of stone sculpture from the early cross-inscribed stones to the High Crosses of the ninth and tenth centuries.

- *Introduction*: Briefly refer to the importance of stone in pre-Christian Ireland – Ogham stones and their transition to early Christian cross-inscribed stones.
- *Point 1*: Discuss the early Christian stones. Draw and describe, e.g. the Reask Pillar.
- *Point 2*: The first appearance of figures, decoration and cross shape. Draw and describe, e.g. Fahan Mura Slab or Duvillaun Slab.
- *Point 3*: The development of the early cross. Draw and describe, e.g. the Carndonagh Cross.
- *Point 4*: The early High Crosses – how they were constructed, their function, and their relationship with the metalwork of the time. Draw and describe, e.g. the Ahenny Crosses.
- *Point 5*: The crosses of the Scriptures – their elaborate decoration, the unique style of carving, and the theme of the stories found on their panels. Draw and describe, e.g. the Cross of Moone or Muiredach.
- *Conclusion*: A brief sentence or two to round off your points.

Question 2 (1995 Higher Level)
Discuss the treatment of the human form on the High Crosses of the early Christian period; mention specific examples in your answer.

- *Introduction*: Briefly describe the development of the High Cross from early cross-inscribed stones. Mention where they were to be found and what their likely function was in the society of the time.
- Describe the crosses of the Scriptures and where they are to be found. Make an outline drawing of the Cross of Moone and the Cross of Muiredach.
- Describe the panels from the Cross of Moone in a general way. Discuss the biblical themes.
- Describe the style of carving and the simple approach to the portrayal of figures. Draw attention to the square bodies, the strange faces with staring eyes, and the turned out feet of the biblical figures and compare these to the more life-like depiction of animals included in some of the scenes.
- Draw and describe in detail one panel from the Cross of Moone.
- Contrast the carved scenes with those on the panels of the Cross of Muiredach.
- Mention the fine detail of the carving in bold rounded relief on the Cross of Muiredach. Draw attention to the number of figures in some of the scenes, but no sense of overcrowding.
- Draw and describe in detail a panel from this cross also.
- *Conclusion*: A brief sentence or two on the unique contribution these elaborate crosses have made to our heritage.

The purpose of this book is to assist Leaving Cert. Art students in the *revision* of Art History and Appreciation.
It is not intended as a full textbook.
Because of the length of the course, topics have been selected to facilitate students in covering some of the more important areas in a short period. This concise factual information is intended to complement previous studies. The black and white drawings are intended to facilitate students, already familiar with the art works, to draw and describe examples for examination purposes.

CHAPTER ONE

PRE-CHRISTIAN IRELAND

STONE AGE (7000–2000 B.C.)

The first human settlers may have come to Ireland around 7000 B.C. This was known as the Mesolithic or Middle Stone Age. These early hunters came to an island where food was plentiful in the rivers and forests. Totally dependent on hunting, these early Irish people settled mostly near river banks or moved about in search of food.

The period which followed, the Neolithic or New Stone Age (3700–2000 B.C.), was a time of great changes. The development of food-producing methods such as harvesting of cereal crops and breeding of animals spread across from the mainland of Europe. By the end of the Neolithic period the first great changes had come upon the landscape of Ireland with extensive clearance of the forests, parts of the land divided into fields, communities occupying the whole island and regular contact with lands overseas. There is evidence enough to suggest that these early people were a highly organised and complex social group. This can be seen from house plans, stone tools, pottery fragments and their great stone tombs.

MEGALITHIC BURIAL MONUMENTS

Very little evidence remains of the lifestyle of farming people of the Stone Age. Their most important legacy to the people of the island today are the remarkable series of megalithic or huge stone burial monuments. These served not only as resting places for the dead or as lasting monuments to ancestors, but also perhaps as symbols of power. The three types of megalithic tomb dating from the Neolithic period are: the portal dolmen, the court cairn and the passage grave.

PORTAL DOLMEN

The portal dolmen is a relatively simple structure but is a most impressive monument. Spectacular examples are found in the Burren at Poulnabrone in County Clare and Kilclooney, near Ardara in County Donegal. In all there are over 170 portal tombs scattered around Ireland.

The design of the tomb is based on a tripod. Two large standing stones and a lower backstone support a large roof stone positioned with its heavier end above the entrance. Single slabs rest against the side and back stones, forming the side chamber. Some portal tombs are set at the end of long cairns; others have small burial chambers opening off the sides of the cairns. These features make them closely linked to the court cairn, and similar stone artifacts and pottery fragments have been found at both [1.1].

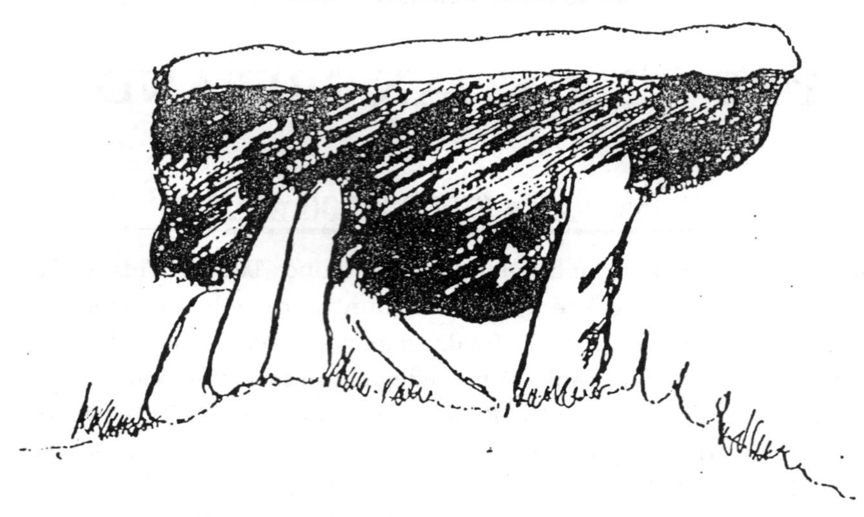

▲ *1.1 Poulnabrone dolmen, Co. Clare*

Court Cairns

Court tombs are probably the earliest of the megalithic tombs to have been constructed in Ireland. Most of these are in the northern half of the country. Court cairns are distinguished by their U or oval-shaped courtyard without a roof. This is set in front of a covered gallery which is the burial chamber and is divided into two or three by protruding stones like door jams. The cairn itself is usually a long triangular shape with the court occupying one end. At Creevykeel, Co. Sligo, burial chambers open off a large court. These burial chambers would have been covered by a long mound. It would seem that these monuments had two functions: the galleries to serve as a tomb; and the court to accommodate some kind of ritual [1.2].

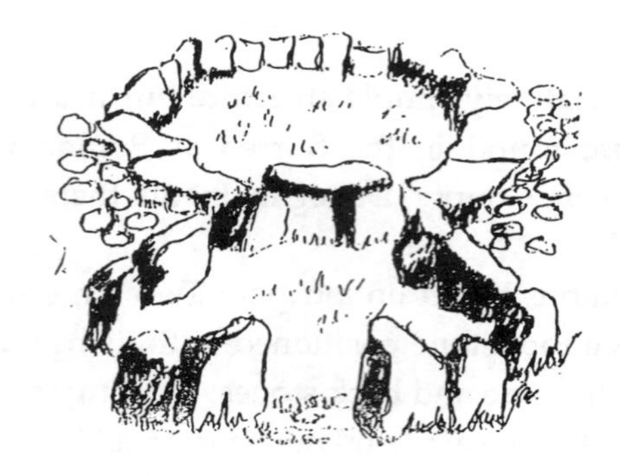

▲ *1.2 Count cairn at Creevykeel, Co. Sligo*

PASSAGE GRAVES AND NEWGRANGE

The most impressive remains of the late Stone Age are the deep and mysterious stone passage graves. Set into the ground above the River Boyne, in a loop that it forms as it meanders on its final stretch across the plains of County Meath, are the finest of these graves, Newgrange and its two satellites, Knowth and Dowth.

Within these graves we find Ireland's earliest examples of human artwork in the form of ornamented stones. Here we find evidence of a highly organised society which used concentric whirls and circles and abstract repeating patterns, about the meaning of which we can only speculate. It is almost certain that these patterns have an astronomical connection, but they may also have had a religious meaning or may have been a form of primitive calendar.

The largest of these graves, Newgrange, probably dates to around 3000 B.C. The mound itself measures about 85 metres in diameter and is 6 metres high at its highest point inside the chamber.

As the name suggests, the tomb consists of a passage and a chamber covered by a large mound or cairn of small rounded stones. This large circular mound is surrounded by a kerb of massive slabs. Situated at a distance of 15 metres or so is a further circle of tall monoliths or standing stones. It has been estimated that there were originally 35 of these stones, but now only 12 are left standing. None of these is decorated.

The most unusual aspect of Newgrange is the roof box which was discovered during excavations in 1963. The box is situated above the entrance and four minutes after sunrise on 21 December (the winter solstice) the sun's rays shine through the gap in the roof box along the passage and reach the floor of the chamber, thus dramatically lighting up the various details of decoration on the side and end of the chambers as well as the roof. The light then narrows and the beam is cut off after seventeen minutes.

The passage itself is 19 metres long with 22 standing stones along the left and 21 along the right. Many of these stones are decorated. The total length of the passage, including the chamber at the back, is 24 metres, making it less than a third of the whole mound. The first part of the passage is roofed by three large slabs. After this the roof is corbelled, that is, slabs are placed on top of each other so that one rests partly on the roof slab beneath it and out from it so there is a gradual rise in height. The stones gradually slope inwards and finish with one large stone or cap on the chamber roof on the outside. The corbelled vault of the chamber is one of the finest of its kind in western Europe. It stands today, without renovation, as it did when it was constructed over 5,000 years ago. The outer edges of the corbels are sloped downwards so that rainwater drains off and into the cairn. This method is shown to be effective in that the passage and chamber at Newgrange remain dry to this day.

A ring of huge kerbstones surrounds the great mound; there are 97 of these. Some are decorated, the most spectacular being of course the entrance stone with its spiral and lozenge ornament. Nobody knows the meaning of these concentric spirals. The vertical line separating the circles appears to be significant. Even more pronounced is the vertical line on kerbstone 52, which is the other richly decorated stone. Kerbstone 52 is at the back of the mound and lines up directly with the entrance stone.

In the chambers at Newgrange and also at Dowth, large stones or basin stones are found. These stones have a sunken shape in the centre and were probably used to hold bones or perhaps cremated remains of the dead. During excavations stone and bone beads were found which were typical offerings to be placed with the dead.

It is certain that Newgrange was used as a burial place. Other functions are not so clear. The art on the stones will remain a mystery, but one thing is certain: this is not art for art's sake.

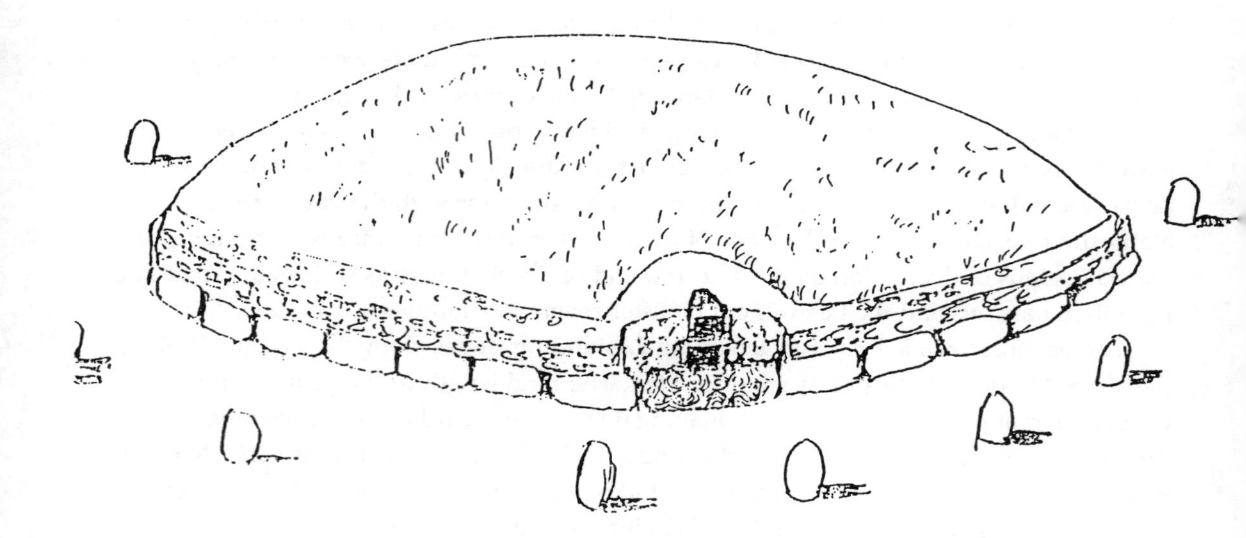

▲ *1.3 Newgrange passage grave*

This is a cairn or a mound of stones covering a passage which leads to a chamber in the shape of a cross. The passage and chamber measures 24 metres at its highest point. The mound is circled by 97 large kerbstones. Some are decorated. Twelve of the original 35 orthothats or huge standing stones remain around the tomb.

Note the recessed entrance, shaped like this after excavations to allow access to visitors. The quartz stone wall surrounding the tomb above the kerbstone was replaced in its original form after these excavations in 1963.

▲ *1.4 Entrance stone*

The entrance stone, with its passage entrance and roof box, has an opening on the roof box which forms a gap allowing the winter solstice sunrise to penetrate deep into the passage. The vertical line in the centre divides the spirals into 3 left-handed and 4 right-handed sections.

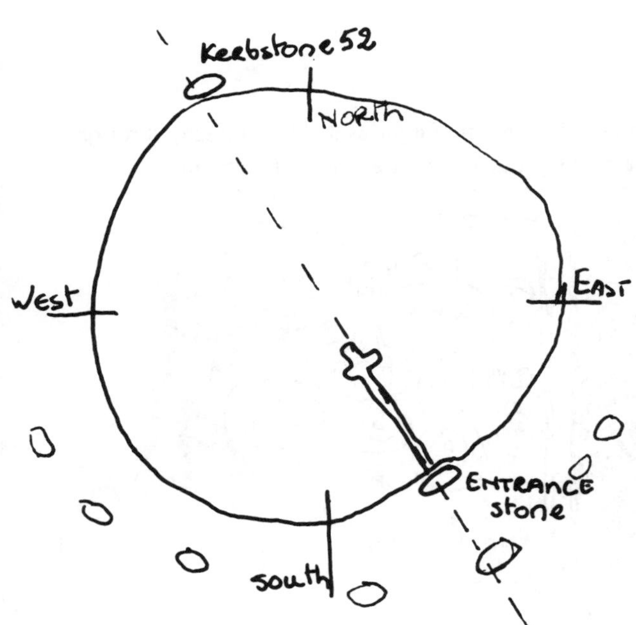

◀ *1.5 Ground plan of Newgrange*

Notice the close relationship between art and astronomy. The broken line shows the bearing of the rising sun. The astronomical line-up is the most important aspect: it lines up not only with the entrance stone, but also with the standing stone in front of the entrance and kerbstone 52 which is at the point opposite the entrance.

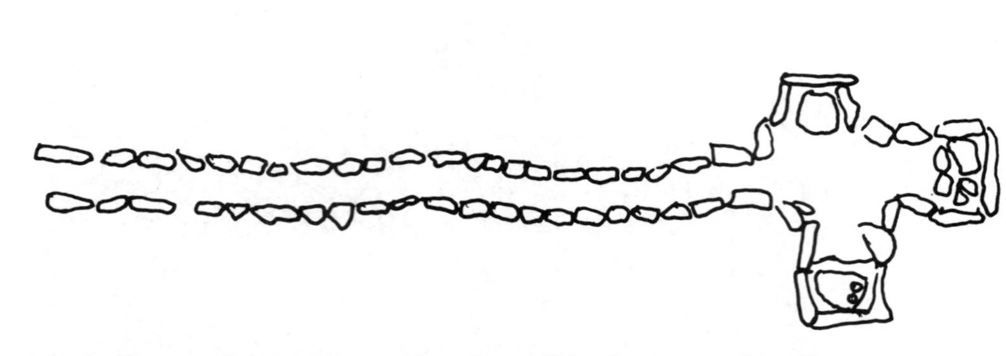

▲ *1.6 Plan of passage showing the cruciform shape of the chambers at the end*

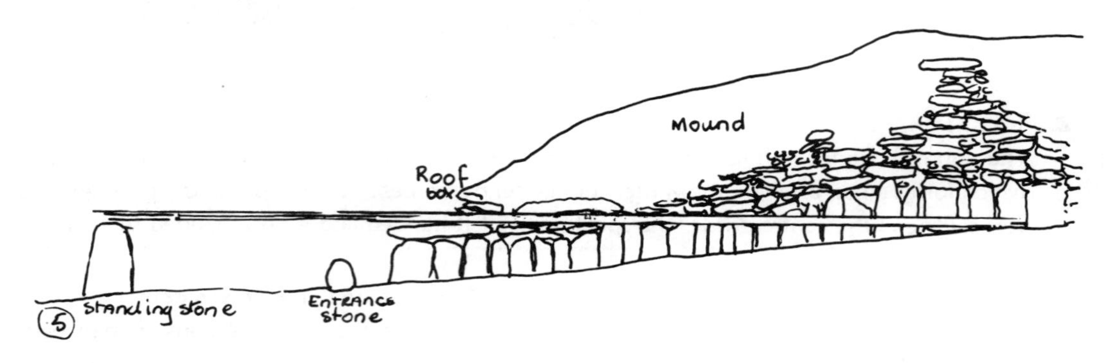

▲ *1.7 Section of the tomb*

The diagram shows a section of the tomb. The stream of light as it shines directly through the entrance box is to allow a narrow stream of light to project deep into the chamber.

▲ *1.8 Kerbstone 52*

This stone is found at the back of the mound on a direct line opposite the entrance stone. It has an even more pronounced vertical line and has some markings similar to those on the entrance stone.

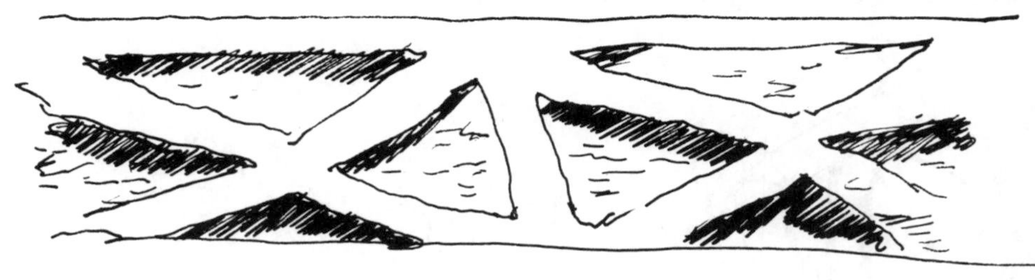

▲ *1.9 Detail of pattern on the lintel above the roof box*

▲ *1.10 Three-spiral pattern*
This pattern is found on the standing stone in the chamber looking towards the passage.

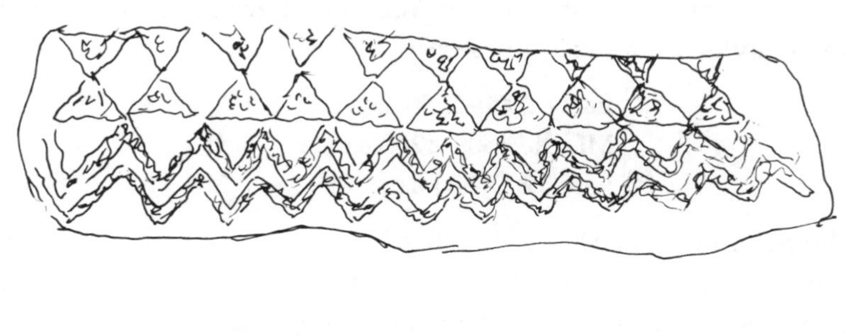

▲ *1.11 Corbel stones in the roof*
Detail of patterns found on the corbel stones in the roof of the chamber.

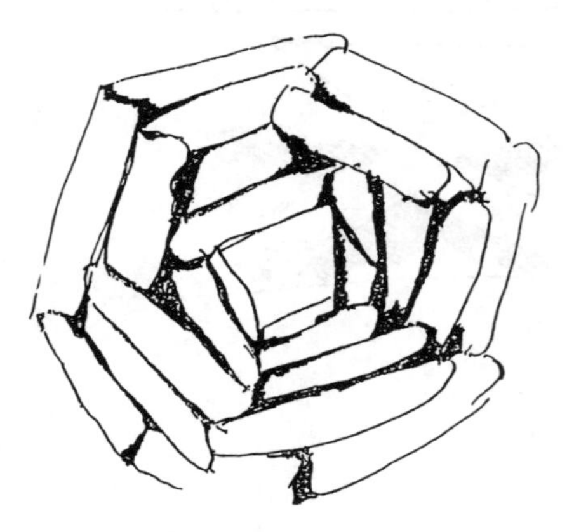

▲ *1.12 Corbel vault looking up towards the roof*

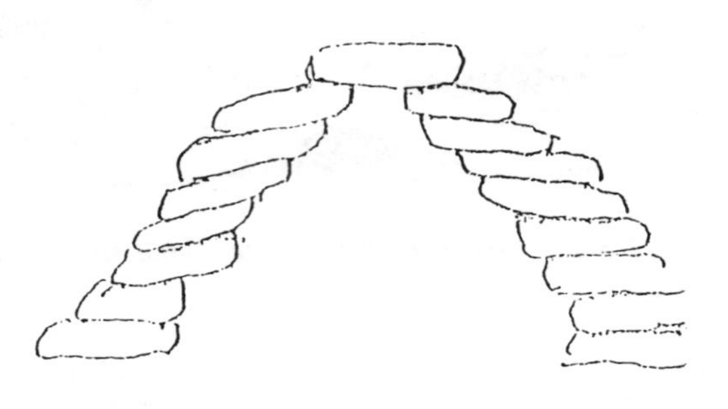

▲ *1.13 Corbel vault*

BRONZE AGE (2000–500 B.C.)

It was not until at least four thousand years after the first people settled on the island in 7000 B.C. that there is any evidence to suggest artistic activity for its own sake in Ireland. The Neolithic people decorated their tombs with a variety of patterns, but it would seem that these were for religious rather than artistic reasons. It was with the onset of the Bronze Age that art and craftsmanship as we know it can be said to have begun.

There is no sharp division between the late Stone Age and the early Bronze Age, but there is general agreement that the Bronze Age started around 2000 B.C. and lasted until 500 B.C. It can be divided into three phases:

Early 2000–1500 B.C.
Middle 1500–1200 B.C.
Late 1200–500 B.C.

During the period up to 2000 B.C. a style of pottery and metalwork which developed near the Danube in central Europe found its way to Ireland through travel and trade. These people are often referred to as the Beaker people and probably had with them a small number of skilled craftsmen. The Shannon estuary formed an important access route for various influences from abroad.

The raw material needed for the new skill of metalworking was readily available in the hills of Ireland. Copper was found at Mount Gabriel in west Cork, silver at the Silvermines in County Tipperary, and alluvial gold was panned from the streams and rivers in the Wicklow hills.

The National Museum of Ireland in Dublin has one of the largest and finest collections of Bronze Age gold ornaments in the world. Many spectacular pieces of gold jewellery in the collection have been found over the years, particularly in the bogs of Ireland. Sadly, many found objects are also known to have been lost or destroyed. Given the quantity and quality of the objects from this era, it is not surprising that it has been called Ireland's first Golden Age. Bronze objects of high artistic quality have been found. These are mainly tools, weapons, shields and trumpets. Pottery such as urns were used to contain the remains of cremated dead. Some artwork on stone is also dated to the Bronze Age; this mainly takes the form of dots in concentric circles. Single standing stones and standing stone circles are found around the country.

Ornament from the Bronze Age has several distinct features. It is abstract and geometric and the techniques of the worker in copper and bronze were also used by the goldsmith. Nuggets of gold or metal were beaten into thin sheets. Gold wire was made by cutting a narrow strip and twisting it; this was then used to cover leather thonging to make necklaces or for stitching two pieces together. Wider thicker pieces were twisted to make torcs (neck ornaments), earrings or girdles. Gold was also used to cover lead objects such as the lead pendant or Bulla from the Bog of Allen.

Methods of decoration used during the Bronze Age included:

repoussé—hammering a design on the reverse of thin gold objects;
incision—cutting a design into the front;
twisting and flange twisting.

In both bronze and gold objects repoussé was a common method of decoration. The thin sheet of gold which was ideal for this method was hammered on the reverse. Compasses were used to apply the decoration on discs, gorget terminals and other circular objects. Casting techniques were also employed involving the pouring of molten gold.

Probably the earliest examples of Irish gold ornaments are thin gold discs [1.14] of various sizes. These were decorated using the repoussé method and have usually a cross encircled by concentric bands of chevrons (zigzags) and dots.

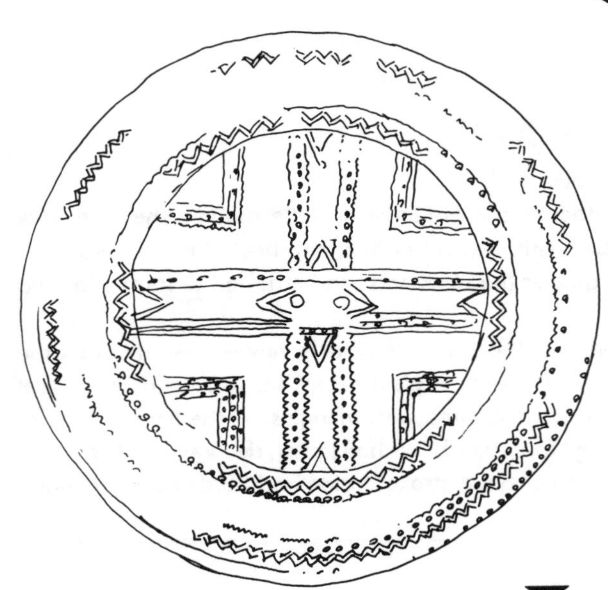

1.14 Gold Disc, Early Bronze Age (c.2000 B.C.)

Thin gold discs like this were cut from a thin sheet of beaten gold. They were decorated in repoussé by hammering and punching a series of ridges, dots and chevrons. Small holes near the centre suggest that these were once sewn to a garment. They are usually found in pairs.

Around 1500 B.C. the repoussé method gave way to a new technique, that of *incision* or *cutting into the front* of the object. The gold lunula is a particularly Irish ornament from this time [1.15]. These lunulae were crescent or half-moon shaped, thus the name lunula or little moon, and were made from thin sheets of gold. Normally there is a fine incised pattern of triangles, lozenges and chevrons near the ends of the crescent and all around the edges. This ornament of the finest quality was executed to the highest standards. It can only be appreciated properly on close examination. The National Museum of Ireland has 45 lunulae in its collection.

The period from 1200 B.C. onwards was a very prolific time for gold ornaments and many gold hoards are dated to that period. These include earrings [1.16], armlets, anklets and twisted ornaments called torcs. Gold torcs [1.17] were made from long strips of gold which were sometimes flattened at the edges into thin flanges before *twisting*. Torcs of various forms were made throughout the Bronze Age with *bar twisted, flange twisted* and *ribbon twisted* being the most common.

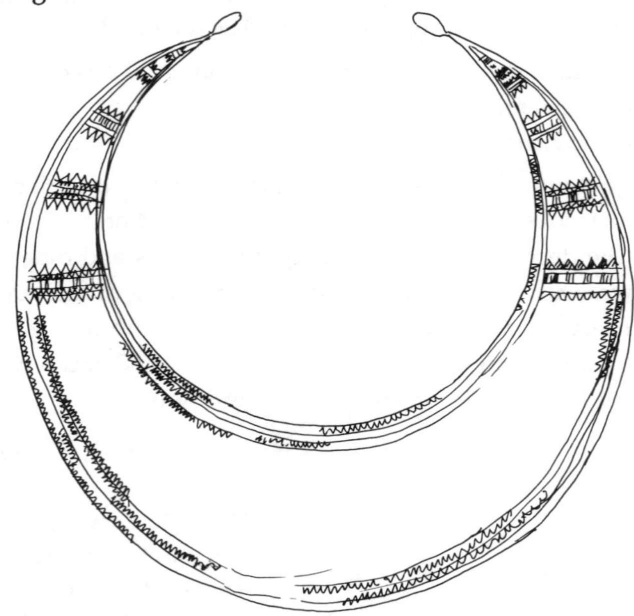

▲ *1.15 Gold lunula, Early Bronze Age (c.1800 B.C.)*

The cresent shape gives these objects their name of lunula or 'little moon'. They are neck ornaments. This one from Ross, Co. Westmeath, was cut from a thin sheet of hammered gold. The paddle-shaped ends are of slightly greater thickness and can be turned to form a locking device.

All the decoration is incised or cut in from the front; the plate is, however, so thin that the designs can be clearly seen from the back. The front is plain except for two bands of parallel lines which run around the border; these are decorated with triangles. At the narrow ends of the lunula the decoration is formed by four bands of horizontal decoration. These are composed of two pairs of parallel lines with chevron strokes inside and bordered by triangles above and below.

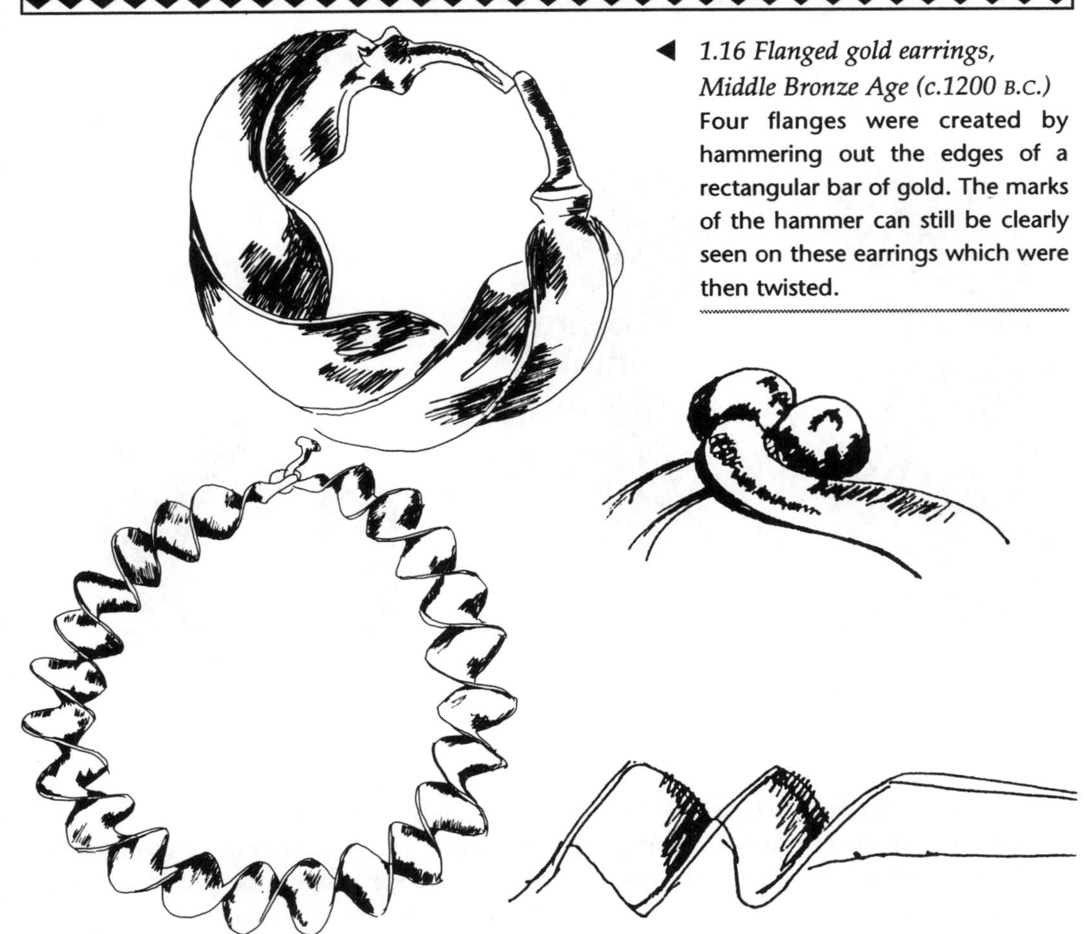

◀ *1.16 Flanged gold earrings, Middle Bronze Age (c.1200 B.C.)*
Four flanges were created by hammering out the edges of a rectangular bar of gold. The marks of the hammer can still be clearly seen on these earrings which were then twisted.

▲ *1.17 Gold ribbon torc, Late Bronze Age (c.1100 B.C.)*
To form an ornament like this gold torc from Belfast, a strap of gold was beaten to reduce its thickness at both sides. The ribbon was then twisted with the narrow ends worked into rounded knobs to form an intricate locking device.

After the lunula the most spectacular ornaments of the Bronze Age are the gorgets from the late period. Like the lunula this is a crescent-shaped collar. The most splendid example is the Gleninsheen gorget [1.18] which was found in a rock crevice in the Burren, Co. Clare. The crescent shape of the collar is decorated all over with raised ridges using the repoussé technique. These ridges are separated by *rope moulding*. The ends of the collar are fixed to discs which have patterns of concentric circles and repoussé dots. These discs were attached to the collar by *sewing with gold thread*. Gorgets are unique to Ireland.

Other ornaments of the late Bronze Age are gold lock rings [1.19] or tress rings, which are believed to have been hair rings. These display a very high level of workmanship. In some the surface is covered with individual gold wires soldered together without a backing. In others the surface of sheet gold is drawn with a compass while the metal was still flat.

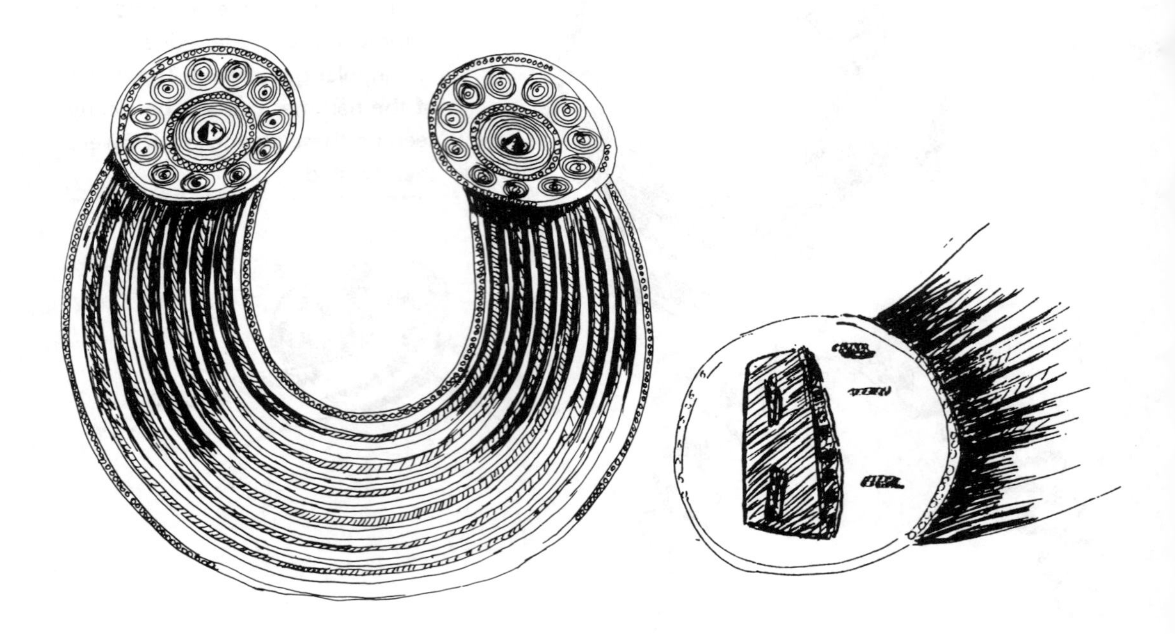

▲ *1.18 Gold collar from Gleninsheen, Co. Clare, Late Bronze Age (c.700 B.C.)*
The gorget is one of Ireland's most impressive neck ornaments. It consists of a cresent-shaped sheet of gold with a disc at both ends. To finish the raw edges of the collar, a narrow strip of gold was rolled all around the edge. The cresent shape has a series of raised ribs between which are placed a series of thinner ribs of rope moulding. All have been formed with repoussé tools.

The collar is attached to the disc by inserting the edge into a slit in the under disc and attaching by means of gold wire stitching. The construction of the terminal discs is very simple. Two circular plates, one larger than the other, have been fitted together by overlapping one over the other and pressing the edges together. Both discs are decorated in a similar way. In the centre is a cone-shaped spike surrounded by concentric circles. Around this is a circle of raised bosses and then a ring of circles, each with a central boss and concentric circles. A further ring of bosses surrounds the outside.

Almost all the gorgets found in Ireland have been found in the counties bordering the area of the Shannon estuary. Although it may have been an imitation of a northern European fashion, the gorget is unique to Ireland.

The gold dress fastener (fibula) is an Irish version of a northern European model. The Irish model consists of two hollow cone-like shapes attached to a curved bow. These were probably worn on the chest to fasten two sides of a garment together. The Clones dress fastener [1.20] is a particularly fine example. The cone-shaped terminals are decorated with a series of small concentric circles surrounding a central dot.

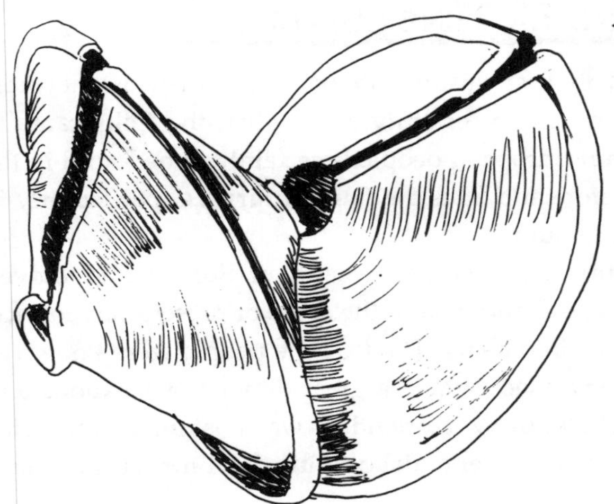

◄ *1.19 Gold hair rings, Late Bronze Age (c.600 B.C.)*

These objects, considered to be for holding hair in place, are some of the finest creations of the Irish goldsmith. They are constructed from four main pieces. Two cones are held together with a circular binding strip and a central tube designed with small bosses on the inside for gripping the hair. The grooves on the surface of the cone are made with wire closely bound together and finely soldered.

1.20 Gold dress fastener ►

Dress fasteners are like double buttons made in metal. They were designed for two buttonholes in a garment. The gold dress fastener from Clones, Co. Monaghan, is the largest of all the Irish fasteners and may only have been used for ceremonial purposes.

A connecting bow joins two cone-shaped bases, both elaborately decorated. Around the base of the bow there are small hatched triangles and on the outside surfaces of the terminals there are freely scattered circles of little engraved pits surrounded by concentric circles.

A much smaller but similar object is known as a sleeve fastener. These fasteners were sometimes cast in one piece and after casting, the terminals were hammered into the required shape. A particular feature of these little ornaments is the remarkable skill and ingenuity required for their production.

The later Bronze Age is famous for the huge quantity, quality and variety of its goldwork. The work had developed over a period of 1,500 years from simple and unsophisticated beginnings and had now reached the height of its achievement. Although outside influences did play a part in its development, goldwork produced in Ireland during the Bronze Age reached the highest standard known to Europe at the time.

Iron Age and La Tène culture

The Iron Age is probably the period in Irish history about which there is the most speculation and the least certainty. There is no certainty as to when the Celts came to Ireland, but the influence of these central European people is certainly to be found in the artwork of the period in Ireland just before and after the first century B.C. particularly in the north and north-western part of the country.

By the mid-fifth century the centre of power and wealth in Europe had moved northwards and westwards to the Rhineland and next to the areas of present day France. This was where the La Tène culture came into being. The La Tène people were known as the Celts. This culture was named after a place where a great deposit of weapons and other objects was found in Lake Neuchâtel in Switzerland. It was customary for Celtic people to throw objects into lakes as part of a ceremonial offering. La Tène has become a prime example of a European Celtic site.

This culture reached far beyond La Tène. It had contact with many areas including the Mediterranean and the East, including Greece. This contact is reflected in the style of artwork associated with this time. The art form was varied but repetitive and very decorative. Motifs were borrowed from Eastern and Greek ideas with special emphasis on plant forms such as the honeysuckle, and these together with flowing tendrils were blended into a distinctive style of abstract and curvilinear patterns. This style which developed in central Europe around 300 B.C. was known as the Waldalgesheim style and it was an offshoot of this which reached Ireland. Iron was commmonly used at the time for implements and weapons. Bronze was used more for ornamental objects. Gold was also used for ornament.

It is not certain when and where these Celtic peoples first came to Ireland. It is believed to have been around the first century A.D. The Iron Age/La Tène era in Ireland is represented more by an art form rather than historical facts.

The Irish La Tène artifacts are largely a continuation of the Bronze Age objects but with new style motifs added. The Irish La Tène was unique and continued to develop long after European examples had become obsolete. The Celtic people also brought with them skills which were added to the metalwork of the time, such as soldering and enamelling.

Many items from this time which were made of iron have not been very well preserved, as over the years gold was considered by dealers to be the only valuable find. However, some very fine swords and scabbards have been found in various parts of Ireland but mainly in County Antrim. Several bronze trumpets were found, but only one now survives. This is a splendid object with a long large curved stem. The mouth of the trumpet is decorated in the repoussé technique with a curvilinear pattern. This is called the Loughnashade trumpet [1.21] after where it was found in County Armagh.

Also in bronze is an object known as the Petrie crown [1.22] after George Petrie, a famous collector of the nineteenth century, who had this in his possession. This object may have been a crown. Circular discs are mounted on a band of metal, with conical horns rising from behind the discs. Small holes around the band suggest that fabric may have been stitched to it. All the pieces are decorated in a curvilinear low relief design. This was produced by cutting away the metal rather than casting or hammering.

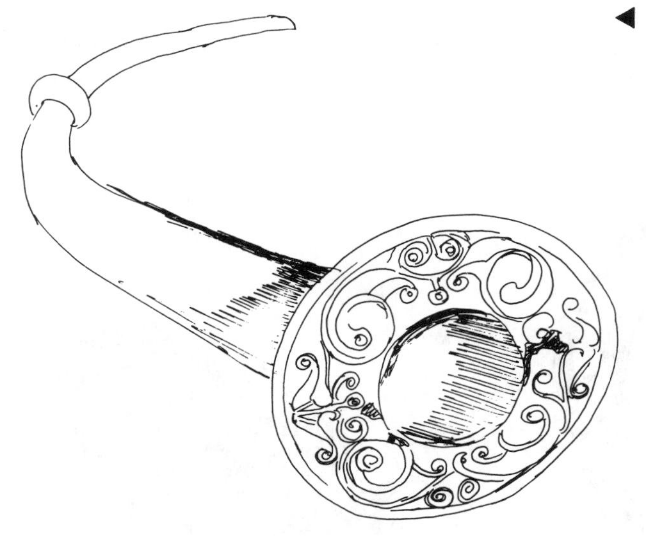

1.21 Bronze trumpet, Ultimate La Tène period (first century A.D.)
This curved trumpet found at Loughnashade, Co. Armagh, was made by rolling a tube of bronze and riveting the sides to a strip on the inside. A ring halfway down the tube divides the object into a tube ending in a mouthpiece and an elongated conical form. The mouthpiece is decorated by a rimmed circular disc. The design executed in repoussé is controlled and regular. Linear curves and spiral bosses are all in high relief with larger spirals ending in curvilinear forms.

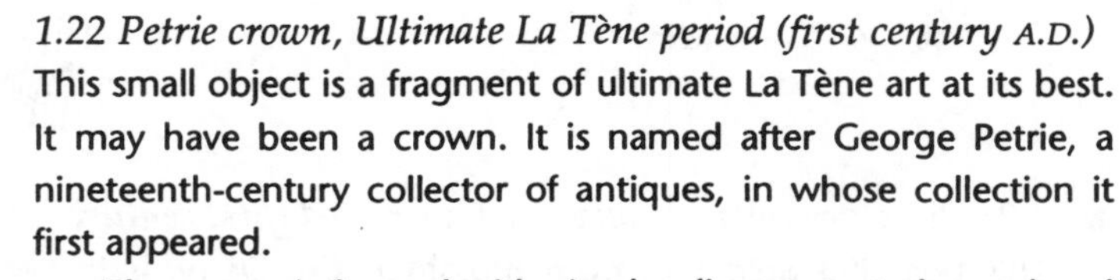

1.22 Petrie crown, Ultimate La Tène period (first century A.D.)
This small object is a fragment of ultimate La Tène art at its best. It may have been a crown. It is named after George Petrie, a nineteenth-century collector of antiques, in whose collection it first appeared.

The crown is formed with circular discs mounted on a band of metal with conical horns rising from behind the discs. This band has a row of small holes which suggest fabric may have been stitched to it.

The cut away designs are composed of spiral designs and trumpet curves ending in stylised birdheads. The disc attached to the horn is concave in shape with trumpet curves sweeping out from the centre where there is a setting for a bead. The disc on the left is similar, but the curves follow a different pattern and the central boss contains a stud of red enamel.

The horn was made by folding a sheet of bronze into a conical shape and riveting the edges to an under sheet of copper. The design was cut away after the horn was in position, as can be seen by the design which continues over the rivets. Curves sweep up and out from the base of the horn ending in beautiful birdheads. From behind further curves sweep to the front of the upper part of the horn where the tip is missing.

An important hoard was found at Broighter, Co. Derry, and forms the richest collection of gold objects of the Iron Age to be found in Ireland. The hoard consists of a little boat with oars and a mast, a bowl, two chain necklaces, two twisted necklaces and a collar ornamented in repoussé work. Unfortunately most of these objects were already damaged by the plough when found.

The splendid Broighter collar [1.23] is made from two thin sheets of gold rolled into hollow tubes. Its repoussé designs of trumpet patterns and flowing tendrils were executed while still flat.

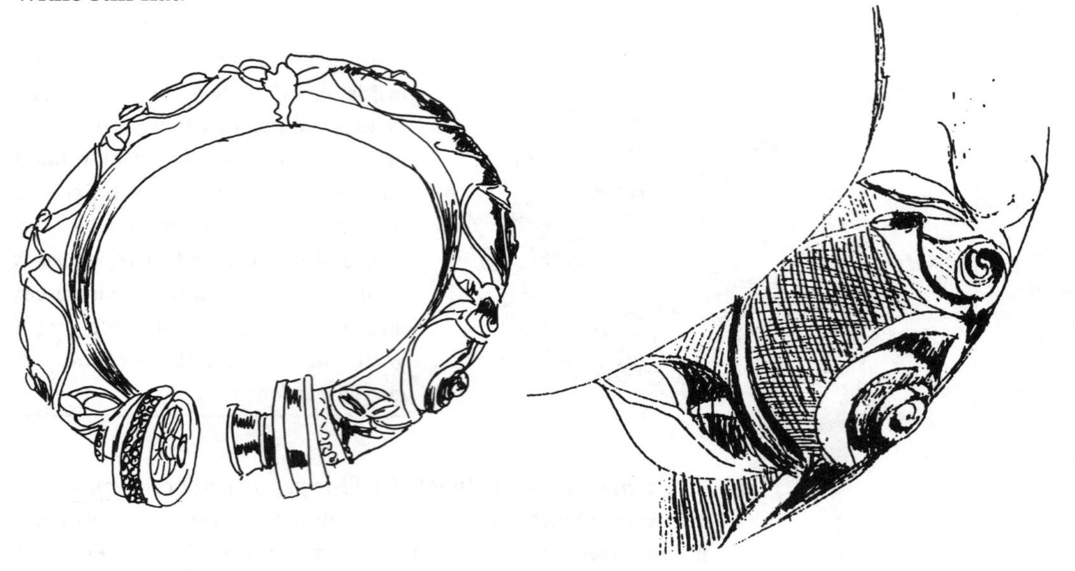

▲ *1.23 Broighter collar, Insular La Tène period (first century A.D.)*
This beautiful gold torc from Broighter, Co. Derry, is in two half-hoops with a decorative fastener. It is most elaborately made. The design made in repoussé was worked down the centre of two flat pieces of gold, leaving broad plain margins. The design itself is based on foliage and leaf motifs. At the centres, where the curves meet, well-formed raised spiral bosses are clipped on giving the appearance of flower heads. The plain spaces in between the repoussé designs are decorated with fine concentric lines formed with a compass, thus bringing together the traditional earlier method of decoration with the new, more decorative La Tène style.

The decorated sheets of gold were rolled into tubes and soldered together. The tubes were filled with hot wax to heat the metal before bending into hoops. An elaborate locking device was attached to the front end of each hoop in the form of a cylindrical drum decorated by bands of gold. The two parts of the collar may have been joined by a linking tube or a decorative hinge. Detail showing La Tène-style ornament with the background roughened with the earlier style compass-drawn arcs.

The Turoe stone in County Galway [1.24] is the best known of the carved pillar stones. The design on this can be compared to the metalwork of the time. It is an almost cylindrical block of granite with the top and the sides decorated with a well-executed design of spirals, trumpets, circles and one single triskele.

Our knowledge of this era is derived from archaeological sources and to a certain extent from the myths and heroic sagas of Cuchulainn, Queen Maeve and the mighty Fionn Mac Cuhaill court at Tara.

One fort from this time still stands today on the Aran Islands. Dun Aengus stands on the Aran island of Inishmore. The magnificent fort is set 280 feet above sea level. It is composed of three rings of strong walls with an abbatis and thousands of upright standing stone pillars to keep invaders out surrounding them.

▲ *1.24 Turoe stone, La Tène period (c.50 B.C.)*

The techniques of metal ornamentation were also applied by Irish La Tène craftsmen to stone and bone.

A famous standing stone at Turoe, Co. Galway, shows an exceptional skill in stoneworking. This lavishly decorated granite monolith could only have been carried out by native craftsmen as it is made of native stone and because of its huge size could not have been easily moved. It is carefully decorated and smoothed. The decoration in low relief suggests that the artist was imitating, not repoussé, but work in which the design was made by cutting away the background.

The undulating whirl of tendril and trumpet ornament covers the stone completely, but it is carefully planned to have four sides. A single triskele, a three-legged device of trumpet curves, appears in the centre of one of the panels. Around the base of the stone is found a more geometric pattern similar to a Greek step pattern.

▲ *1.25 Expanded drawing of the ornament of the Turoe stone showing that although the pattern continues around the stone it is planned to have four distinct sides*

Exam Questions

1990 Ordinary level

1. Describe and discuss the passage grave at Newgrange, Co. Meath. Use sketches and diagrams to illustrate its structure and decoration.

1991 Ordinary level

1. Describe any stone carving of the pre-Christian period and discuss the nature of its decoration.

1992 Ordinary level

1. Discuss the use of gold in the pre-Christian era in Ireland and describe some such objects from the period. Use sketches and diagrams to illustrate your points.

1993 Ordinary level

1. Objects in gold, silver and bronze for practical and religious use and for personal adornment were made in Ireland from the Bronze Age to the Christian Age. Select any *one* such object and discuss its design and the techniques used in its making.

1994 Ordinary level

1. Give a detailed illustrated account of the decoration found on the kerbstone and inside the passage grave at Newgrange. Refer briefly in your answer to the structure of the passage grave.

1990 Higher level

1. Give a detailed account of an important passage grave of the megalithic period and explain how it differs from such other stone tombs as the dolmen and the court cairn. Use sketches and diagrams to illustrate your answer.

1991 Higher level

1. The dominant influence during the Iron Age was the La Tène culture. Explain what you understand by the term La Tène and describe some examples of Irish metalwork and stonework from the La Tène period.

1992 Higher level

1. During the Bronze Age (2000–500 B.C.) gold ornaments of remarkable quality were produced in Ireland. Discuss, with the aid of sketches and diagrams, the nature and function of these ornaments and the techniques used in their production.

1993 Higher level

1. Much of our knowledge of the Neolithic period in Ireland derives from the stone graves or megalithic tombs located throughout the country.
   (i) Describe, with the aid of sketches and diagrams, a stone tomb such as the dolmen, the court cairn and the passage grave.
   (ii) Describe the decoration on these tombs and say what these tombs tell us about the people who built them.

1994 Higher level

1. Describe, with the aid of sketches and diagrams, the important features of *either* carved stonework *or* metalwork of the pre-Christian period in Ireland and suggest how these features might be of interest to a modern designer.

1995 Higher level

1. Discuss the use of line in Irish megalithic art with reference to *any* passage grave you have studied.
2. Trace the development of metalwork in Ireland from pre-Christian times to the end of the early Christian period. Refer in your answer to the purpose of the metal objects, the materials from which they were made, and the manner of their decoration.

CHAPTER TWO

Early Christian Ireland

Introduction to Christianity

The coming of St Patrick in A.D. 432 is the accepted date for the change to Christianity in Ireland. Ireland is the only country in western Europe to which Christianity came without Roman conquest. This meant that Irish Christianity was adapted on to and blended imperceptibly with the old pagan ways. Although the Romans never invaded Ireland, it is certain that their influence reached here through trade and contact with Roman colonies such as Britain. One feature of the period was the development of a form of writing based on the Roman alphabet known as 'Ogham'. This period of Romanisation led naturally to the introduction of Christianity, by then the official religion of the empire, to Ireland in the fifth century, but we have very little knowledge of the process by which the pre-literate pagan society of the Iron Age developed into the civilisation of the Early Christian period when Ireland earned its title of the island of 'Saints and Scholars'.

The establishment of Christianity in Ireland marks the beginning of a great period in Irish Art. Christianity and the Roman learning which it brought were a dynamic force. The merging of Roman designs on brooches, jewellery and the use of precious stones inset in metal with native traditions was to produce many magnificent objects and manuscripts. Early Christian Irish art can be divided into two phases.

The first phase was from the fifth to the mid-eighth century. This was the time of the early monastic settlements. Few objects remain from this era except some pins and brooches and the first decoration of capital letters in manuscripts as seen in the Cathach. The eighth century saw the dramatic development of Irish art with the early stone crosses and the Book of Durrow.

The second phase was from the mid-eighth century to the ninth. This was the Golden Age of Irish art when technical skill reached the height of its perfection and treasures such as the Tara brooch and the Book of Kells were produced. The ninth century was the time of the great stone crosses such as the crosses of Monasterboice and Moone.

While St Patrick was not the first man to bring Christianity to Ireland, he and other missionaries established small communities ruled over by their own bishop. This system, however, gradually changed and during the sixth and seventh centuries a shift towards monastic foundations took place. The result was a Church organisation very different from that in neighbouring Britain or continental Europe. The Church in Ireland recognised the authority of the abbot of the monastery more than the bishop of the diocese.

The monastic communities were founded by saints such as Colmcille, Brigid of Kildare, Ciaran of Clonmacnoise, Brendan of Clonfert and Enda of Aran. The abbot of the monastery was heir to the founding saint and succession from father to son was common. These abbots were often laymen, as were many of their members. As well as being centres of learning, the monasteries were strong economically while also maintaining their religious function. The abbots of leading monasteries had a high social standing and strong connections with the secular rulers whose residences were the ring forts or raths and crannogs. The masters of these raths were the main patrons of artistic production for hundreds of years.

EARLY IRISH ARCHITECTURE

Early Irish monasteries were usually enclosed within circular walls. Larger communities often had two surrounding walls, with the centre being the area of more sanctity. The outer space was the area of economic activity, where the everyday work of food production, craft, metalwork and trade took place.

The monastic enclosure [2.1] usually surrounded a cemetery and a church. Buildings were usually constructed of wood or wattles and circular in shape. The abbot's house was near the church and it was surrounded by little huts known as beehive huts occupied by other monks and followers.

Very few of these early sites have survived. The early structures were made of wood and their churches have all been rebuilt over the centuries.

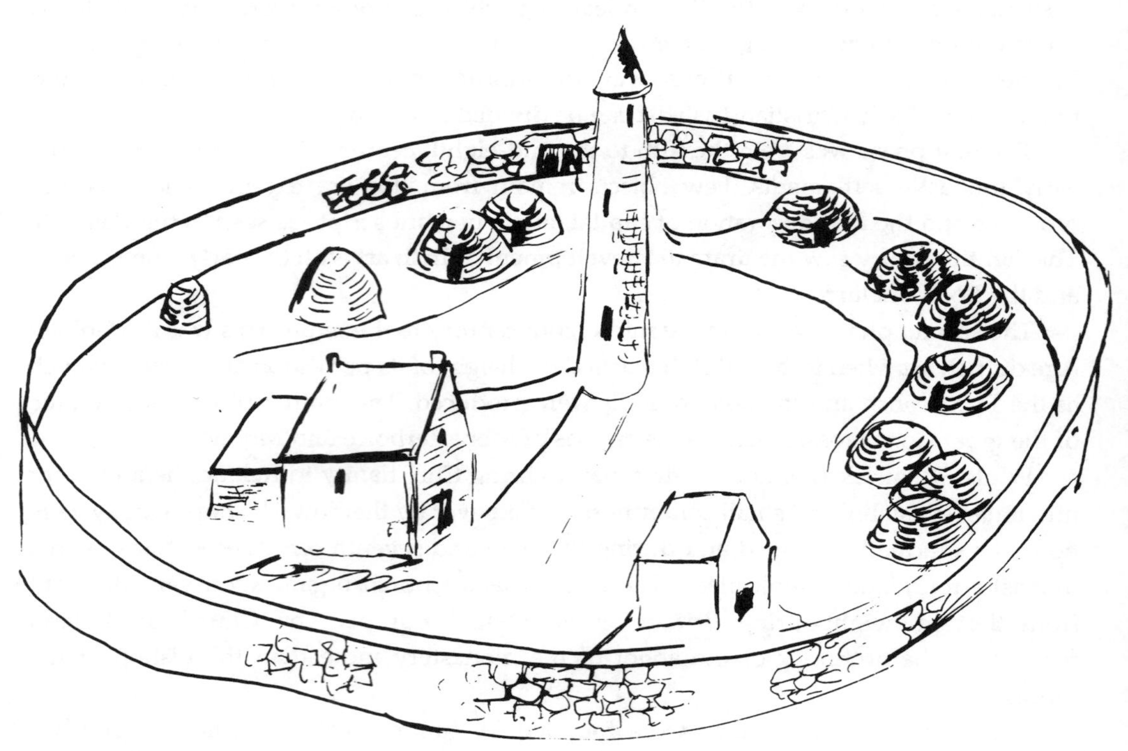

▲ *2.1 Monastic enclosure*

SKELLIG MICHAEL, CO. KERRY

▲ 2.2 *Beehive huts on Skellig Michael, Co. Kerry*

The stone huts built on Skellig Michael Island seven miles off the coast of Kerry are a well-preserved little monastic settlement. Perched high on a tiny rocky island which rises to a sharp peak, it is dedicated to St Michael the patron saint of high places. Much of the monastery remains to be seen today. Stone steps rise steeply from the landing area to a height of 180 m where the little stone church of St Michael is surrounded by six beehive huts [2.2]. These little huts used the same corbel method of construction as found in Newgrange built 3,000 years before. The two small oratories are built in the same style, but these have adapted the corbel to suit the rectangular shape. Both have one window and a low doorway. It is not easy to put a date on these beehive huts. They may be ninth century when the monastery was known to be inhabited, or as late as the eleventh century, the time of the monks' departure from their exposed isolated retreat.

GALLARUS ORATORY

▲ 2.3 *Gallarus oratory, Co. Kerry*

Beehive huts are dotted around the coast on the tip of the Dingle Peninsula, where also is found the little church known as Gallarus oratory. [2.3] Here again the corbel is used in the rectangular shape and the danger of the roof collapsing on the longer sides is overcome by the careful selection of well-shaped stones which fitted together and have remained as strong and dry today as they did when built sometime between the eighth and twelfth century. The walls slope inwards for strength and the little church has a low door and one window on the gable walls.

Round Towers

▲ *2.4 Round tower at Ardmore, Co. Waterford*

Round towers which first made their appearance around the tenth century were normally located to the west of the monastery with their doors facing those of the church.

A most striking feature of many monasteries, they were presumed to be bell towers but they were not equipped with hanging bells, and it may be supposed that they were an imported idea adapted to native skills in stone building. They were probably a mark of status as the monasteries grew in wealth and sophistication.

The round tower was tall, slender and tapering, with a cone-shaped corbelled cap. They have usually four windows at the top, with one window for each storey below. Each of these windows faces a different direction. The towers may have been used to store valuables or as places of refuge as the height of the doorway—two or three metres from the ground—would suggest. The doorway was reached from outside by a ladder which could be drawn inside. Internally they had wooden floors also reached by ladder. The eleventh-century round tower at Glendalough is 31.40 m high. The little church is known as St Kevin's kitchen and was built about a century later. Some well-known round towers can be found at Clonmacnoise, Co. Offaly, Glendalough, Co. Wicklow, Monasterboice, Co. Louth, and Ardmore, Co. Waterford [2.4].

Manuscripts (sixth to eighth century)

Christianity is a religion of the book, and the Irish, like every other Christian community, had to learn to read and write the Scriptures. The earliest missionaries to Ireland would have brought with them books written in the standard scripts of the fourth and fifth centuries, that of the 'uncial script'. Curiously, the first Irish manuscripts are not written in this, but in the distinctively Irish hand of the 'half uncial'. This Irish hand attained great beauty and perfection and was to be taken abroad by the Irish missionaries to England and Scotland in the sixth and early seventh centuries, where it became the national script of these countries. Missionaries and scholars produced small gospel and missal books which could easily be carried. These were written in the 'miniscule' script. Larger luxury productions used on the altar on special occasions were written in the solemn letter forms of the 'majuscule' script.

In the period between the late seventh and early ninth centuries manuscripts which were masterpieces of calligraphy and painting were produced in Ireland and by Irish monks abroad, surpassing anything produced in the rest of Europe.

Copying the texts was considered an act of devotion. Manuscripts were produced in a room called a scriptorium and considerable wealth was required by the monasteries for the production of luxury books. A large herd of calves was required for the production of vellum; and colours were expensive and often had to be imported from abroad. Traditionally, books were kept in leather satchels which were hung on the walls, but special books were elaborately bound and sometimes stored in ornate metal boxes or shrines. The shrine of the Book of Durrow was lost from Trinity College in 1690 and the cover of the Book of Kells was stolen in 1007, no doubt by the Vikings who were more interested in ornate metalwork than in books. Two leather satchels and several shrines survive today.

On the west coast of Scotland is a little monastery founded by the first Irish missionary about whom there is the most detailed information. Colmcille (or Columba) founded the monastery of Iona in A.D. 563. Iona became the centre of a far-flung community that included monasteries at Durrow, Co. Offaly, and Derry, Co. Derry. Scribal activity was of the greatest importance to Colmcille and he and his followers have come to be particularly associated with manuscript production. The scriptorium at Iona is generally considered to have been responsible for the production of the most lavish of surviving Irish manuscripts, the Book of Kells.

THE CATHACH (SIXTH CENTURY)

The earliest surviving Irish manuscript, now in the library of the Royal Irish Academy in Dublin, is the psalter known as the Cathach of St Columba.

The name 'Cathach' means battle book and it earned its name when Colmcille took it into a battle fought over the first recorded breach of copyright. In the year 561 the tale is that Colmcille took a rare and valuable copy of the psalms from St Finian and copied them out in his own hand in the night. Finian appealed to the High King of Tara who ruled against Colmcille who took up the cause in battle. The battle was fought near Sligo and ended with the death of 3,000 men. Colmcille's offence was considered so grave that he was exiled to Iona.

▲ *2.5 Capital letters from the Cathach*
These letters show the adaptation of motifs from La Téne metalwork. The letters are surrounded by dots.

The beginning of the book is missing and its decoration is confined to the first letter of each paragraph. It shows a very important feature of early Christian art, that of the adaptation of the old Celtic motifs used in metalwork to script. Another important feature of the Cathach is the use of stylised animal ornament which was to remain a particularly distinctive feature of Irish manuscript illumination during the next centuries. The book is in black and white, with a small amount of colour such as red and yellow used here and there.

▲ *2.6 Capital letter showing the use of stylised animal ornament*
A new type of stylised animal ornament from the Cathach which was to form a vital part of early Christian ornament. The tail on the letter Q forms a spiral which becomes the head of an animal with an open mouth.

BOOK OF DURROW (SEVENTH CENTURY)

The Book of Durrow was probably intended for use on an altar as it is too large to be carried around easily. It is traditionally associated with the Columban monastery and was probably produced in a scriptorium there in the mid-seventh century.

The book contains the four gospels and some other material. The script is in the Irish majuscule hand with pages decorated in red, yellow, green and deep brown against a background of black or the plain vellum page. Some pages open with an ornamental capital letter, others are pages of pure decoration known as carpet pages [2.8 (a) & (b)]. Just before each gospel is a symbol of the evangelist [2.7] who wrote it, in a style that shows the full development of the beast in early Irish manuscripts.

The beast in Irish manuscript illumination had its origins in the great variety of animal ornament associated with the Nordic and Germanic tribes of northern Europe. It made its way to Ireland through England and so is similar to those in Anglo-Saxon manuscripts. Its introduction to Ireland brought the second important feature of early Christian art.

The third important feature of early Christian art which first makes its appearance in the Book of Durrow are the interlaced bands. These were to form a very important component of early Christian Irish art. Many of the pages have thick bands of this interlacing which are accentuated by double lines around the edges. However, the strongest characteristic of the Book of Durrow is the space allowed around the ornament. Large areas of the vellum are left undecorated making a strong contrast between itself and the later highly ornate Book of Kells.

▲ *2.7 The lion, symbol of St John (later St Mark)*
Before each gospel there is a symbol of the evangelist who wrote it. Here we see the development of the stylised beast of Celtic ornament. In the seventh century Bible St John was represented by the lion, which in later interpretations became the symbol of St Mark. In the Book of Durrow this symbol of the lion introduces the gospel of St John. It is framed by a band of broad ribbon interlace ornament which may be eastern Mediterranean in origin.

▲ *2.8 Carpet pages*

The carpet page follows the evangelist page. The whole of this left-hand page is given over to ornament.

(a) folio 191v

This design is a combination of La Tène motifs including spirals and triskeles as seen on the Turoe stone and Mediterranean broad ribbon interlace. It is obvious from this type of design that the Book of Durrow was produced in a place where metalwork was practised.

▲ *(b) folio 192v*

This page is a masterpiece of design. Animal ornament in panels surround a roundel of broad ribbon interlace. Above and below are two panels of animals painted in reds, greens and yellows on a black background. Each has a long snake-like body which curls around so that it bites its own back leg with long jaws and open mouth. These interlace with other similar beasts. On either side of the roundel is a panel of three dog-like creatures with feet entwined and each biting the other's back. An undecorated square surrounds the roundel.

BOOK OF KELLS (c.800 A.D.)

The most famous of all Irish gospel books dates from the mid-eighth century, a century or more after the Book of Durrow. It is not certain where the sumptuously decorated Book of Kells was produced, but it is presumed to have been at the Columban island monastery of Iona in Scotland. It may have been produced to commemorate the centenary of the death of Colmcille (A.D. 597). It was honoured as the great gospel book of Columba during the middle ages.

It is thought to have come to Ireland with valuables and relics at the beginning of the ninth century when the community moved to found the monastery of Kells after a particularly disastrous Viking raid on Iona.

▲ *2.14 Capital U*

Angels guard the capital which begins the word *una* in the centre of the Resurrection page. *Una* means day number one, or Sunday, the first day of the week. The angels on each corner are painted in gleaming white. In the right-hand corner of the page a fierce monster is cast out by the power of good over evil.

The manuscript contains the four gospels in the Irish majuscule script, brilliantly illustrated. As well as being larger and more elaborate than previous manuscripts, the Book of Kells has new features such as drawings between the lines of quite naturalistic animals, and introduces new colours and figural scenes not seen before, such as the Virgin and Child and the Arrest and Temptation of Christ. Five main colours are used in the book as well as the browns and blacks which are used to fill in the background of the full-page illustrations. The colours are:

Red which was made from red lead and has kept its brightness very well.

Yellow which was made from egg-white and a mineral found in the ground. It is called orpiment. This colour has a shiny surface and looks like gold. It was used extensively throughout the book.

Green was made from copper and has an emerald colour. This colour has also lasted well but has an acidity which sometimes eats through the page.

Purple and *Blue* may have been imported into Ireland. Purple probably came from a leaf plant found in Mediterranean countries such as Italy. Several shades of this colour have been used.

Blue is thought to have come from the precious stone called *lapis lazuli* found in the Himalayas in India. This colour is found in some of the ornate capital letters [2.14].

Some pages of the manuscript are missing and all but two of the remaining 680 pages are decorated. The ornament varies from an endless variety of decorated initials and humorous marginal drawings to pages fully covered with the most detailed illustrations and designs in strong and brilliant colours. To an already wide variety of colours is added the new technique of covering one colour with a thin wash of another.

The four main artists have been named as:

The Illustrator—responsible for the Virgin and Child [2.11], the Arrest of Christ [2.12], and the Temptation.

The Portraitist—responsible for the portraits of Christ [2.13], Matthew and John.

The Goldsmith—responsible for the fine pages introducing the four gospels and the famous Chi-Rho page [2.9]. This name has been given because the work resembles the metalwork of the time in its fineness of detail. Yellow was substituted for gold.

The second master was responsible for the cats and kittens [2.10] on the end of the Chi-Rho page and the charming depictions of animals and everyday life found in the margins and between the lines [2.15].

◄ *2.9 The Chi-Rho page*

This fascinating page is packed with detail. It is the last and perhaps the finest page of the book. A large letter 'X' forms a magnificent sweeping design and is surrounded by the most minute detail of abstract patterns and tiny human and animal figures. The animal figures include an otter with a fish in his mouth. Near the otter are two cats with kittens. On the top right-hand corner is a butterfly with spreading wings tucked away between the spiral designs and the side of the letter 'X'.

Apart from animal and human figure designs the page is rich in abstract design of circles, spirals and triskeles. All are blended with interlacing and golden yellow is one of the most dominant colours.

The other letters in the design are 'P' and 'I'. The letter 'P' is entertwined with the letter 'I' and ends with a human head.

2.10 Detail from the Chi-Rho page
Two kittens have climbed on to their mother's back while two others play with the sacred host. On their right is an otter catching fish. The fish was an early symbol for Christ the Saviour. The cats are almost naturalistic but the otter is quite stylised.

2.11 Birth of Christ
On this famous Christmas page a solemn Mary is seated on an ornate throne with a wise unbaby-like Jesus on her knee. The child's face is turned to his mother's, with one hand on her breast. The page illustrates a great event, the birth of someone very special. Four angels celebrate this great occasion: two above the chair are pointing to Mary, while two others peep out from behind, on the lower corners, suggesting the mystery and wonder of Christ's birth. The colours are skilfully blended, mingling several shades of purple with emerald green. The purple indicates royalty. In a box to the right of the picture are six human figures: these represent the people that Christ came on earth to save.

◀ *2.12 Arrest of Jesus*

Enclosed in an arch representing the Garden of Gethsemane two figures grab Christ. At the top facing each other, two fierce monsters snarl, with tongues intertwined, suggesting the violence and evil of the occasion. Jesus is portrayed as calm and solemn with arms outstretched in surrender. His beautifully folded red gown, face, hands and hair are perfectly symmetrical. As with the other paintings in the book, the scene is completely stylised and no attempt is made at realistic human depictions of sacred figures.

2.13 Portrait of Christ ▶

Near the beginning of the Book of Kells is a full-page portrait of Christ. There are two other portraits, one of St Matthew and the other of St John.

Christ in a brilliant red gown is shown seated on a throne, with one hand raised in blessing, the other holding a book bound in red. Above his head is a cross and behind him are two peacocks, which in the art of this period suggested life everlasting. Vine leaves and grapes grow from vases in which the birds are standing, each with a little white disc on its breast. This can be taken to symbolise the Eucharist. Surrounding the central figure of Christ are smaller figures of men and angels.

The colours in this painting are particularly well preserved. Around the figure of Christ in red and purple is an arch of interlacing and forming a frame around the scene is a broad band of ribbon interlacing linking roundels of red, blue and yellow.

▲ *2.15 Dog guarding a syllable*

The scribes often included little animals in between the lines as they wrote. Cats and dogs can be found chasing across the page or a little animal such as a mouse playing with the sacred host runs down through the script. This was a way for the scribe to express a sense of humour. Birds are often found on certain words or fish and scorpion-like creatures surround words. Animals are sometimes used instead of brackets. Occasionally the scribe could not fit the whole word on to the line and in that case the syllable would be placed over the line tucked under an animal's leg or under a bird's wing.

The Book of Kells was sent to Dublin for safe-keeping in 1654 and presented to Trinity College Dublin in 1661 where it can still be seen today.

METALWORK (EIGHTH–TWELFTH CENTURY)

The establishment of a monastery in Iona by Columba in 563 was an important event in the civilisation of Ireland. From Iona the Irish missionaries contributed and drew on cultural developments in Britain. The Anglo-Saxons had invaded Britain and brought with them the animal art of northern Europe. Britain had also been occupied by the Romans. During the Christian era a new artistic tradition developed in Ireland which fused Germanic art with traditions taken from the Roman world and the various traditions around the Mediterranean. All these traditions were fused to ultimate La Tène art. This style was found in manuscript illumination, the Book of Durrow being the first major example, and the link between the style of manuscripts and metalwork of the late seventh and eighth centuries is very close.

About the year A.D. 600 fine Irish craftmanship had changed considerably from that of the later Iron Age. Solid silver objects had appeared, enamel was used more and a new technique of millefiori glass had been adopted. This was a method of producing motifs by covering a cane of glass with layers of different coloured glass and cutting into short lengths. Sometimes lengths of coloured glass were laid together and fused, before cutting and setting into the metalwork.

New types of objects had become fashionable, such as large pins for fastening garments and penannular brooches. There were probably workshops all over the country, but some are known to have been at the monastic site at Armagh and at Ballinderry crannog, Co. Offaly. A small group of penannular brooches, of which the Ballinderry brooch [2.16] is the finest, survive from that time. The penannular brooch, so called because of the gap in the ring, was developed from a Roman military-style brooch found in northern Britain.

It is clear that motifs used in metalwork were also considered suitable for manuscripts, such as the imitation of gold. The colouring used in manuscripts is approached in metalwork by coloured enamels and in the range of new techniques introduced in the seventh century. Eighth-century metalwork shows an astonishing range of techniques, a love of sumptuous, all-over decorations, and a combination of local and borrowed techniques imitating various effects found in other traditions. New techniques of gold filigree, gilding and silvering, *kerbschnitt*, die-stamping and a variety of new colours in glass and enamel were added to the native skills of bronze casting, engraving and colouring with red enamel.

The early eighth century is the era known as the Golden Age and is a time of perfection in Irish art. Objects with a dazzling array of techniques, such as the Tara brooch [2.19] and the Ardagh chalice [2.18], seem to have suddenly made their appearance. However, these and other splendid pieces were found by chance and who knows what other objects have been lost from that time.

BALLINDERRY BROOCH, CO. OFFALY (A.D. 600)

Millefiori glass is inlaid in a little plate on the terminals of the Ballinderry brooch, along with sunken areas of red enamel. The ring is decorated with bands of lines, hatchings and herringbone design.

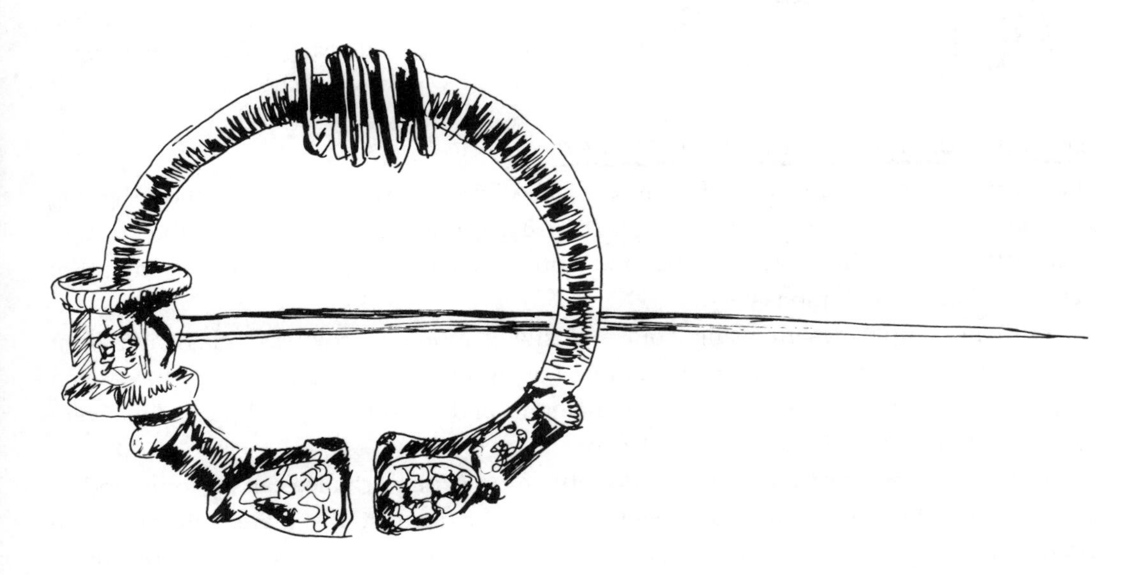

▲ *2.16 Ballinderry brooch*

RINNAGAN CRUCIFIXION PLAQUE (LATE SEVENTH CENTURY)

St John's crucifixion plaque was found in County Roscommon at Rinnagan, an ancient site on Lough Ree, near Athlone. It is one of the earliest examples of the crucifixion scene and dates to the late seventh century. This magnificent bronze plaque was originally gilded and was probably pinned to wood, serving as a book cover. This is suggested by the numerous small holes which surround the piece.

2.17 St John's crucifixion plaque, Rinnagan, Co. Roscommon

The scene is dominated by the central figure of Christ. The nailed feet point downwards. With arms outstretched and nailed to the cross, it resembles Christ on the stone cross at Carndonagh, Co. Donegal.

The design is a combination of herringbone pattern, spirals and zigzags. This is an unusual form of decoration and is not found elsewhere on pieces of this time. The ornament on the garments is of the La Tène style. On the figure of Christ a cluster of scrolls form a centrepiece on the chest and the long-sleeved garment has interlace at the wrists.

Around Christ are smaller figures of angels, the lance bearer and the sponge bearer. The angels attending Christ have arms and legs, two pairs of wings and spiral designs at the points where the wings are attached.

ARDAGH CHALICE (EARLY EIGHTH CENTURY)

One of the richest discoveries of early Christian Irish art was made by a boy digging potatoes near Ardagh, Co. Limerick, in 1868. This has become known as the Ardagh chalice. With it he found four brooches and a bronze chalice. They must have been part of the collection of a rich monastery.

With its simple design using gold and silver, moulded coloured glass and light engraving, the silver chalice is the finest piece of eighth-century metalwork to have been found in Ireland to date. A wide range of materials and considerable technical skills were combined to produce this work of perfection.

The balance and restrained formal dignity of the Ardagh chalice can be compared to the Book of Durrow, where the designs are set off against the plain vellum of the manuscript. In the chalice also, large areas of silver are free of decoration, but where decoration is used, it is sumptuous. It involves plain interlace and animal interlace, scrolls, plaits and frets in gold wire filigree. Other techniques used are engraving, casting, enamelling and *cloisonné*, a method of enamelling which separates the colours with thin strips of metal.

▲ *2.18 Ardagh chalice*

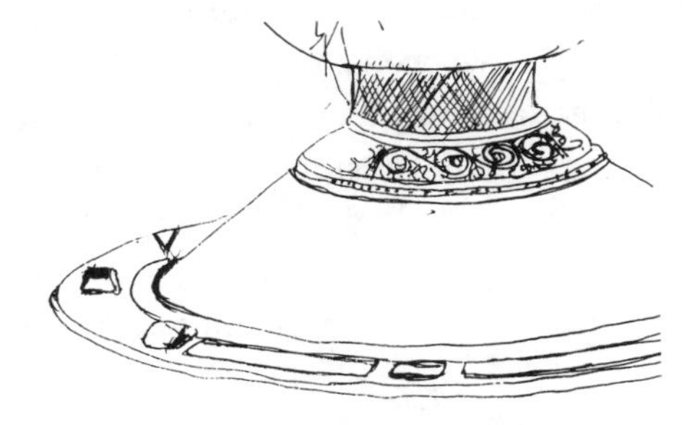

Complex gold filigree work forms a band around the chalice and this is broken by red and blue glass studs. Under this band, engraved lightly into the silver, are the names of all the apostles except Judas.

The handles on both sides are a concentrated area of rich colours and patterns. They are decorated with coloured glass panels in red, blue, green and yellow, in between which are tiny panels of complex and skilled gold filigree work. In the centre of each side is a cross within a roundel. The design is simple but it is richly decorated using spirals of gold wire filigree work, coloured glass and a *cloisonné* enamelled stud in the centre.

The bowl of the chalice is joined to the base by a thick bronze stem. The stem is heavily gilded (a thin layer of gold impressed on to the metal), and here the decoration is the most intricate and involved of all. The base is formed by a cone-shaped foot around which is a decorated flange for extra stability. This flange has square blocks of blue glass separated by panels of interlace and geometric ornament.

In the centre of the underside of the base is a circular crystal surrounded by gold filigree and green enamels. The outer edge of the flange underside is divided into eight, with six copper studs and two silver.

TARA BROOCH (EIGHTH CENTURY)

The Tara brooch is a form of the penannular brooch which passed originally into Irish jewellery from a Roman design. These brooches have no particular Christian connection and were as likely to have been made for the personal adornment of a queen or king as for that of a bishop. There are many examples of this type of brooch in Irish art but the Tara brooch, although one of the smallest, is the finest of them. It is a ring brooch and has no gap through which the pin can pass and so is pseudo-penannular. Chain and loops are needed for fastening in a brooch like this. The famous brooch was not actually found at Tara but on the seashore at Bettystown, Co. Meath, near where a cliff had collapsed due to the erosion of the sea. A jeweller who had it for some time named it the 'Tara' brooch and the name has remained.

If the Ardagh chalice can be compared to the Book of Durrow, the Tara brooch can be well compared to the Book of Kells. As in the manuscript, the little brooch is crowded with detailed decoration front and back. It is quite small, but has an astonishing amount of minute skilful work in the form of detailed ornament which, like that of the Book of Kells, fits into a very small space.

The Tara brooch is close in style to the Ardagh chalice and, like the chalice, design, technique and materials are of the highest quality. It belongs to the same period and may even have come from the same workshop.

The Tara brooch is a perfect example of eighth-century metal craftsmanship in that every skill available to metalwork of the time is to be found on its small surface.

DERRYNAFLAN HOARD (EIGHTH CENTURY)

One of the most interesting discoveries of recent years was the finding of a hoard of liturgical vessels at the ancient monastery of Derrynaflan, Co. Tipperary. The hoard contained a chalice [2.21] very similar in design to the Ardagh chalice, suggesting that there may have been a tradition of this kind of design in the Irish Church. The hoard also contained a silver paten [2.20] and a beautiful strainer-ladle.

The paten is considered to be one of the finest expressions of Irish art and, like the closely related Ardagh chalice, shows an astonishing range of techniques such as filigree, enamelling, casting, engraving, stamping of thin gold and knitting of wire mesh. Both were probably made in the mid to late eighth century.

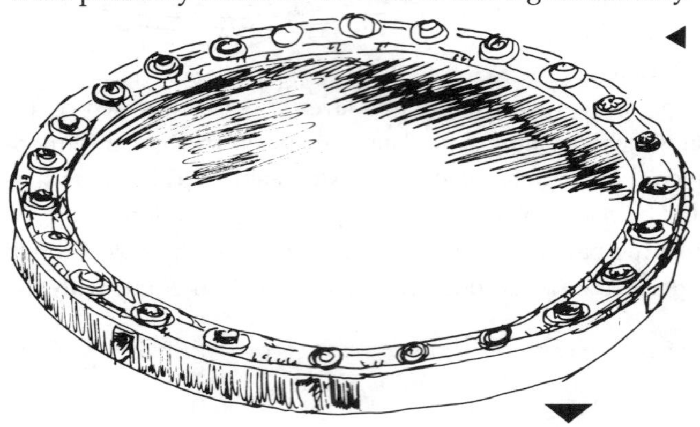

2.20 Derrynaflan paten (eighth century)

The Derrynaflan paten is similar in many of its details to the Ardagh chalice. On the rim are found cast glass studs, filigree gold animal interlace, engraving and knitted wire mesh all around the edges, making this an object of great beauty.

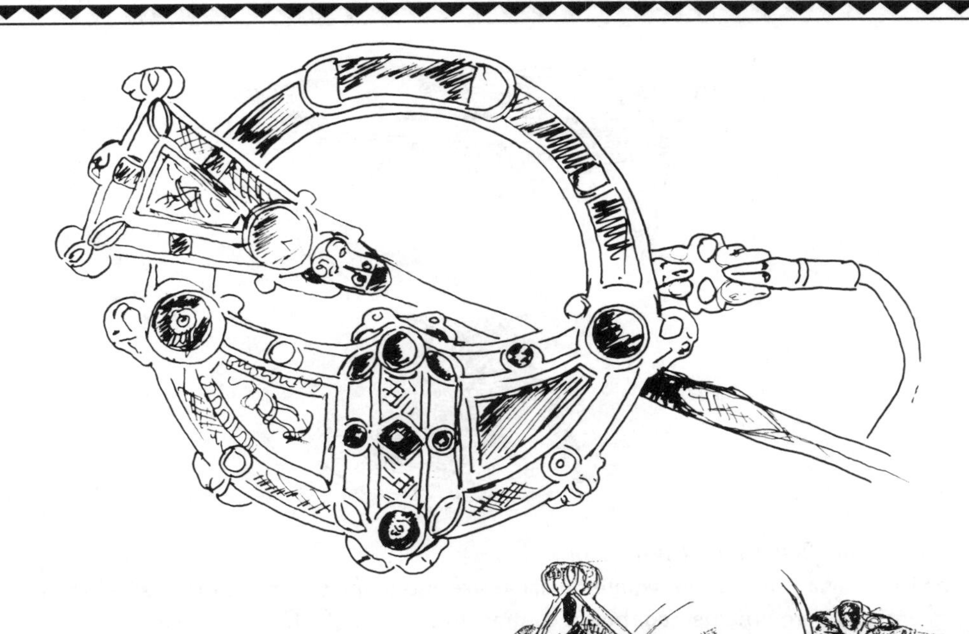

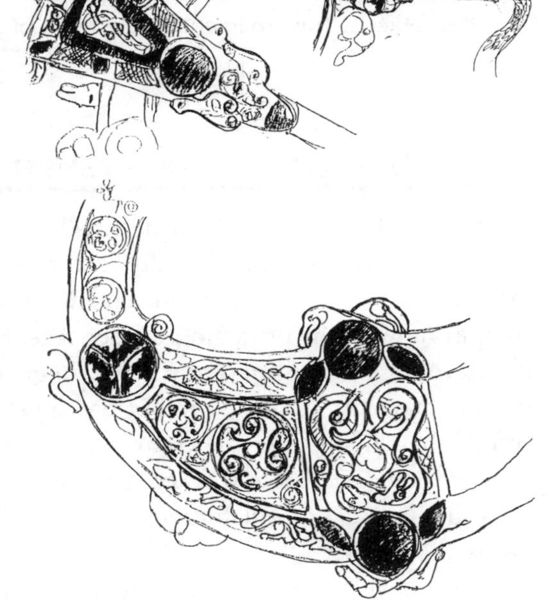

▲ *2.19 Tara brooch*
This spendid piece of craftsmanship consists of a closed ring in silver with an ornamental pin attached by a loose ring. Attached to one side is a mesh chain, which suggests it may have been one of a pair originally joined together across the back of the shoulders.

A number of panels of decoration on the front are now empty, but those that remain show a remarkable fineness and delicacy of work. Beasts, with pronounced eyes and lips that curl and intertwine, in raised gold thread filigree work, fill the tiny spaces. At key points in the design there are glass and amber studs.

On the back of the brooch are two plates. Here a La Tène design is dark against a silver background. Recent laboratory work has shown that the dark outlines were made of silvered copper, which when first made would have glowed copper red against a silver background. The chain is attached to the brooch by two animal heads at each end of a little plate. Two human heads lie in the centre of this plate. These human faces are of purple glass.

Cast and gilded *kerbschnitt* ornament appears on the shaft and head of the pin. It also occurs on both the inner and outer edges of the ring. *Kerbschnitt* is a method of casting which imitates wood carving.

▲ *2.21 Derrynaflan chalice (ninth century)*
The Derrynaflan chalice looks quite similar in size and shape to the Ardagh chalice. The handles, rim and stem are ornamented, but in contrast to the Ardagh chalice there is no enamel on the Derrynaflan chalice. It had become popular in the ninth century not to use coloured enamel on silver objects. The ornament on the rim is of gold filigree and amber, with gold on the stem.

METALWORK (ELEVENTH AND TWELFTH CENTURY)

Artistic production in Ireland declined considerably during the late eighth and ninth centuries, only the great stone crosses of the ninth and tenth centuries comparing with the preceding Golden Age. However, the eleventh and twelfth centuries saw a great revival in craftsmanship. In this period of peace between the end of the Vikings and the coming of the Normans, stoneworkers and metalworkers produced works of art equalling, if not outshining, the masterpieces of the earlier years.

Almost all the fine metalwork of this period is associated with the Church. They were mainly highly ornamented shrines or reliquaries connected with early Irish saints. Shrines like the Cross of Cong [2.22], the Book Shrine of the Cathach and Shrine of St Patrick's bell [2.23] were made to hold relics or objects associated with the saints, such as books or bells, while objects like the Shrine of St Lachtin's arm [2.24] may have been made to hold the bones of a saint.

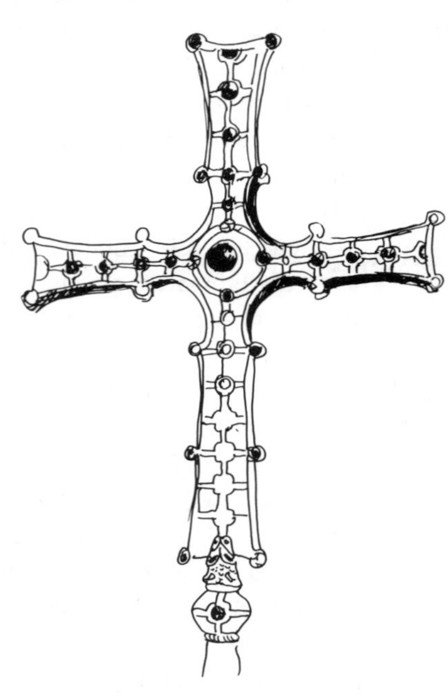

▲ *2.22 Cross of Cong*

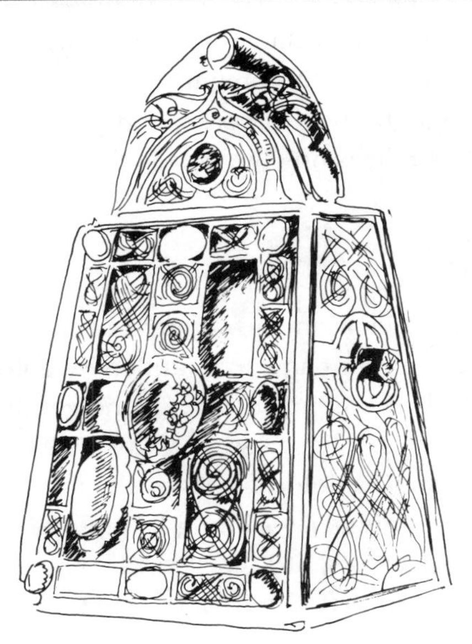

◀ 2.23 *Shrine of St Patrick's bell*

Great care was lavished on the creation and decoration of these sacred objects. In the Irish Christian Church croziers were held in great reverence and the Lismore crozier and the Clonmacnoise crozier [2.25], produced in Ireland, are the finest in Europe of this time.

One of the most notable features of the metalwork of this time is the blend of Scandinavian influences, seen particularly in the use of animal imagery, with native Irish work.

▲ 2.24 *Shrine of St Lactin's arm*

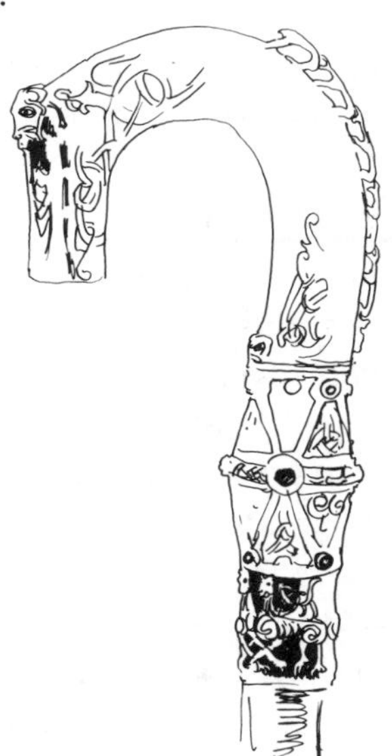

◀ 2.25 *Clonmacnoise crozier*

The scale and craftsmanship of the objects show that the arts were highly patronised by the rich and well-to-do clans and royalty of the time. Documentary evidence indicates that in 1122 Turlough O'Connor, King of Connaught, was in possession of a fragment of the true cross. The shrine made for this precious relic is now known as the Cross of Cong and is one of Ireland's most important shrines.

Cross of Cong (early twelfth century)

This magnificent processional cross was made to enshrine a fragment of the true cross which is protected by a crystal rock set in a silver mount and surrounded by gold filigree in the centre of the cross. A splendid tubular silver edging surrounds the gently curved outline of the cross punctuated by bossed rivets. The cross surface is divided into ornamented sections of cast bronze thread-like snakes holding animal shapes.

The staff and the cross are linked together by animal jaws biting the base of the cross. These animals have scaled heads, pointed ribbed snouts, little curved ears and blue glass eyes. Below these heads is an ornate knob similar to that found on the croziers.

Shrine of St Patrick's Bell (early twelfth century)

The Urnes style was named after a small Norwegian church. The term Urnes is used, however, to cover a wide variety of designs. Urnes ornament made its impression on Irish metalwork around 1100. The Shrine of St Patrick's bell, which was made for the safe-keeping of the iron bell of St Patrick, is one of the best examples of the style. The shrine has a tapering body and a curved top. The front is covered with a gilt silver frame in which there were originally 30 gold filigree panels. These contain a variety of intertwined, single or animal pairs forming regular figure eight shapes. A large rock crystal now occupies the centre space, but some of the other panels remain empty. On the back is a series of interlocking crosses pierced into a silver frame against a bronze background. The sides are decorated with panels of animal interlace separated by a circular cross. Rings on the sides of the shrine suggest that it was meant to be carried.

Shrine of St Lachtin's Arm (early twelfth century)

The shrine has a wooden centre and is covered with cast and engraved panels in the shape of an arm and hand with fingers bent over. This shrine was cast in one piece and the engraving of animal interlace was once inlaid with silver. In the palm of the hand is a triangular gilt silver plaque ornamented with spiralled plant decoration. Silver and niello (a compound of metal sulphides inlaid into silver to give a dark background against the light of the silver) and decorated bands of silver filigree form the base.

Clonmacnoise Crozier (early twelfth century)

The crozier was formed by two tubular lengths of bronze wrapped around a wooden staff finishing with a curved crook. The crook is hollow and cast in one piece with animal interlace in silver, edged with niello inlay down the sides. On the front of the crook is a grotesque bearded human head with staring eyes decorated with silver niello. Behind this human head is a crest running down the curve of the crook. The crest is formed by a series of dog-like animals, some of which have now broken off.

The base of the crook is formed front and back with grotesque animal heads in the Urnes style. Under the base is a band on which there are two pairs of cat-like animals who stand with arched backs and legs entertwined and decorated with silver and niello. The large clawed legs spring from a spiralled upper body and the tails twist to form an interlace pattern.

CARVED STONE CROSSES INCLUDING HIGH CROSSES (SIXTH–TWELFTH CENTURY)

In early Christian Ireland there was no great tradition of building or carving in stone. Standing stones were a feature of pre-Christian Ireland and the tradition continued into the first Christian symbols of the cross. The natural shape of the stone itself was not changed and the carving was applied only to the surface of the stone—perhaps this was because of an early fear which existed in pre-Christian Ireland of interfering with the 'spirit' of the stone. No exact dating can be made on the early cross-incribed pillars, a large number of which are found along the west coast or on islands, but the sites suggest an early dating. The crosses engraved on the pillars are of a wide variety, but a Greek cross in a circle is quite a common occurrence. A Greek cross is found on the reverse face of the Duvilluan slab, Co. Mayo [2.26], and a rare early representation of the crucifixion is engraved on the front. A Maltese cross is found on the Reask pillar, Co. Kerry [2.27]; this is supported by lines and spirals of Celtic decoration. An interesting combination of ogham, the very early form of script in Ireland, and imagery, in the form of a Greek cross, is found on the Aiglish pillar [2.28] in County Kerry. Large numbers of engraved grave slabs survive near important monasteries like Clonmacnoise, where a cross design is accompanied by a beautifully engraved inscription.

▲ *2.26 Duvillaun slab, Co. Mayo*

▲ *2.27 Reask pillar, Co. Kerry*

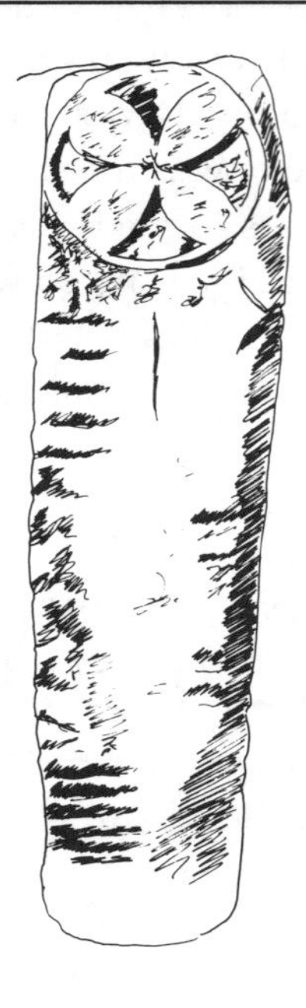

◀ *2.28 Aiglish pillar, Co. Kerry*

◀ *2.29 Cardonagh cross, Co. Donegal (seventh century)*
The Cardonagh cross is decorated all over with broad ribbon interlace edged with a double line similar to that found in the Book of Durrow. On one side this is combined with figures. This is the first cross to be cut in a cruciform shape.

2.30 Fahan Mura slab, Co. Donegal (seventh century) ▶

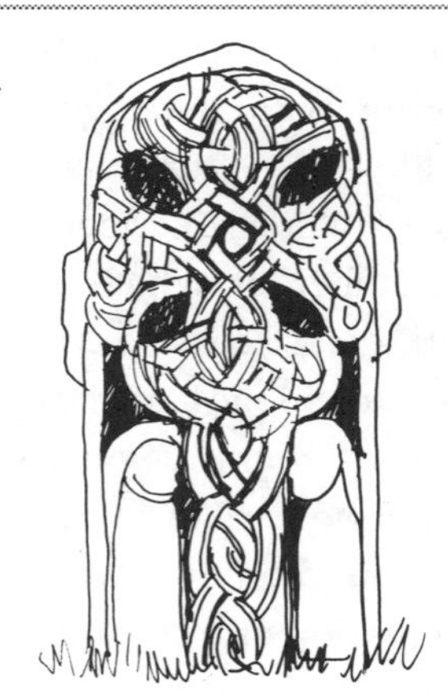

The first free standing cross appears to have been in Donegal. At Carndonagh, Co. Donegal [2.29], the idea of the Christian cross incribed on a pillar goes further and the cross itself is cut out of the stone. Near by the Fahan Mura slab [2.30] has little shoulders in the place of arms and bears the only early inscription in Greek in Ireland. Both crosses are carved with broad ribbon interlace similar to that in the Book of Durrow and are dated to the seventh century.

HIGH CROSSES

The first free standing ringed crosses appeared in the eighth century and were a completely new departure in Irish art. The best examples of the earliest group are found only a few miles apart in County Kilkenny and at Ahenny, Co. Tipperary [2.31]. The two highly ornamented crosses at Ahenny make no attempt at biblical or figurative scenes, and are decorated mainly in abstract ornament found in metalwork of the time.

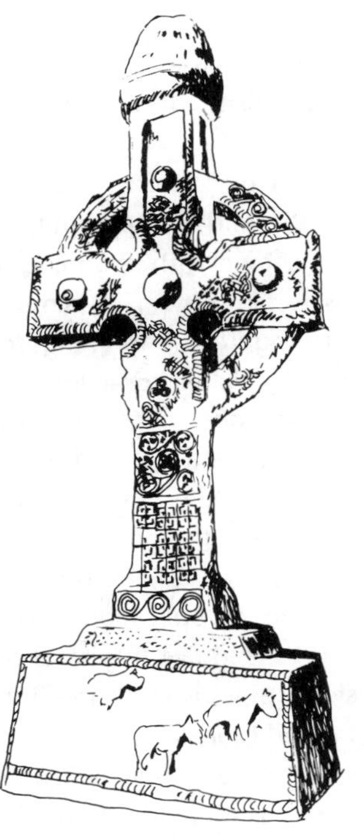

2.31 North cross at Ahenny (eighth century)

The north cross at Ahenny is one of a pair of famous crosses which stand in a graveyard in County Tipperary on a remote hillside. The crosses are quite short with a widely spaced ring and wide base. A large portion of the shaft is above the ring and the north cross retains an unusual conical-shaped cap. Both crosses are decorated with motifs seen in metalwork of the time. These include interlace, Celtic spirals and geometric patterns. The rounded bosses at the joints have no function in stone, but are similar to rivets found on metal which suggest that it might have been inspired by an object in metal. One of the most distinctive features of the crosses is the high relief rope moulding which runs around the edges of the ring and cross shapes.

Throughout the ninth and tenth centuries there were astonishing developments in stone carved crosses. The crosses became larger and more complex in structure, and the shafts were divided into orderly depictions of biblical scenes. The ring, which is the most distinctive feature of the crosses, circles the intersection of shaft and arms. The angles are softened by arcs in the cross itself, and in the arcs are little volutes or rolls. At the top of the cross is a cap which often takes the shape of a church. These ringed crosses have become one of the best-known symbols of early Christian Ireland.

Most of the crosses of the Scriptures, about 30 in all, are grouped together around the River Barrow near the cross of Moone [2.32] and Castledermot, but one of the best-preserved examples is at Monasterboice, Co. Louth, with Muiredach's cross [2.33], so called because of an inscription on the base.

Finally, a late group of crosses including the Dysart O Dea [2.34] appeared after a century or so of little or no stone carving. These late crosses show a completely different style, with the ringed wheel-head gone and a simple figure, usually of Christ or a bishop, in a strong and prominent position on the upper part.

2.32 Scriptural Cross of Moone, Co. Kildare (ninth century)

The tall and slender, tapering cross of Moone is one of the earliest to introduce biblical scenes. This elegant granite cross has a narrow ring and is missing its capstone. It is covered on four sides with figurative scenes from the Old and New Testaments which occupy only the base. These follow a logical order starting with the Fall of Man on the east side and continuing around. The Bible stories found on the high crosses are the stories which were popular in religious lessons at the end of the eighth century. These scenes are shown with charming simplicity and the cross is famous for its simple square and rectangular figures. A long figure of Daniel is surrounded by six fearsome lions who bite at his body in the lions' den. This scene and the intervention of the angel in the Sacrifice of Isaac by Abraham on the east face [a] show how God intervenes to save the good from destruction. In the same way the Flight of the Holy Family into Egypt and the Multiplication of Five Loaves and Two Fishes to feed five thousand people, on the south side [b], show divine intervention. A square-bodied Mary with turned out feet rides a reasonably life-like donkey; a head peeping from behind Mary's shoulder is Jesus; and Joseph, square bodied but with a beard and walking feet, leads the little group. The miracle of the loaves and fishes is reduced to five circles for the bread and two fishes and, added in on the side, two eels. On the west face the crucifixion scene occupies a triangular section above the base, while underneath are Christ's apostles standing in three neat rows of simple square-bodied little men with turned out toes and strange faces with staring eyes and big noses [c].

(a) East face (detail)
Daniel in the lions' den; The sacrifice of Abraham; Adam and Eve.

▲ *(b) South face (detail)*
Multiplication of the loaves and fishes; Flight into Egypt; Three children in a fiery furnace.

▲ *(c) West face (detail) The Twelve Apostles*

▲ *2.33 Muiredach's cross at Monasterboice, Co. Louth (early tenth century)*

The cross of Muiredach is a massive six metres tall. It is a most impressive achievement for its time. The west face is devoted to the crucifixion and scenes from Christ's life, the last panel showing a scene depicting the Arrest of Christ who wears a brooch similar to the Tara brooch to denote his royal status. At the base of this side, two cats carved in high relief sit in front of an inscription in Irish that invites us to pray for Muiredach under whose direction this cross was made [a]. The west face has scenes from the Old Testament, but the most impressive is the depiction of the Last Judgment which is spread all over the surface of the crosshead. The scene is extremely rich in detail. God sits in the centre with the souls of the good on his right turned to him, while David plays his harp. On God's left a devil with a three-pronged trident herds the souls of the damned whose faces are turned away. Below the feet of God is a scene showing Michael the Archangel with scales, weighing souls, with a devil waiting below. It is interesting that this was carved about two hundred years before scenes like this appeared on European Romanesque churches. The fine detail with which the figures on this cross were carved is evident from the carving under the arm of the cross which has suffered less from weathering than the faces of the cross [b]. All the carving is executed in bold rounded relief, and despite the number of figures and the amount of detail there is no sense of overcrowding in the well-ordered panels.

▲ *2.34 High cross at Dysart O Dea, Co. Clare*

EXAM QUESTIONS

1990 Ordinary level

2. Give an account of any work in stone or metal of the early Christian period (432–1170) and describe its decoration.

   or

   The Book of Kells is decorated with various types of ornament. Describe how the artists used human and animal forms to decorate the book.

1991 Ordinary level

2. Discuss how the human figure is shown in any of the carved panels on either the Cross of Moone or the Cross of Muiredach (tenth century).

1992 Ordinary level

2. (a) Write about any *one* page of a Christian manuscript.

   or

   (b) Write an account of an important piece of metalwork from the Christian period—a brooch, a chalice or a cross.

1993 Ordinary level

2. How does the apparently early Carndonagh cross differ from the later Cross of Moone?

   or

   Write as fully as you can about either cross. Use diagrams and sketches.

   or

   The Book of Kells is considered to be the greatest achievement of manuscript art of the Christian period. Describe the use of colour and the nature of the design on any *one* page of the book.

1994 Ordinary level

2. Write as fully as you can about the Ardagh chalice describing its design and ornamentation and the materials used. What do you think are its distinctive features?

1995 Ordinary level

1. Give an account of any stone High Cross which is decorated with figures. Describe its basic shape and carved decoration.

   or

   Discuss the techniques used, and the ornamentation of any important piece of metalwork from the Christian period. Use sketches to illustrate your points.

1990 Higher level

2. Discuss the treatment of a biblical scene in a manuscript book *or* on the surface of a High Cross of the early Christian period (A.D. 432–1170).

   or

   Describe, with reference to design and ornamentation, either the Cross of Cong (twelfth century) or St Patrick's Bell Shrine (twelfth century). How does the style of decoration you have described differ from that to be found on the metalwork of an earlier phase of Christian art?

1991 Higher level

Give an account of the architecture of the Early Christian period in Ireland, referring in your answer to the structure and function of early architectural forms such as beehive huts, oratories and round towers.

or

The carved panels on the high crosses of the ninth and tenth centuries could be regarded as a form of visual religious instruction. Discuss this statement with reference to the carvings on *one* or *two* crosses of the period.

1992 Higher level

2. Give an account of the development of stone sculpture from the early cross-inscribed stone slabs to the high crosses of the ninth and tenth centuries.

   or

   Describe and discuss (a) the Book of Durrow or (b) the Book of Kells, making reference in your answer to use of colour, script and the nature of the decoration on either of these illuminated manuscripts.

1993 Higher level

2. The monasteries of the Early Christian era in Ireland were important centres of artistic activity. Discuss this statement with reference to specific examples of stonework and metalwork from this period.

1994 Higher level

2. Trace the development of Irish illuminated manuscripts from the Cathach (sixth century) to the Book of Kells (eighth century), referring in your answer to examples of decoration from the manuscripts you describe.

   or

   Give an account of any metalwork shrine of the early Christian period.

1995 Higher level

2. Trace the development of metalwork in Ireland from pre-Christian times to the end of the early Christian period. Refer in your answer to the purpose of the metal objects, the materials from which they were made and the manner of their decoration.

   or

   Discuss the treatment of the human form on the High Crosses of the early Christian period; mention specific examples in your answer.

CHAPTER THREE

Eighteenth-Century Georgian Ireland

Plantations, rebellion and war dominated the seventeenth century in Ireland. Because of this, building in Ireland took the form of fortified castles rather than elegant mansions which were found in England and elsewhere in Europe.

The period after the Battle of the Boyne (1690) was, however, a period of relative tranquillity. The old Irish aristocracy who had supported James II were defeated and fled to France, never to return. The victorious William III, determined to end all future rebellions, reduced the native Catholic population to a position from which they could not revolt. The penal laws were then enacted which prevented any Catholic from rising to a position of power or from holding public office. These laws put the few converted Irish and the English settlers into a privileged position and soon led to a prosperous Protestant landed gentry who were very anxious to display signs of their wealth and power. In the period of peace which was to last nearly ninety years fashionable houses and public buildings sprang up in town and country alike which were some of the most beautiful and elaborate the country had ever seen.

This was a wonderful time for the arts of decoration and architecture in Ireland. Architects and all kinds of craftsmen were brought from the continent of Europe. European influences, particularly from Italy, began to show in the new buildings. The builders and craft workers were themselves Irish, but the style was Italian.

Andrea Palladio was an Italian sixteenth-century architect. He had studied classical remains and had published a book on his findings. This and other books on ancient Rome became the source of inspiration for a style of architecture which became very fashionable in England. Palladianism spread to Ireland in the early eighteenth century, making its first appearance in large country houses.

Palladian Period (1700–1760)

Irish Country Houses or Great Houses

In the first half of the eighteenth century an enormous number of great houses were built around the Irish countryside. The following are a sample of the major ones.

Castletown, Co. Kildare (1720s) designed by several architects including Edward Lovett Pearce. Also designed by the same architect: Bellamont Forest, Co. Cavan.
Russborough House, Co. Wicklow (1741) designed by Richard Castle (Casells). Also designed by Richard Castle: Carton, Co. Kildare and Westport House, Co. Mayo.

PUBLIC BUILDINGS

Parliament House (Bank of Ireland) 1729 designed by Edward Lovett Pearce
Trinity College Dublin (1752–1791)
Provost's house designed by John Smith
Chapel & Examination Hall designed by William Chambers
Dining hall designed by Richard Castle

NEOCLASSICAL PERIOD (LATE EIGHTEENTH CENTURY)

Charlemont House 1767 (Municipal Gallery of Art) designed by William Chambers
Casino, Marino (1758) designed by William Chambers
Custom House (1781) designed by James Gandon
The Four Courts (1786) designed by James Gandon
Portico, Parliament House (1785) designed by James Gandon

ARCHITECTS OF THE EIGHTEENTH CENTURY

Edward Lovett Pearce (1699–1733)
Richard Cassells (1729–1751)
William Chambers (1723–1796)
James Gandon (1743–1823)

IRISH GEORGIAN COUNTRY HOUSES

Eighteenth-century architecture in Ireland and England went through two periods. The first up to 1760 was associated with the Palladian style. In the latter half of the century the style changed to a Neoclassical style. Russborough, Carton and Castletown houses are outstanding examples of Irish Palladian mansions.

CASTLETOWN HOUSE, CO. KILDARE (1722)

Castletown [3.1] is a large and palatial mansion situated in a huge demesne outside Celbridge, Co. Kildare. It was the first and is still the grandest of Ireland's Palladian country houses. It has been described as 'the finest house Ireland ever saw'. It was designed by several architects including Sir Edward Lovett Pearce, who was the foremost architect of the time, for William Conolly, the Speaker of the Irish House of Commons.

Edward Lovett Pearce had travelled in Italy and had seen the work of Andrea Palladio. It was Pearce who added the Palladian Ionic colonnaded curtained walls with twin pavilions to each end of the central block of Castletown House. This was the first Palladian scheme in the country and was to be a source of inspiration to many other houses. Speaker Conolly died in 1729 and the house remained unfinished for many years.

▲ *3.1 Castletown House, Co. Kildare*

Inside, the entrance hall [3.2], designed by Edward Lovett Pearce, has two storeys and a black and white chequered floor. Ionic columns, the same as those on the outside, surround the lower floor. The ceiling is coved and decorated with baskets of fruit and flowers in carved wood.

The stairs are cantilevered and made of Portland stone. The walls are decorated with swirling stucco (plasterwork) of Chinese dragons, shells, flowers and masks by the Francini brothers, Paul and Philip, from Italy.

▲ *3.2 Entrance hall, Castletown*

The Long Gallery [3.3] is a magnificent room. It is almost 24 m by 7 m. Small wall paintings grace the blue walls, and over the two large doors a large semicircular painting depicts Aurora, the goddess of dawn. In the niche between the doors stands a statue of Diana. Classic patterns in plasterwork decorate the overdoors. The ceiling is of an early style, heavily ornate and divided into large compartments. The three original glass chandeliers in blue and pink glass which were made to order in Venice still hang. Four large sheets of mirrored glass which came from France hang on the walls, but the exquisite furniture which once graced the room when it was a living-room in the 1770s has long disappeared. An amount of restoration has been done to this and other rooms in Castletown by the Irish Georgian Society.

▲ *3.3 The long gallery, Castletown*

RUSSBOROUGH HOUSE, CO. WICKLOW (1741)

Russborough [3.4] is the best preserved of Ireland's country houses. The building began in 1741 and took about ten years to complete. The architect was a German, Richard Cassells, who later changed his name to Castle. He became associated with Sir Edward Lovett Pearce and virtually took over his practice when Pearce died in 1733. The house is built in the Palladian style, with central block and pavilions linked by curved Doric colonnades. The main block has a façade of six bays including a portico which does not protrude or reach roof level. Four Corinthian columns support the pediment.

Russborough stands on an embankment, with a large pond and man-made terraces behind and facing a splendid view of water and mountains. It is built of granite from a nearby quarry which shines because of the mica content, especially after rain.

On the inside all the rooms on the ground floor are 6 m in height. The ceilings are coved (curved where wall and ceiling join) which brings the cornice and the frieze down about 1 m and so softens the great height.

The Francini brothers from Italy are presumed to be responsible for the stucco work in the saloon, library and music room. Other important features of the house are the mantelpieces and the floors, some of which are mahogany with satinwood inlay.

The house is home to the fine collection of paintings of Sir Alfred Beit with masterpieces from Holland, Spain, England and Italy on view to the public.

▲ *3.4 Russborough House, Co. Wicklow*

Georgian Town Houses

Towns in the south of Ireland changed considerably with developments during the eighteenth century. In Dublin and Cork the newly appointed Wide Streets Commission (which was Europe's first official planning authority) cleared and straightened many streets. Town planning was particularly strong in the eighteenth century in England, and Ireland followed suit. Large towns including Dublin saw the development of churches, schools, hospitals and market houses. Later in the century the spacious and elegant red bricked squares and streets appeared as a result of private developments. Landowners teamed up with speculators. For example, Lord Fitzwilliam of Merrion released his lands and Merrion Square was developed. Many of these streets still bear the names of families like Fitzwilliam and Mountjoy in Dublin and Pery in Limerick. Large towns in Ireland often have a square of Georgian houses or a tree-lined Georgian street running down the centre.

During the eighteenth century the Irish Parliament sat in Dublin and prosperity increased. Dublin became a fashionable and elegant city. After the Act of Union in 1800 when the Irish Parliament was abolished, much of the wealth was transferred to London and Dublin went into a decline. However, because of the lack of industrial or commercial development, which was of course one of the reasons for the grinding poverty of nineteenth-century working-class Dublin, the heart of the city retained its tall and elegant red bricked streets and squares, although some were used as tenement houses and fell badly into disrepair. The character of Dublin city centre, however, is still essentially Georgian and elegant.

Originally privately owned, town houses are now better known as public buildings. These great town houses were, like the public buildings, built of stone. The Earl of Kildare commissioned Richard Castle to build his town house on the southern, unfashionable side of the river. As a result the northside became unfashionable and most of the houses became tenements. Kildare House is now Leinster House.

Charlemont House was the last of the great town houses inhabited by its original owners. In 1933 it was formally opened as the Municipal Gallery of Modern Art.

▲ *3.5 Georgian terraced houses, Dublin*

Dublin's terraced houses [3.5] present a uniformly austere façade. Rows of plain red bricked houses are broken only by the variation in doorways [3.6], different fanlights over the doors and patterns on the first-floor balconies. The reasons for this are more than just fashion. One of the powers of the Wide Streets Commission was to impose uniformity on buildings, and eighteenth-century town planners liked uniformity. Also, Planning Acts at

▲ *3.6 Georgian doors in Dublin*

the end of the sixteenth century had decreed that town buildings be of brick because of the danger of fire with wood. Fire precautions also decreed that the front wall of the house should extend 18 inches above the eaves of the roof and form a parapet, to prevent sparks from setting fire to the roof.

Most of the houses were built with English brick brought over in ships to the port as ballast, although on some the first floor was faced in granite.

Inside the plain façades, Georgian houses vary considerably depending on the wealth of the owner. Ely House, Ely Square, has a large plain exterior, but inside there is a remarkable stairway, the balustrade of which is decorated with animals and ends with a life-sized figure of Hercules.

The typical Georgian interior has a fanlight over the door lighting the hallway which leads the entrant straight to the stairs and to the reception rooms on the first floor. The hall is paved in stone, often in black and white squares. The front and back drawing-rooms are on the first floor. Doors to the main rooms are surmounted by sometimes ornate and very elaborate plaster overdoors. Each room has a cornice, usually about a foot deep, with a plain or decorated frieze running all around. Drawing-room ceilings are usually more ornate than those in dining-rooms, but the richness of the stucco work and decoration in general depended on the wealth of the owner. Terraced houses tended to be built in threes. An owner would build one house for himself and let the other two. The houses for letting tended to be smaller and have plainer interiors. Many of these houses are on view to the public in that they have become offices, and some are museums.

PUBLIC BUILDINGS

TRINITY COLLEGE, DUBLIN

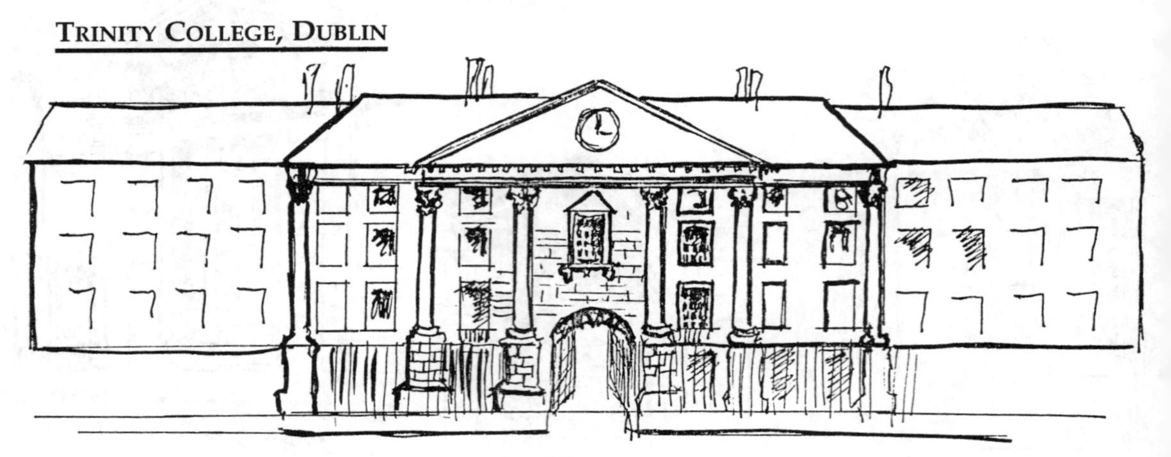

▲ *3.7 Trinity College, Dublin*

The Palladian period in Dublin produced many fine public buildings. The Houses of Parliament [3.8] (now the Bank of Ireland) and Trinity College Dublin [3.7] are two fine examples. Queen Elizabeth I established the College of the Holy and Undivided Trinity near Dublin, and over the years the city grew around it. Most of Trinity College's public buildings are essentially eighteenth century in layout and atmosphere. The west front and Parliament Square were built between 1752 and 1760. The main façade is of granite block with Portland stone columns resting on granite blockwork plinths. The west front or Parliament Square façade has a portico with six columns in the classical Corinthian style. Inside the main gate is a fine classical square with green lawns, trees and cobblestones. On either side of the green are the Chapel and the Public Theatre designed by one of the foremost architects of the later Georgian period, William Chambers. Both these buildings have fine examples of neoclassical plasterwork by one of Dublin's foremost stuccodores, Michael Stapleton. Richard Castle was responsible for the design of the dining-hall next

▲ *3.8 Bank of Ireland, former Parliament House, Dublin*

to the chapel, which was completed in 1791, some forty years after his death. Still used for its original purpose, the Provost of Trinity College lives in one of Dublin's grandest Georgian houses.

PARLIAMENT HOUSE (BANK OF IRELAND)

Facing Trinity College in College Green is the semicircular façade of one of Dublin's finest and best-known landmarks. Many well-known architects had a hand in its design, but Parliament House [3.8] was begun by Edward Lovett Pearce. It was the earliest large-scale Palladian public building in Britain or Ireland, but Pearce unfortunately did not live to see his most important work completed as he died in 1733 at the age of 34. The splendid piazza forecourt is surrounded on three sides by Ionic colonnades. Like other large public buildings of the time, it is built of limestone from Portland in Devon.

Apart from the piazza forecourt the most spectacular of Pearce's designs is the House of Lords. This design remains and can be seen today looking much the same as it did in the eighteenth century. Large tapestries on either side of the room represent *The Glorious Battle of the Boyne* and the *Siege of Derry*. A great Waterford crystal chandelier hanging from the ceiling was made with over 1,000 pieces of glass. The original fireplace of carved oak still stands. William Gandon designed a separate entrance to the House of Lords in the latter half of the century and linked it to Pearce's colonnaded forecourt with a curved screen wall. Later, when the bank took over the building, a similar wall was built on the west side and at the same time matching pilasters were added to Gandon's screen wall to balance the whole effect.

STUCCO (PLASTERWORK)

STUCCODORES

1st half of the eighteenth century
Freehand workers before moulding

LA FRANCINI BROTHERS, PAUL AND PHILIP

From Italy, came to Ireland to work on:
Carton House, Co. Kildare;
Castletown House, Co. Kildare;
Russborough House, Co. Wicklow;
Riverstown House, Co. Cork (copies of the plasterwork from the walls and ceilings at Árus an Uachtaráin).

ROBERT WEST IRELAND'S MOST DISTINGUISHED STUCCODORE

No. 20 Dominick St, Dublin, built for himself. High relief of birds, fruit, girls and musical instruments.

LATER HALF OF THE EIGHTEENTH CENTURY

The Adams brothers, Robert and James, from England, produced low relief moulded plasterwork. Mechanically reproduced in Ireland by skilled stuccodores such as:

MICHAEL STAPLETON/ARCHITECT/MASTER PLASTERER WHO PRODUCED:

Lucan House (Italian Embassy) with blue and white delicate plasterwork;
Trinity College examination hall and chapel;
Belvedere House richly coloured, low relief plasterwork.

PLASTERWORK

Plasterwork called 'stucco' work after the Italian word 'stuccodore' meaning plasterer, was very popular in fine Irish houses, in town and country alike. Some very fine eighteeenth-century plasterwork is to be found in Irish Georgian houses, some of the finest being in Dublin's terraced houses which can often be glimpsed at night when office lights show what were once upstairs drawing-rooms. Styles in plasterwork changed considerably in the period 1725 to 1800.

The earliest style around 1725, called the *compartmented* style involved the division of the ceiling into ornamented geometric shapes. The word ceiling comes from the use of plaster to 'seal' or 'ceil' along roof beams to keep out draughts.

Around 1740–1760 the Francini brothers introduced the human figure into plasterwork. Most of this type of work is plain white with high relief figures, flowers and garlands. They worked in the Rococo manner, a style associated with swirling ornament. Baroque and later Rococo were styles fashionable in most of Europe during the eighteenth century.

Robert West was an Irish stuccodore, working in the Rococo manner, who produced some of the finest plasterwork in Dublin. He is best known for his superb plaster free standing birds.

From 1780 to 1800 the Neoclassical style made much use of moulds to produce low relief, delicate but somewhat repetitive work in the Adam style. Robert Adam was an English architect and furniture designer who developed a style popular in the 1760s in Britain. The Adam style did, however, require skilled craftsmen and Michael Stapleton, who inherited Robert West's practice, is most associated with its development in Ireland. A master plasterer and architect, he is responsible for some very sophisticated delicate work in this style. He used moulds but also some freehand work. This kind of plasterwork looks very well picked out in colour.

FRANCINI BROTHERS AND STUCCO IN IRISH COUNTRY HOUSES

Paul and Philip Francini, stuccodores, were brought to Ireland in 1738 by the Earl of Kildare. For him they executed the great saloon ceiling in the Baroque style at Carton House, Co. Kildare, depicting the courtship of the gods which is the finest of its kind in the country. Their example was to influence profoundly the existing school of Irish stuccodores, whose magnificent work is to be found on staircases and ceilings of many Dublin houses. Work frequently attributed to 'the Italians' is more than likely the work of one of their many Irish followers. Superb examples of Lafrancini work is to be found also at Castletown, Russborough and Riverstown houses.

CASTLETOWN HOUSE, CO. KILDARE

A cantilevered Portland stone staircase was built at Castletown in 1760 under the direction of Simon Vierpyl. The walls are decorated in an exuberant Rococo manner by the Lafrancini. Shells, garlands of flowers, Chinese dragons and masks are included in the decoration. A large picture of a boar hunt is framed by plasterwork using garlands, fruit and little putti.

RUSSBOROUGH HOUSE, CO. WICKLOW

Russborough has some of the finest plasterwork in Ireland. Records of the work on the house were destroyed during the destruction of the Four Courts during the Civil War, but it can almost certainly be assumed that the plasterwork on the ceilings of the saloon, library and music room is the work of the Francini brothers. The saloon ceiling in true Rococo manner has garlands of flowers and little putti. The library also reflects the ornamentation of their work of the period. Although some has broken off over the years, there is still superb plasterwork on the ceiling over the stairway.

RIVERSTOWN HOUSE, CO. CORK

Riverstown House was the seat of Dr Jemmett Brown, Bishop of Cork, who rebuilt it in 1745.
Francini room: The meaning in some of the images in plasterwork by the Francini brothers at Riverstown is not all that clear. It has however been explained as personifications of subjects such as Liberty [3.9], a figure in classical drapery, who inverts a pot over an urn from which a plant is growing.

Over the mantel the figure of Marcus Curtius [3.10], an unarmed soldier with flying cloak and mounted on a horse which rears towards flames and smoke, personifies Heroic Virtue. Images representing other classical virtues cover the walls of this magnificent dining-room, but its crowning glory is the ceiling [3.11] which represents Time rescuing Truth from the assaults of Discord and Envy. This is a translation into plaster of a painted ceiling by Nicholas Poussin now in the Louvre. The vigorous and aged

▲ *3.9 Liberty, Lafrancini plasterwork from Riverstown House, Co. Cork*

◀ *3.10 'Marcus Curtius', Lafrancini plasterwork from Riverstown House, Co. Cork*

▲ *3.11 Lafrancini ceiling from Riverstown House, Co. Cork*

winged figure of Time carries the beautifully modelled form of Truth away towards the clouds from Discord, who is armed with a dagger and flaming torch, and Envy who is entwined with snakes. Above, a winged boy displays a sickle and circle, symbols of Time and Immortality. Copies of this plasterwork were taken for the President of Ireland at Áras an Uachtaráin, Dublin, in 1948.

Robert West

The principal Irish stuccodore of the early eighteenth century was Robert West. One of the best examples of his work is No. 20 Dominick St, Dublin, which he built for himself. Inside the plain brick fronted façade of this terraced house is a riot of extraordinarily rich and imaginative Rococo plasterwork. On the stairs [3.12] up to the reception rooms are the almost three-dimensional birds for which he is famous, free standing, with wings outstretched on asymmetrical perches, over 40 cm from the wall surface. At each corner of the ceiling above are pairs of girls whose heads and shoulders emerge from cone-shaped pockets surrounded by swirling lines, clusters of fruit and musical instruments.

▲ *3.12 Plasterwork by Robert West in 20 Lower Dominick St, Dublin*

MICHAEL STAPLETON

Works by Michael Stapleton, the late eighteenth-century architect, are to be found in many Dublin buildings including Trinity College and Lucan House, now the Italian Embassy. A feature of his work are delicately modelled plaster medallions surrounded by lace-like geometric patterns. Michael Stapleton's work is seen at its imaginative best in the splendid plasterwork of Belvedere House. The walls and ceilings of this house are covered with a rich display of coloured plasterwork. The ceilings show a remarkable variety of intricate decoration. Colour dominates the stairs. The ceiling is blue with white lacework and modelled centrepieces. The walls are yellow with pale green inset panels. The lacework and figures in the medallions are white, but the frieze and medallion backgrounds are russet. In spite of all this colour and pattern the effect is still one of elegance and taste.

NEOCLASSICISM

Palladianism quite suddenly went out of fashion in England. In addition to engravings of old Rome now in circulation, architects gained inspiration from travelling in Italy. Young gentlemen visited Rome as part of the 'grand tour' which often lasted several years. Architects were now less inclined to rely on Palladio's interpretation of Roman buildings. A book called *Antiquities of Athens* was published in England full of drawings and reconstructions of Greek buildings. This book showed the ancient world to be rich and varied and less bound by rules than that suggested by Palladio. The Neoclassical movement followed the publication of this book. The change was gradual in Ireland, with some architects still following the Palladian guidelines.

Richard Castle died in 1751 and after his death no other architect dominated the building style in Dublin. The character of Dublin, with its graceful red bricked streets and squares, owes more to its rich and influential families than it did to any architect's influence.

John Smyth who designed the Provost's house at Trinity College kept Palladianism alive for some time. He looked directly to the work of Palladio in Italy for his inspiration. Other architects did not, however, adhere so strictly to this tradition.

BLUE COAT SCHOOL, DUBLIN

Thomas Ivory designed the Blue Coat School in Dublin [3.13]. Originally King's Hospital, the school has now moved to Palmerstown. The old building has been aquired by the Incorporated Law Society and is in the process of restoration. The building has quite a different spirit from that of Palladianism. The three buildings are separate although joined by a wall. The same rusticated stonework and round headed windows are common to all, but the main building and wings contain new and unfamiliar details, for example, blank niches on the main floor and windows without mouldings. This complements the essential Palladian quality of the main building with its Ionic columns and pediment. As

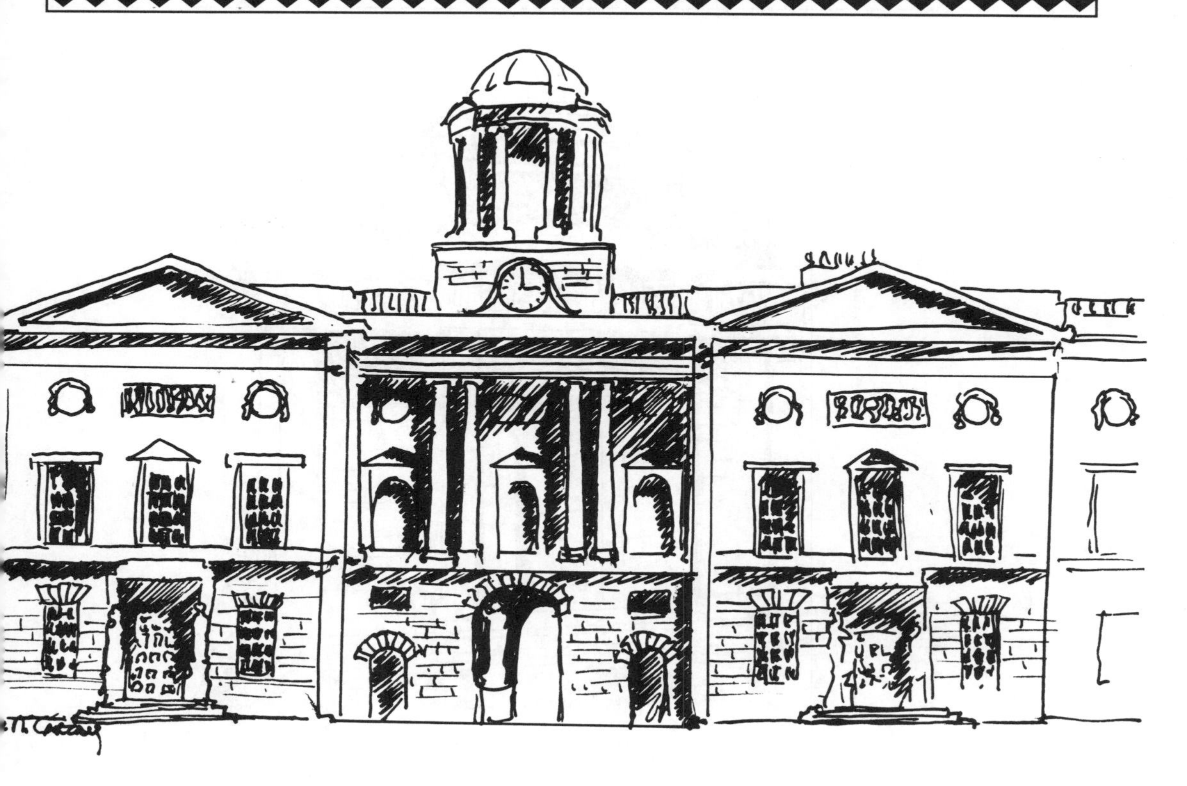

▲ *3.13 Blue Coat School, Dublin*

a result the building as a whole is more monumental and at the same time more decorative than others of an earlier period.

The details on this school herald the onset of the new style. James Caulfeild, was a young Irishman who spent many years in Italy. Considered to have been one of the most enlightened and cultivated men of his day, Lord Charlemont absorbed much of the classical influence during his travels and befriended many young architects, painters and stuccodores. Charlemont commissioned the most prominent London architect of the day, Sir William Chambers, to design both his town house and country house. The town house is now the Municipal Gallery of Art. His country house perished in a fire, but the villa designed in the grounds remains at Marino in Dublin.

THE CASINO AT MARINO

The Casino [3.14] was built in the 1760s and is a unique creation of architectural skill. The building itself had probably very little function and was certainly very expensive to create. However, it is a gem of architectural design. From the outside it appears to be a Greek temple design with one storey, but in fact the inside is cleverly constructed to hold three storeys and a basement. In plan it consists of a Greek cross inscribed in a Doric colonnade. The second storey is cleverly camouflaged behind the large door, of which

3.14 *Casino at Marino, Dublin* ▶

only half opens. The windows of curved glass are designed to reflect the exterior and hide the internal walls which run across them. On the roof the Grecian funerary urns function as chimneys and the columns are hollow to allow rain to run down and collect in tanks as a supply for the house. On the exterior, lions guard the four corners.

The interiors are masterpieces of design. All the rooms are very small but proportioned to avoid any sense of crowding. Ceilings are beautifully ornate with plasterwork by Cipriani. Magnificent parquet floors, using exotic woods patterned and geometric in design, cover the hall and main reception room which faces towards the sea.

William Chambers never actually visited Ireland and so the work on the Casino was carried out by Simon Vierpyl, who was responsible for the carvings on the exterior and overseeing the building. The design of the funerary urns on the parapet were used again in the work of James Gandon who was at that time assistant to Simon Vierpyl, but who was later to make his own mark in Dublin.

CUSTOM HOUSE, DUBLIN

The English architect James Gandon (1743–1823) was born in London and trained in the office of William Chambers. In 1781 he was summoned to Dublin to build a new Custom House [3.15]. The site was nearly a mile closer to the mouth of the river and the ground was at that time quite marshy. For that reason the building proved complicated and expensive.

▲ *3.15 Custom House, Dublin, by James Gandon*

The long south façade faces the river in a continuous line broken only by its protruding central and end bays. It is this that gives the building its strength and character. The columns on the central and end bays are both free standing and recessed to add further variety. A dome on top of the central bay is similar to one designed by Sir Christopher Wren in Greenwich, London. On the Custom House it is supported by a columned drum and could in fact be considered too dominant for the building.

Most of the carving on this building is by Edward Smyth. On the skyline are funerary urns similar to those found at the Casino. The royal arms grace the four corners while on the pediment are the figures of Hibernia and Britannia embracing. But the most popular and best-known carvings from the Custom House are the riverine heads set in the keystones above the doors and windows on the ground floor. These represent fourteen of the main rivers of Ireland. The keystone over the main door facing the river represents the Liffey and is the only female figure of the series [3.16].

The Custom House was burned by Republican forces in 1921, and rebuilt. The stone used on parts of the building is native Irish limestone and is slighty darker than the original limestone from Portland in Devon. The building is crowned by an enormous statue of Commerce by Edward Smyth which stands on top of the dome overlooking the river and Dublin.

James Gandon remained in Ireland to design among other buildings the Four Courts. This was his second great building on the north bank of the Liffey. This great granite building was also the victim of damage, this time during the Civil War in

▲ *3.16 Keystone representing 'The Liffey' from the Custom House*

Ireland. It was burned by Free State troops in 1922. It was rebuilt, its original façade restored, but the interior is lost forever and its beauty can only now be appreciated from Gandon's original drawings.

James Gandon is also responsible for the portico which was added to the separate entrance to the House of Lords on Edward Lovett Pearce's Parliament House. The portico with Corinthian-style columns was linked to the main front of Parliament House by a curved screen wall, plain except for niches.

Later, when Parliament House was expanded to the west, a second screen wall was added to match that of Gandon's. The present Bank of Ireland was designed over many years by different people, but it is still a monument to good taste and is one of Dublin's finest landmarks.

EXAM QUESTIONS

1990 Ordinary level

Describe and discuss any major public building of the Georgian period referring to its structure and decoration. Illustrate.

1991 Ordinary level

3. Give a detailed account of one of the following:
   (i) The Custom House, Dublin. (Gandon)
   (ii) The Casino at Marino, Dublin. (W. Chambers)
   (iii) A typical terrace of Georgian houses.

1992 Ordinary level

3. Give an account of any public building *or* dwelling house of the Georgian period from any part of Ireland. Identify in your answer the features which are characteristic of the period.

1993 Ordinary level

2. Describe the façade (front wall) of a terraced town house of the Georgian period referring in your answer to the detail of its doorway and windows and its decorative features.

1994 Ordinary level

3. Describe the interior of a building of the Georgian period referring in your answer to the design and location of the plasterwork (stucco) and to any other characteristic Georgian features.

1995 Ordinary level

Describe any important House of the Georgian period and discuss its ornamentation and its decorative features. Use sketches to illustrate your points.

1990 Higher level

3. Write as fully as you can on *one* of the following:
   Castletown House, Co. Kildare (eighteenth century); Bank of Ireland, College Green, Dublin (eighteenth century).

1991 Higher level

3. The use of classical elements was a distinguishing feature of Georgian architecture. Describe a major Georgian building with which you are familiar and indicate the classical elements used in its construction.

1992 Higher level

3. Describe the interior design, the decoration and the furnishings of any great house or a terraced town house of the Georgian period.

1993 Higher level

3. Describe an important Irish building by *one* of the following architects:
   (1) William Chambers (1723–96)
   (2) Richard Castle (Cassels) (*c.*1690–1751)
   (3) Thomas Ivory (*c.*1732–86)
   (4) James Gandon (1743–1823).

1994 Higher level

3. The eighteenth century, a time of peace and prosperity in Ireland, has left a legacy of fine domestic architecture. Discuss this statement with reference to a great house *or* a street/square of terraced town houses of the Georgian period.

1995 Higher level

3. 'No element of interior decoration more vividly expresses the wealth, gaiety and vitality of the Georgian period than the exquisite plasterwork which adorns so many of the houses.' (Kevin Corrigan Kearns) Explain, with reference to at least *one* example, how plasterwork was used in the decoration of Georgian houses.

CHAPTER FOUR

Nineteenth and Twentieth-Century Irish Artists

Nathaniel Hone (1831–1917)
Walter Osborne (1859–1903)
Roderic O'Conor (1860–1940)
William Orpen (1878–1931)
William Leech (1881–1968)
Jack B. Yeats (1871–1957)
Mary Swanzy (1882–1978)
Mainie Jellett (1896–1943)

Stained Glass
Harry Clark (1890–1931)

Painting in Ireland (late 19th–early 20th Century)

It was common for Irish painters to go to art schools in England during the late eighteenth and early nineteenth centuries. However, in the late nineteenth century and early twentieth century this practice became rare. The only two major painters to do so were John Butler Yeats the elder and William Orpen. It was at this time that Irish art enjoyed a period of immense enrichment. There was a mood of development and growth and it became much more common for Irish painters to bypass England and complete their training abroad. On the continent, particularly in France, young Irish students were to come under the influence of leading artists and movements of the time.

Nathaniel Hone first went to Paris in 1853 and remained there for many years. When he returned to Ireland in 1872 many young painters followed his example and went to study in Paris, Antwerp and Brittany. This trend continued for many years and by the end of the century there was an established pattern of travelling to Paris. Many of Ireland's best-known artists went there to study. Some attended the official École des Beaux Arts but most attended private studios or *ateliers*.

The real education for Irish students began when they went to the countryside. During the summer they left the cities and joined groups of artist colonies painting out of doors. In the village of Barbizon in the forest of Fontainbleu, and in Brittany at Concarneau and Quimperlé, Irish artists met with many other nationalities to 'paint from nature' which was the great passion of young artists of the day. Mingling with Americans, English and Scandinavian as well as French these young students from Ireland were part of a wide and influential movement and were no longer an isolated group.

Painting in the sunshine of France with the colour and brightness of Brittany, the work of the Irish artists was transformed by the use of colour. Many of these paintings are small in scale and are of humble subjects such as woodlands, farmyards, market places and harbour scenes, but have a strong feeling of intimacy. The village people of Brittany in their distinctive costumes were a favourite theme and most of the Irish painters delighted in portraying old people, young girls in white bonnets and children in colourful caps and aprons to add richness to the landscape of the area.

Some Irish artists visited France and left; others remained, settling in a particular colony where they worked for years. There were many trends in painting in France at the time and the work of the Irish students was varied, reflecting this. There was still the Academic tradition, the naturalistic landscape of the Barbizon school, *plein air*-ism, Realism and Impressionism. Irish artists tended to work first in a realistic manner, but later artists such as Osborne, O'Conor and Leech produced some splendid work in the Impressionist style.

NATHANIEL HONE (1831–1917)

Nathaniel Hone was a member of an artistic family and grand-nephew of the eighteenth-century painter of the same name. He trained as an engineer but gave this up to study art in Paris.

Most of his later paintings are landscapes, very often enlivened with animals and occasionally with figures. In France he was influenced by the painter Gustav Courbet who was taking a new and quite revolutionary direction into Realism. His closest links were, however, with another French artist, Camille Corot. Hone became a close friend of one of Corot's followers at the Barbizon school of landscape painting. At Barbizon he learned to appreciate colour and tone in the landscape and apply it in strong and confident brushwork to the painting of Irish subjects on his return.

Hone's paintings completed in France are similar to those he worked on when he returned to his farm in County Dublin, but the finish is perhaps more polished in these later Irish works. One of his finest pieces is *Pastures at Malahide* [4.1]. Cows in the foreground of the painting sit quietly grazing against a low horizon. This allows for a large amount of space to be given to the rich sky full of white clouds. The atmosphere is one of peace and tranquillity, but typically Irish with a feeling of impending rain.

▲ *4.1 Pastures at Malahide (Nathaniel Hone) National Gallery of Ireland, Dublin*

WALTER OSBORNE (1859–1903)

Because of his death at a young age Walter Osborne has been somewhat overlooked everywhere outside of Ireland. The unfortunate result is that he is seen only as a painter in the Irish context.

The son of a Dublin painter in whose studio he spent some time, he won a scholarship to study in Antwerp. On completion of his studies he went with some friends to Brittany which had become very popular with artists who were attracted by the native costumes, customs and picturesque landscape. Here he made contacts with other artists and absorbed all kinds of influences. *Apple gathering Quimperlé* [4.2] is one of his best-known paintings. It is painted in lush silvery greens with Osborne's natural sympathy for children seen in the two children, in their rough aprons and white bonnets, who are typical of the models he chose for his painting of the time.

Returning from France he spent some time in England where under the influence of French *plein air* painting (painting in the open air) he worked in small rural communities.

Although exhibiting regularly in Liverpool and Birmingham, Osborne continued to exhibit in the Royal Academy in Dublin and gradually began to change his schedule to work more often in Ireland. He found his subjects in the streets of Dublin and in the towns north of the county. He returned to Ireland as much for family commitments as for any

▲ 4.2 *Apple Gathering Quimperlé (Walter Osborne) National Gallery of Ireland, Dublin*
In this early painting the landscape is confidently handled but the figures still retain a certain awkwardness. In the background the rooftops of the town and the church spire are painted in subtle shades of grey.

other reason. His parents were quite elderly and not in full health. His sister Violet had married and gone to Canada where a year later she died in childbirth. The child, also called Violet, returned to her grandparents in Dublin which placed a burden of responsibility on the artist. He turned from his preferred genre of landscape to portrait painting which offered the best hope of making money.

He kept in touch with English and continental art exhibitions and movements and by 1903 was a well-known and loved figure in Dublin society. The influence of his new lifestyle is shown in his portraits of children and his family. With a natural sympathy for children, he painted his niece Violet Stockley and her friends from the time the little girl

▲ *4.3 The Dolls' School (Walter Osborne) National Gallery of Ireland, Dublin*
This scene is one of great intimacy and charm. The little girl sits on the bed deep in childish communication with the dolls which are arranged around the side and end of the bed. The little group are all turned away from the spectator showing the painter's sensitivity to the child engrossed in the game. The delicacy of the watercolour captures the mood of intimacy and gently picks out colour in the dolls, complementing the subtle tones of the bed cover.

▲ *4.4 The Goldfish Bowl (Walter Osborne) Crawford Gallery of Art, Cork*
The little girl is Violet Stockley, the painter's niece. The painting of the white dress clearly shows the influence of French Impressionism in the range of colours. The blues, pinks and purples of the shadows make the whiteness of the cloth particularly striking against the blurred outlines of the orange fish.

came to live with them. One of his most charming watercolours is *The Dolls' School* [4.3] in which the little girl is sitting on her bed playing with her dolls. She also features in *The Goldfish Bowl* [4.4]. The influence of French Impressionist painters Renoir and Monet are obvious in these final works, particularly in the loose handling of the brushwork and in the use of colour in both light and shade.

He was probably at the height of his powers as a painter and on the brink of some greater achievements when he died suddenly of pneumonia in April 1903 at the age of 43.

RODERIC O'CONOR (1860–1940)

Roderic O'Conor left Ireland as a young man and spent most of his life in France. He never really associated with Irish artists there and it seems only exhibited once among them. This meant that he was virtually forgotten in Ireland and until very recently was recognised only for his association with the French artist Paul Gauguin. He is, however, one of the most interesting of the Irish artists because he became totally integrated with French painters.

O'Conor was born in County Roscommon and was connected to an ancient and well-known O'Conor family in the area. He studied in Dublin and Antwerp but went very soon to Paris which he obviously felt was a better artistic centre. His life as a student lasted in all about ten years.

His development as an artist was similar to that of his Irish contemporaries until his late twenties. It was in France that he quickly found a new direction and began to paint landscapes in a bold Impressionist manner. Some of his canvases from this time display a surprisingly advanced style painted in strong loose brushwork and bright colours that capture the heat and glare of the sunny French countryside. Other Irish artists had passed through the *plein air* stage and Realism, but O'Conor seemed to throw off his Antwerp training and go straight to Impressionism.

Events in Paris at the time which would have had a considerable influence on O'Conor were the last Impressionist exhibition in 1886, Gauguin's exhibition of many of his Breton paintings and most particularly Van Gogh's paintings which were on exhibit at the Salon des Indépendants in 1889. It is possible that O'Conor met Van Gogh in Paris at that time. Van Gogh died in 1890 and after his death his Provençal paintings were exhibited, having created a great impression on some of the more advanced French artists. O'Conor was one of the first foreign artists to appreciate the work of Van Gogh which had a profound effect on him and which was reflected in his own work for the next ten years or so.

These next ten years were spent in Brittany where O'Conor painted landscapes and seascapes. Some of these are painted in strong bold colours with a strong use of stripes as in *A Field of Corn, Pont Aven* [4.5]. Here also he painted a series of portraits of Breton women in traditional costume. He painted these in solid rounded forms, sitting or absorbed in their work. Sometimes he painted the background in strong bold stripes, and in *Breton Peasant Knitting* [4.6] he has continued the stripes around the stooped form of her

▲ *4.5 A Field of Corn, Pont Aven (Roderic O'Conor) Ulster Museum, Belfast*
In this tiny landscape O'Conor has used vivid colours to give the effect of a rolling countryside under a burning sun. The sunlight has a dazzling intensity with contrasts of bright yellows in the cornfield, the striped red and green of the hillside and the pale blue and green of the sky.

body. A gentler more sensitive portrait is that of a *Young Breton Girl (La Jeune Breton)* [4.7] in profile who gazes into a glow of light. The soft brush strokes contribute to the peaceful mood created in this work.

O'Conor's link with Paul Gauguin began when he joined a community of artists which had established itself around Gauguin in Pont Aven in Brittany. O'Conor joined this group after the leader had already left for his first trip to Tahiti, but the spirit he created in the group remained, and when the artist returned the following year the two

4.6 Breton Peasant Knitting (Roderic O'Conor)
The old woman is bent over her knitting, the needles almost clicking before our eyes. The stripes follow the contours of her body linking the figure to her work. Her gnarled face is striped as are her hands in the same reds and greens of the knitting making them inseparable.

4.7 La Jeune Breton (Roderic O'Conor) National Gallery of Ireland, Dublin
This is one of O'Conor's earliest Breton pictures. Dated 1890, it may have been painted during his first visit. The painting is quiet and contemplative, with the model's hands clasped in front. One side of the background is strongly illuminated, the other in shade, with the colours contrasting between soft reds and golds in the light and blues in the shade. A gentle blue-green shadow covers the underside of the bonnet.

became friends. Although he was deeply impressed by Gauguin, O'Conor's work remained unique and independent and is more comparable to a group of artists working in France known as *Les Fauves*. One of his best-known works from Pont Aven is *The Farm at Lezaven* [4.8] featuring a sunlit farmhouse, where the studio shared by some of the artists is glimpsed against a glowing sky through dark trees. The field and wild flowers are painted in harmonious reds, greens, pinks, violets and oranges.

O'Conor's subject matter included landscape, figure painting and still life with no aspect dominating. Using pure colours and influenced by Van Gogh, he was at his most expressive in his landscapes and particularly his seascapes using thick paint and a striped application of paint in a strong and exaggerated fashion.

In the next decade his colours changed to a more muted palette. His style, whilst still expressive, became more subdued. Throughout the early twentieth century he maintained his independence from any group or movement. For some years he did not exhibit though he painted continuously. Because of his family connections in Ireland he never had to worry about money, having private means. In his later years he married a much younger woman, had a studio in the south of France, and had one exhibition in 1937. He died in 1940.

▲ *4.8 The Farm at Lezaven (Roderic O'Conor) National Gallery of Ireland, Dublin*

This is a gentler landscape than the burning striped canvases of a year or two earlier. The brush strokes are smaller and thinner and the effect is one of the rich profusion of summer rather than a burning intensity. The picture creates a sense of pattern, with the dark green and purple uprights of the trees breaking the bright horizontal shapes of the pink and purple flowers and layers of greens in the undergrowth.

WILLIAM ORPEN (1878–1931)

William Orpen had a great influence on Irish painting in the twentieth century. Although an artist of considerable importance himself, his influence as a teacher in the Metropolitan School of Art in Dublin was overpowering and he moulded a generation of students, many of whom became successful painters in their own right.

He began his own training in the Metropolitan School of Art at the age of 11 in 1890 and remained there until 1897 when he went to the Slade in London where his talent was developed under the direction of Henry Tonks. These years in London were very successful for Orpen and a time when he got to know many people who were later to become important names in London's art establishment.

His early pictures are mainly interiors based on the Dutch tradition but are more realistic. One of his favourite devices of the period is a convex Arnolfini mirror. In *The Mirror* [4.9] he uses the mirror to reflect the artist in the painting. The panelling on the wall behind the figure is clearly based on a Velasquez painting, *Las Meninas*.

From 1900 to 1906 he produced many other fine masterpieces in which the influence of Velasquez, whom he saw on a trip to Spain, showed in his work. At this time he was working with a model called Lottie Stafford, a washerwoman from Chelsea, whose strong arms and, as he described, her 'wonderful swan-like neck' are seen in *The Wash House* [4.10].

4.9 The Mirror (William Orpen) Tate Gallery, London

This picture shows a number of influences. Apart from the mirror inspired by the Arnolfini wedding portrait and the background panelling derived from a Velasquez painting, he clearly borrows the idea of the pose of the figure from Whistler's painting of his mother. It shows the artist's desire to capture the precision and minute detail of the Dutch seventeenth-century paintings.

▲ *4.10 The Wash House (William Orpen) National Gallery of Ireland, Dublin*
The painting of one of his finest models, Lottie Stafford, a washerwoman, shows the artist's superb draughtsmanship and confident painting technique.

In the first ten years of his working life he painted some beautiful nude figures. He maintained that a nude must also be a person and he never simply painted flesh or a pretty figure, but always made sure the character and feelings of the sitter were represented.

Orpen never studied abroad like many of his fellow countrymen, but he did travel extensively in Europe and developed a *plein air* style of his own. Some of his finest painting comes from the summers spent at Howth Head during the time he was teaching in the Metropolitan School of Art in Dublin between 1908 and 1912. The pebbly beaches and rocky cliffs inspired one of his masterpieces of the period, a family relaxing in *Midday on the Beach,* and the superb painting of his wife Grace on a hilltop against a wide sweep of sea and sky in *Summer Afternoon* [4.11].

▲ *4.11 Summer Afternoon (William Orpen)*
This is one of the most eloquent of the final group of Howth pictures. The artist's wife Grace stands gazing dreamily out to sea. The bright sinking sunlight is reflected on her shoulder, contrasting with the glistening pinks and yellows in the shadows of her white dress. The sky is one of the most perfect renderings of Irish cloud formations in Orpen's work.

This was reputedly a time of great contentment in his life and he wrote later of these days before the First World War recalling 'the wonderful and ever changing vista of Dublin Bay'.

At the start of the Great War, Orpen was in England having become a fashionable society portrait painter which paid well and allowed him to have a good life but which was putting a heavy strain on his marriage.

He left this to become a war artist. He never expressed any of the revulsion he felt at the horror of the trenches, but rather concentrated on snow covered scenes or ground covered with wild flowers of which he made a collection.

After the war he rarely returned to Ireland. The experience of the war had led him to drink and he had met and fallen in love with a Belgian model with whom he remained in Paris. Later on he burned himself out and his portraiture lost its spontaneity.

During the last ten years of his life he published two books, one a collection of stories of himself and Ireland, and the other a memoir of the First World War called *Onlookers in France*.

WILLIAM LEECH (1881–1968)

William John Leech always considered himself an Irish painter although his parents' move to London meant that he had less connection with and probably rarely visited Ireland in his mature years. However, during his long career he exhibited about 300 paintings in the Royal Hibernian Academy in Dublin.

He was born in Dublin, the third son of a professor of law at Trinity College. In 1898 he enrolled at the Metropolitan School of Art, but because the teaching was so poor there, after a year transferred to the Royal Hibernian Academy School. At that time Walter Osborne was there as a visiting teacher and, according to Leech, 'had enthusiasm and could teach'. He studied at the school for three years and exhibited his first picture, a Swiss landscape, at 18 years of age.

Leech came from an established Anglo-Irish Protestant family who supported his ambition to be as painter. When he went to study in Paris his father put him in lodgings and gave him a small allowance. He studied at the Académy Julien for the next three years and, like other students from his own country who had been there before him, found he learned as much from his fellow students as he did from the painters who taught there. He said himself that all he had to do in Paris was to continue with what Osborne had taught him.

In 1903 he moved to the walled town of Concarneau in Brittany. This was just the time that O'Conor was leaving Pont Aven. This move was to have a very important effect on his career. The old town with its harbour and fishing boats completely absorbed him and the colourful markets and local costumes prompted much of his work, as the other artists before him. His paintings from this time are full of colour and sunlight. Some of his works were studies of different times of the day and his interest in vivid sunlight against contrasting deep shadow remained with him even after he left Brittany. It has been said that Leech retained a special love and nostalgia for the landscape and friends of his youth from his period in Brittany all his life. He remained there until 1908. It was in France at this time that he met and later married Elizabeth Saurin Kerlin, a young American-born artist with a similar style of painting to his own. It may have been Elizabeth who posed for one of his best-known works *In a Convent Garden* [4.12]. It features a young nun in the traditional Breton wedding costume who walks deep in thought through the long-stemmed flowers of the enclosed garden. She was also the model for two other fine paintings, *The Sunshade* and *The Goose Girl* [4.13]. The couple separated after two years of marriage.

In 1917 Leech went to the south of France with a friend and there he painted a number of paintings *en plein air* of cactus plants and aloes. This period of his life ended when he was drafted in 1918 and spent the last months of the war in a detention camp.

When he returned to his parents' home in London after the war, depressed and penniless, he turned to portraiture to get himself painting again. It was through portraiture that he met May Bottrell with whom he began a lasting relationship. He painted her many times but in 1940 he painted her in a relaxed pose against the window of their flat in London. He considered it 'one of my best things'.

▲ *4.12 In a Convent Garden (William Leech) National Gallery of Ireland, Dublin*
The figure is portrayed in a delicate sensitive manner in a dress of different shades of white. The painting is one of sunlight and glowing colour. The young novice is depicted among the bright greens and yellows of the grass and tall lilies painted in thick swabs of paint. This pool of sunlight is surrounded by areas of shadow forming a frame around the central area.

▲ *4.13 The Goose Girl, Quimperlé (William Leech) National Gallery of Ireland, Dublin*
The painting was probably painted sometime between 1910 and 1914. It is unsigned and Leech rarely dated his paintings. The picture has something of an Impressionist touch in the way the light filters through the trees and distant hazy landscape. The feeling of a summer's day is wonderfully captured in the soft shadows of the violet and orange flower-covered meadow which is repeated in the girl's dress. There are no other Quimperlé paintings and the broken mosaic pattern is not quite typical of Leech.

In 1953 after the death of May's husband the couple married and moved to a small cottage in the country where he had a studio in the garden. May died in 1965 and although he continued to paint views from the cottage, still lifes and self portraits, he was lonely and depressed. He died in 1968 following an accident.

JACK B. YEATS (1871–1957)

Ireland's foremost painter of the twentieth century is Jack B. Yeats. He came from an artistic background. His father John Butler Yeats was a portrait painter and his brother William Butler Yeats became one of Ireland's best-known and loved poets. Jack Yeats always distinctively signed his name Jack B. Yeats to avoid confusion with his father, but to this day one is still mistaken for the other.

John Butler Yeats the elder had given up a career in law in Dublin to study art and had taken his family to London. He returned to Dublin when he had finished and attempted to work as a portrait painter. Although gifted in this area, he was a hopeless businessman, and had a reputation for leaving work unfinished and forgetting to ask for payment. He had a great ability to capture the character of his sitters and drew or painted many of his friends as well as his family as they grew up.

At the time when Jack was born John was again in London trying to earn a living but not succeeding very well and the family were often in poor circumstances. When he was not painting or sketching, the elder Yeats was writing and both his sons inherited these dual gifts. As a young man W. B. painted in watercolours and all his life Jack's preoccupation with words co-existed with his painting. In most of his works there is a considerable narrative element and in later life he wrote novels and books.

Jack was the youngest of the six Yeats children, only four of whom survived childhood. Most of his childhood was spent apart from his parents, brother and sisters, with his grandparents at his mother's home in Sligo. Because of this separation he was able to develop an independence away from the heavy intellectualism of his father's circle of friends. Jack enjoyed the company of his practical Pollexfen relations who were respected and successful businessmen in the town. The atmosphere of the west, with its rugged coastline, mist, rain, constantly changing weather conditions and sense of space and colour, were to enrich and inspire his later work. In his wanderings as a youth he absorbed the dramatic imagery, but he also became familiar with the people and their relationship with their environment. He said: 'A true painter must be part of the land and the life he paints.'

Like the other members of his family he drew constantly from a young age and when he joined the family in London again his talent for comic humour in drawing greatly amused them. He attended various art schools in London but none were as valuable an experience to him as his apprenticeship working as an illustrator for some of London's magazines. He contributed to these for ten years or so, making borders and drawings and as a poster artist for a time in Manchester. He was earning his own living from the age of 17 on.

European art developments appear not to have affected him. He remained detached mentally and physically in his own country where, as he travelled, he observed horse races, country fairs, travelling circuses and the streets of Dublin. He found in Ireland the enchantment and the kind of melancholy that satisfied his own imagination. His art is deeply personal and cannot be formally defined. For some time after he returned to Ireland his painting was realistic and narrative. He chose small incidents like three women on a tram deep in conversation, but even then his brush strokes were soft, with free and fluid paint, giving a light and airy look to the work. For a while, particularly in the 1930s, he came close to Expressionism, but later this was to develop into strong and dramatic painting when his individuality was keenly apparent. In this later period of his life he was drawing heavily on the memories and sketches of his youth. The smallest incident could result in dramatic possibilities in paint for him. Underpinning this work at all times were his powers of keen observation and strong drawing ability, but he was essentially a painter of inner vision and poetry, capturing a world of landscape and memory, half imaginary, half fact. Caught between reality and fantasy, his paintings remain an enigma to the spectator.

His observations of life in Sligo and memories of his youth are the subject of his early work. A memory was to feature as a recurring artistic device in his work as he progressed through his career. He sketched continuously and often returned to this collection of notebooks, filled with people, events and pieces of scenery, for his painting years later.

The simple water colours of his early career, with their narrative quality, changed and deepened over the years. His friendship with J. M. Synge the playwright may have influenced Yeats in his awareness of Irish subjects. He often interpreted Synge's writing and he spent some time in the west of Ireland with him. He remained, however, quite isolated from contemporary artists, working in and out of Ireland even though artists of the time expressed admiration for him. He appears to have ignored his own famous countrymen of the time, having little in common with artists like Osborne, Orpen, Lavery and others.

From about 1900 on he turned to oil paint, developing slowly at first and somewhat heavily. In 1910 he returned to Ireland and the main thrust of his painting was to realistically record what he saw in everyday life and the characters of the country, as in his painting of *The Priest*. Many of these observations are recorded in woodcut prints. The events of 1916 convinced him that he should explore more deeply, rather than merely record what he saw. He moved to Dublin from Wicklow to experience the reality of the Irish character and to be able to express it better. His paintings of the 1920s still retain something of the narrative quality, but modern Ireland and the challenges it was producing were beginning to appear in the atmosphere of these paintings. From this transitional period *The Liffey Swim* [4.14] captures the excitement of this annual event in Dublin. Sporting events were always a subject which interested him but he had abandoned them in favour of quiet landscapes for some time.

Jack Yeats's painting was to erupt in a dramatic manner. His work suddenly developed expressive qualities hitherto only hinted at, making much more use of colour and its potential. It may have been his illness during the Easter Rising of 1916 that led him to deep inward thinking, and around that time he also developed an interest in dreams. He may also have been impressed with the paintings and their use of colour that he saw when he visited Paris in 1922.

Changes developed, with a deeper understanding of light and colour, and gradually took the form of looser brushwork and flowing paint as emotion began to feature in the

▲ *4.14 The Liffey Swim (Jack B. Yeats) National Gallery of Ireland, Dublin*
The intensity of the moment is expertly captured by Yeats. The brush strokes are long and fluid, following the flow of the river and creating a feeling of speed. The crowd lean forward one over the other, each one straining to see the action, with the passengers from the top of the tram adding a final tier to the crowd. The direction of the surging crowd points our attention to the powerful motion of the swimmer, involving us in the spectacle and excitement of the event.

imagery of his work. His style changed completely in his new freedom with oil paint. In spite of these changes, however, there remained inside the artist the same young man who had grown up in Sligo noticing and storing memories for later. By 1930 his observations, gained over many years, were expressed in a dream-like combination of fantasy and reality. He did not discuss the meaning of his work and was often amused at the various interpretations by critics. He felt that the paintings could speak for themselves. He said: 'It doesn't matter who I am or what I am. People may think what they will of my pictures.' He never discussed his painting while it was in progress and no one was allowed to visit his studio to watch him at work.

From about 1940 he painted incessantly until 1955 when he was 84. The 1940s, his most prolific period, produced up to one hundred paintings a year. These were larger in scale and more expressive than before. His paintings during these years have a deeply personal significance and he relied more and more on memory. *Many Ferries* [4.15] is

▲ *4.15 Many Ferries (Jack B. Yeats) National Gallery of Ireland, Dublin*
This is a narrative painting based on a minor event. A boatman who took Yeats and Synge to the island showed them a fine view of the islands and the sea beyond. The man who recounted his sad story of being a young widower with a large family is represented in the far left of the picture standing on a hill, his story half-suggested in the figures who stand below him. The picture is painted in deep blues and greens contrasting with yellows as the view stretches westwards and into the gleam of the far distant horizon.

based on an incident of 1905 when Yeats and Synge were in Connemara. They visited Dinnish Island at the end of a string of islands which had to be reached by boat. The boatman in the picture told the two his life story. Synge later wrote about it and Yeats made one or two sketches. The colours are deep blue and green with a glow of yellow lighting up the distant sky and the islands. The intensity of paintings like this is reflected in the use of strong colours. Deep vibrant blue is a particular feature of his later work. Given the extraordinary working pace of these years, it is not surprising that he was more interested in getting his ideas on to canvas than taking care with the preparation of his materials. Some of the paintings have technical problems due to the inadequate priming. The overuse of oil has also resulted in paint flaking and cracking.

In 1947, after fifty-three years of happy marriage, his wife Cottie died. He had married Mary Cottenam White, a fellow art student, in 1894. The couple never had any children but Cottie had been his most loyal supporter, always convinced that her husband was a

▲ *4.16 Grief (Jack B. Yeats) National Gallery of Ireland, Dublin*

Grief is one of Yeats's more passionate paintings. With simple imagery he conveys his detestation and total rejection of war. Nothing in the painting is clearly defined, but a white horse and rider can be seen emerging from between two rows of houses surging forward, preceded by figures of what appear to be an angry crowd of fighting men. The figure on the horse has a mask-like face and is surrounded by red as he gestures aggressively. This painting, large by Yeats's standards, is painted in strong blues and blood red, broken by a fiery yellow and orange over the buildings. In the foreground and to the right of the fighting men are the barely discernible figures of an old man and a woman with a child, the victims of war swept up in the clamour and aggression of it all.

man of genius. For some time Yeats was unable to paint but gradually he came to terms with his loss and worked his emotion into his work. Having lived through two wars and one of Ireland's most troubled periods in history, he painted one of his most moving pictures at a time when he was dealing with his own sadness and loneliness. In *Grief* [4.16] he has produced a work of profound emotion, powerfully expressing his deep abhorrence of war. This and some of his finest work was done in his eighties.

Throughout his life he had painted many horses. Though he was never a horseman himself he had a great affection for them. *For the Road* [4.17] expresses this affection and the understanding that can develop between horse and rider. The tunnel with the light at the end and the toss of the horse's mane as he heads towards the rider creates a feeling of hope and optimism.

In his last paintings of 1955, two years before his death, his use of paint becomes fluid and almost abstract. Jack Yeats died in March 1957. Ireland's most renowned painter is now receiving widespread international recognition.

▲ *4.17 For the Road (Jack B. Yeats) National Gallery of Ireland, Dublin*

At the call the horse runs through a tunnel of trees towards the distant rider who stands in a pool of yellow light at the end of the wood. This light brings rider and horse together as it pours along the woodland floor, reflecting on the horse's face and mane as he runs. The yellow contrasts with the dark blue of the trees dashed with red which form strong vertical lines at either side of the picture. The horse itself is painted in slabs of white and green, giving it an almost transparent dream-like appearance.

MARY SWANZY (1882–1978)

Mary Swanzy's work took a long time to reach its own individual self-expression. She began her career as a portrait painter and alternated between modernist and academic styles, coming at last to a style that was truly her own. She painted free landscapes of Ireland, some strongly coloured ones from her time spent in Samoa which show the influence of the Fauve movement in France; other styles included the Cubist manner, and she also painted in an Impressionist style. Some of her landscapes are similar in style to William Leech's, but her colours are stronger and her work shows a more decisive, less traditional technique. The modern period in Paris does not seem to have given her very much, but she undoubtedly benefited from the intellectual stimulation and contacts with many artists she met there.

Swanzy was born in Dublin, the daughter of an eminent opthalmic surgeon. Her upper-class background gave her a self-assurance that allowed her to feel equally at home either at study in Paris or travelling in the South Seas. Some of her South Seas pictures have been compared to Gauguin's. She came in contact with Cubism in Paris and visited the Gertrude Stein establishment where she must have come across Picasso's work, but appears not to have been moved by this early work.

In 1913 she held her first solo exhibition in Dublin and the next year some of her work was shown in Paris. She travelled a great deal after the death of both her parents and showed her work from her travels in an exhibition in Dublin in 1922. After this she spent a great deal of time visiting Samoa, California and Hawaii.

Throughout the forties she continued to exhibit in Dublin; then in 1968, after a long absence, she staged a large retrospective exhibition in the Municipal Gallery in Dublin. She was painting up to a few years before she died at the age of 96.

▲ *4.18 Boats at Rest, private collection*

This is a boldly painted Impressionist work, with strong slabs of colour forming reflections in the water. The rich colours of the old wooden boat throw an eggshell blue and red glow over the surface of the painting, sending ripples of colour and white diagonally across the work.

MAINIE JELLETT (1896–1943)

The 1920s was a time in Ireland when many painters gathered in Dublin. The Irish way of life was a theme popular with many artists who were establishing themselves as regular exhibitors at the Royal Hibernian Academy. Other artists were part of a school of thought which sought to incorporate the ideas of modernism in Europe into their work. The Irish art world had some difficulty accepting these ideas in a new state struggling to establish its own cultural identity

In modern Irish painting Mainie Jellett and Evie Hone, who worked closely with her, were the great innovators. Mainie Jellett studied in Dublin and London before moving to Paris to study under André Lhote. In Lhote's studio, Cubism was seen as an extension of all the Western art which had preceded it and, instead of rejecting the older art forms, students were encouraged to visit the Louvre and study the old masters. In later years Jellett said she owed her admiration of the old masters to Lhote.

▲ *4.19 Homage to Fra Angelico, private collection*

In this work Jellett has given the old mixture of symbolical meaning in myth, religion and history a new meaning. The painting manages to capture the devout quality of Fra Angelico's work. The deep question of belief is addressed in a formal rational manner. She made it clear in her own descriptions of her work that, unlike Picasso, she was not interested in exploring the possibilities in the material qualities of objects, but her Cubism had more to do with a spiritual concept related to much older traditions.

Jellett and Hone moved from Lhote's studio after they persuaded Albert Gleize, an exponent of Cubism, to take them to his studio. Jellett was to find Gleize's theory of the spiritual link between shape and colour a continuous source for her work. This spiritual quality and the old masters' religious subject matter was a recurring feature in her work. She interpreted the old myths with a new meaning in a Cubist manner. In *Homage to Fra Angelico* [4.19] she has used the age old image of the Coronation of the Virgin, and in an ordered and balanced harmony builds up the picture symbolically without realism.

Impressionism was played down during the period between the two world wars in favour of a more abstract exploration of tones. Gleize believed that the artist could leave aside the representational form of painting and express ideas in a more abstract or conceptual way. From Gleize the two Irish artists learned the fundamentals of the Cubist theory, and for the next ten years they divided their time between Dublin and Paris.

Jellett's work was not very popular in Dublin, where she was described as having been a 'victim' of the 'artistic malaria of Cubism'. For her and artists like her the only way to overcome the prejudice in Ireland and the narrow point of view of the RHA was international acceptance. Her work was widely praised in London and Paris and featured in the Olympic Games in Amsterdam in 1928, the Irish Art Exhibition in Brussels in 1930 and the New York World Fair in 1939. She began to write and lecture on Cubism, and gradually her success abroad and her reputation as a teacher brought her a belated acceptance in Ireland.

In 1943 she and Evie Hone established the Irish Exhibition of Living Art with other artists, Louis le Brocquy, Jack Hanlon and Norah McGuinness. The artists felt that an annual show was needed to show the strength of modern Irish painting and that the RHA was not providing an opening for those outside its own members. In the years after the Second World War the Exhibition of Living Art became associated with innovation and the RHA with the more traditional approach. Mainie Jellett was chairman of the founding committee for the exhibition in 1943, but was already suffering from the cancer which caused her death in 1944.

STAINED GLASS

Sarah Purser was a painter, a hostess to many of Dublin's intelligentsia and a collector of artworks. She is probably best remembered in Ireland for her associations with the stained glass movement and the establishment of An Túr Gloine (the glass tower). This studio was begun in 1903 and although she designed stained glass herself, her real work was in the administrative and financial work which she continued until her death at 94. The splendid stained glass in many Irish churches is the result of her efforts and the leading stained glass artists employed there over the years. The only artist not to spend any time at An Túr Gloine, who brought a creative impulse unlike any other artist of the early twentieth century to Irish stained glass, was Harry Clark.

HARRY CLARK (1890–1931)

Born just over a century ago Harry Clark is now recognised as a genius of his time. He worked most of his life in Dublin and he worked with an intensity as if he was aware that his life was to be a short one. He was only 41 when he died of tuberculosis.

Throughout his life he was an avid reader and as a result his work had a literary quality. His illustrations are among his finest works. He would have known the work of Aubrey Beardsley as a student in Dublin, but it was not until 1913 that the influence of Beardsley began to work its way into the drawings of the young artist. The influence of Art Nouveau, then popular in France, also began to manifest itself in his work about this time. The influence of Gustav Klimpt was particularly strong and this was to remain a feature of his work throughout his career.

Harry Clark began work in his father's studio where he learned the craft of stained glass from William Nagle. He spent some time in London working in a studio by day and taking classes at night. Severe homesickness caused him to return to Dublin in 1906. He continued to work in his father's studio and attended night classes by Alfred Child at the School of Art. At this time he was drawing and painting for his own satisfaction on the Aran Islands. But his studio work demanded his attention, particularly because it was in competition with An Túr Gloine.

In 1910 he was awarded a scholarship to go to the School of Art to study stained glass. This meant that he could take part in exhibitions and competitions open to day students. In 1912 he submitted six pieces for the national competition in south Kensington and won the only gold medal awarded to Ireland. In the following years he won further gold medals in England and many awards in Ireland.

While still in his mid-twenties he created some of his finest work. The windows of the Honan Chapel in UCC are powerful and vibrant in colour. The seven panels depict the saints of Ireland. On either side of St Patrick are St Brigid and St Colmcille. Patrick in a cloak of rich green raises a hand to bless the shamrock. St Brigid is in one of Clark's favourite colours—blue, which is also used in the window of the Virgin Mary, and the window of St Ita and *St Gobnait* [4.20]. The scarlet of St Finbarr's window reflects on the stone floor below, reminding the viewer of some of the magnificent glass of the medieval Gothic cathedrals on the continent. Clark himself visited Chartres Cathedral a year before his work on the chapel and is said to have been enthralled by the glass.

His studio produced a huge volume of work considering his short life. In his time Church art was often vulgar and tasteless and the stained glass tended to be particularly so. Although he produced many windows for churches all around Ireland and England and some of his clients may have been demanding or hard to please, his work never descended to commercial or debased artwork and fortunately he was highly regarded and accepted by the Church.

His *Eve of St Agnes's window* is in the Hugh Lane Gallery in Dublin. This window is subtle and rich in detail, with some of the panels like tiny flashing jewels. The strange elongated figures give the work an almost fairy tale-like appearance, in contrast to the solemn glow of the Honan windows.

Whether in stained glass or in his magnificent illustrations, Harry Clark's work has become increasingly sought after.

▲ *4.20 St Gobnait (Harry Clark) Honan Chapel, UCC*

St Gobnait is the patron saint of Ballyvourney, Co. Cork, where she lived in the sixth century and a strong cult developed around her. In the long slender fingers of her right hand she holds the wooden crozier of an abbess. In her left hand she holds a model of her abbey.

The face, turned elegantly in profile, is pale and beautifully painted, her deep red hair falling below her waist. She wears a collar which covers her neck completely and is finely pleated all the way. This is the first time Clark uses this motif which was to become a regular feature in his work.

According to legend robbers tried to break into the abbey one night but were driven away by Gobnait's bees. The robbers are creeping along behind her at the bottom of the panel, the first of whom turns showing his terrified face as he is confronted by a bee larger than his head.

The saint's tunic is blue and divided into a series of beautifully patterned lozenge shapes. One of the lozenges bears the initials of the artist and the date 1916. On another is a miniature gravestone that bears the inscription 'H.C. RIP'. The figures of the curly haired robber, Gobnait herself and a young novice at her side are some of Harry Clark's finest works in glass.

CONTEMPORARY ARTISTS IN IRELAND

Jack B. Yeats's painting was a personal response, rather than a following of any international style. This was to have far reaching effects on the general direction of Irish painting which followed the Second World War. Painters who emerged during this period tended to work in an individual, semi-abstract, expressive mode. This was the direction of painters in the 1950s and 1960s and to some extent its influence is significant even now. Some of the more important artists in this poetic genre were Louis le Brocquy, Patrick Collins and others including Tony O'Malley. Common threads can be perceived in the work of these artists which includes a preference for muted colours and soft-edged shapes. All of the artists were influenced by their rural roots.

Reflection on the past is a common feature and visual expression in their work tends to be subtle. There is a far deeper core to their work than mere observation of nature; it is a more poetic interpretation, where the image goes inside the subject to reflect its hidden depths.

Perhaps Irish sculpture suffered somewhat from economic conditions. Sculptors are less numerous from that period of modern Ireland. Oisín Kelly is one of a few notable sculptors who worked in figurative sculpture in this poetic mode.

Artists in the 1960s continued in the semi-abstract vein. Abstract Expressionism was also influencing Irish painting but most artists in Ireland tended to avoid the pure abstract and remained with figurative subject matter. Rural motifs remained prominent subject matter and many artists like Brian Bourke continued to work with landscape.

During the 1970s a shift was apparent and more Irish artists turned to look at international modes. The semi-abstract styles were replaced by many with the new and more hard-edged abstract styles. This was the new Ireland of the high rise buildings and a European outlook. Sculpture received a particular boost due to the building boom and industrialisation. Corporate bodies promoted sculpture with commissions for sculptures in new premises and corporations and county councils commissioned public sculptures for cities and towns around the country. Sculpture was designed to be an intrinsic part of the building rather than a decorative afterthought. Exponents of abstract Minimalism received many such commissions and stone or steel abstract sculptures appeared in public places, creating dialogue and in some cases controversy with a public not always ready for the hard-edged non-objective approach.

The Rosc exhibitions held every four years since 1967 brought international names to Dublin, making the public more art conscious and influencing a new generation of art students. A new wave of artists has emerged in recent years, as many as they are varied. Groups including New Expressionists, Photo-Realists and Abstractionists have exhibited nationally and internationally.

A school of sculptors emerged in Cork, which included the sculptors Eilish O'Connell and Vivienne Roche, working in steel.

The Irish art world today is varied and self-confident. Galleries and small outlets for art may be found in quite small towns as well as the cities, and groups of artists, Irish and non-Irish, have tended to gather in areas throughout the country. These are accepted and considered to add colour and vitality to the locality where once they might have been considered freaks or cranks.

TONY O'MALLEY (1913–)

Tony O'Malley came to painting at a relatively late age and never thought of himself as an artist until he was almost middle aged. He is now probably Ireland's most loved living painter. His work could not be described as abstract but more the essence of something. Abstraction for its own sake has never interested him. He prefers painting in an abstract form, which allows him to go beneath the surface beyond appearances and express his mind, giving deeper meaning and power to his work.

Tony O'Malley was born in County Kilkenny in 1913. As a teenager he sketched quite a bit but never had any formal lessons. Having left school at 18 he worked for a time in the bank, but was given leave of absence to serve in the army during the emergency. Here he became unwell with the beginnings of TB and later after his return to the bank developed full TB. After treatment and periods of rest in his home town of Callan, during which he started drawing and painting, he went to a sanatorium in Kilkenny where he spent some years.

After his release from the sanatorium in 1950 he worked with great intensity enjoying the outside world again. He was back at work and painting for the love of it. He greatly admired Cézanne and Van Gogh and other French painters. He reacted to their spirit, which to him suggested a sense of freedom and release. He spent the 1950s on the east coast in places like Enniscorthy and Arklow. He painted to please himself, places he liked, still life and people. He painted his mother who was bedridden for some time. *Portrait of the Artist's Mother* [4.21] was painted around this time.

4.21 Portrait of the Artist's Mother (Tony O'Malley) private collection ▶

Margaret O'Malley was confined to bed for some years before she died at 84 in 1954. She had four children of whom Tony was the eldest. He painted several pictures of her, mostly of her sitting up in bed. Some of these paintings were made after her death. Deeply attached to her, her death left him very depressed for some time. In this painting he suggests the fragility of the old lady who closes her eyes against the lights of a car passing her window, the grid of the window casting a pattern over her figure and bed clothes. It is painted in yellows, pinks and whites, with the handling of paint quite dry. The small scale of the work and the way the figure fills up the whole frame conveys a sense of intimacy.

In 1955 and 1957 he visited St Ives in Cornwall and it was here that the possibilities of abstraction as a means of expression were opened up to him. Memory began to play a part in his paintings and an intuitive quality replaced the more observational and descriptive work. He spent these holiday times working in the studio where Peter Lanyon and some other artists, moderns of that time, welcomed and accepted him. Some of the painters he met in Cornwall probably influenced his work, but his style never became abstract like theirs. In *Landscape with figure, Clare Island* [4.22] he has painted himself bearded in a fisherman's jersey similar to those worn at St Ives. Clare Island was his father's birthplace and he always enjoyed spending time there as a child. He liked the people and their ways. He was shortly to leave Ireland and settle in Cornwall for the next thirty years and many of his early St Ives paintings deal with his own identity which was strongly bound up with Clare Island.

▲ *4.22 Landscape with Figure, Clare Island (Tony O'Malley) Collection Betty O'Malley*
The painting is one of stark simplicity in a warm range of browns and reds, using flat blocks of colour to model the face. The flat plane of the island rises up behind him, a row of houses ranged along its ridge.

From 1960, having retired from the bank, he was living and painting in Cornwall. St Ives was at that time the centre of abstract painting and to some extent the capital of post-war British art. He found the freedom and liberation which had not been available to him in Ireland. He had never felt at home in the Irish art world which he found conservative and inward looking.

Winter was often the subject of his painting and several works are entitled *Winter Silence* or *Silent Winter*, and *Van Gogh, Winter* (from a dream) in which the artist identifies with Van Gogh. The winter of the soul, as well as the season itself, is suggested in the cold blues and greys of these paintings. He chose winter again in a painting dedicated to his friend and fellow artist, entitled *Hawk and Quarry in Winter* [4.23]. This lonely and evocative painting recalls the death of Peter Lanyon who died in a gliding accident in August 1964.

▲ *4.23 Hawk and Quarry in Winter, in Memory of Peter Lanyon (Tony O'Malley)*
Crawford Gallery, Cork
The expressive importance of winter in O'Malley's work is seen in several of his pictures. Peter Lanyon died in August but O'Malley's commemoration of him is a winter picture, painted in cold, white and dark greys. He noticed a hawk one day swooping into a quarry and it brought to mind the gliding accident which had killed his friend. O'Malley chose to paint a place rather than a person for this picture.This was appropriate for Peter Lanyon who was an abstract painter but with a strong sense of place.

O'Malley developed a particular painting technique, handling materials in an individual way. In his paintings on board he often makes cuts and incisions and on others uses found objects and textured material. He enjoys the craft of making a painting and still experiments a lot. He likes to paint on board because he can work into and use its surface like 'ploughing a field'.

The 1970s was the decade that brought many changes to O'Malley's life. In 1970 he met Jane Harris, an artist from Montreal working in St Ives. Like O'Malley she was a dedicated painter. They shared a studio and married in 1973. Jane's family lived in the

Bahamas and they made several visits there which resulted in a new light and colour in his work. Both liked the nomadic life and it was after his marriage that he began to return to Ireland each summer. In 1977 he bought a plot of land outside Callan.

His time was divided between the Bahamas and Ireland and his painting responded not so much to the image of both places but to the colour and light associated with each. His Cornish and Irish paintings are low in tone, but his Bahamian pictures are light and airy and warmer in colour range. *Bahamian Butterfly* [4.24] has a feeling of lightness, rhythm and pattern in its bright cheerful colours, capturing the feeling of a butterfly in flight.

Tony O'Malley began to receive critical attention in Ireland in the mid-seventies and built up to a big exhibition in the Douglas Hyde Gallery in 1984 when he was in his seventies. Since that time his work has been seen all around Ireland and England. He now lives and works in Callan, Co. Kilkenny.

▲ *4.24 Bahamian Butterfly (Tony O'Malley) private collection*
This bright and lively work is painted in pinks, yellows and blues. The cheerful abstract pattern suggests the markings on a butterfly's wings. The artist has scored and incised into the paint and the board on which it is painted, adding to the energy of the surface.

BRIAN BOURKE (1936–)

Brian Bourke is best known for his landscapes and his mocking self-portraits which are many and varied. A lively expressive line runs through his work, creating an energy and restlessness. His colours are bold and vivid, and a bizarre and humorous element is never far from his drawings and paintings. His style has also translated well into sculpture which was a new discipline for him.

He did not complete his first year in the National College of Art in Dublin. He found the system unsatisfactory and moved to London, briefly attending Goldsmith's College and St Martin's School, but short of money he left to find work. He still distrusts art colleges, finding them 'dangerous places for genuinely talented people'.

In London of the 1950s he studied the old masters and life drawing with the aid of his girlfriend who smuggled him into life drawing classes. He worked at various jobs building up a discipline of hard work. He spent two years as an assistant in an operating theatre which was a valuable lesson in anatomy for an artist.

He returned to Dublin in 1959. Two central themes emerged in his art, which continue to occupy him, landscape and portraiture. He spent a short while in Germany during which time his landscapes became more spacious, with skies developing a greater importance. In 1967 he won first prize in the Irish Exhibition of Living Art for artists under 35.

4.25 Knockalough (Brian Bourke) ▶
One of a series on this subject, *Knockalough* is painted in swirling vivid colours. It is set in a patterned oval, creating the illusion of looking through a porthole. The colours and strongly shaped clouds conjure up an image of the countryside and the restless Irish weather, but also focus attention on the painted surface itself.

He moved to the west of Ireland in 1975 where the horizons in his landscapes became even more pronounced. The drama of light and weather on plant life and the ever moving skies of the Irish countryside are reflected in his work. His *Knockalough* series [4.25] is richly coloured and display a painterly control, while responding to the mood of the countryside. The abstract brushwork and particularly the coloured borders on the paintings emphasise his skill at bringing an old theme to new life.

In 1988 he produced a series based on the legendary character, Sweeney, and his mad flight around Ireland. *Sweeney in Frantic Flight* [4.26] was seen in Rosc 1988.

Many of the artist's latest works are of mixed media on paper and some of these take the form of a triptych or a quadriptych (3 paintings or 4 paintings together). Vivid colour remains a strong feature of his landscapes.

▲ *4.26 Sweeney in Frantic Flight (Brian Bourke)*

The Sweeney series is based on the legend of an early Irish king who went mad after he opposed the coming of Christianity and was cursed by St Ronan. Under the influence of the curse he roams mad around the world. Bourke became interested in Sweeney after he read Seamus Heaney's translation of Buile Suibhne. The strange wiry figure of Sweeney retains the squiggly drawing line through the colour of the paint and is characteristic of this artist's work.

Oisín Kelly (1915–1981)

Oisín Kelly is one of Ireland's most famous sculptors. He worked both in a realistic and abstract style concerned mainly with ideas native to Ireland and its culture. His work shows an affection and understanding of his subject which is especially noticeable in his sculptures of birds, animals and people. Subtle humour is sometimes found in his work and his religious works are respectful but in an unsentimental manner.

Christened Austin Kelly, the sculptor was born in Dublin in 1915. Like his father before him, he started his working life as a schoolteacher. He spent eighteen years in St Columba's College in Rathfarnham, Dublin. There he initially taught French and Irish, but soon changed his position to that of art master.

After the war he took two terms off teaching and went to study under Henry Moore in Chelsea Polytechnic. Kelly had already been working with the human form, but in Henry Moore's class he was strictly confined to work with the model, learning with absolute realism how to measure with calipers. Moore took the view that students were there to learn anatomy and insisted that they be absolutely accurate working from the model. So it was that Kelly, who went there to study the sculpture of Henry Moore, found an interest in the natural form and developed a style of his own in no way like the work of Henry Moore.

Soon after his time in England, Kelly's work began to develop a spirit of its own. He produced one of his most splendid works, *Step Dancer*, a figure of an Irish dancer carved in wood.

His first Church commission came from Michael Scott the architect in 1949 to make a statue of Our Lady of Fatima for a church in Limerick. In this charming wood carving he portrays Mary as a young girl. After this he was asked to make statues, crucifixes and relief carvings all over Ireland.

In his religious sculptures Kelly often reverted back to medieval works and adapted them to produce beautiful Madonnas reflecting both tenderness and majesty. He returned also in his crucifixes to the old penal form of the cross, carving crucifixes which are not a mere copy of things past, but more a refinding of an old theme in a new spirit. His crosses showed all the symbols found on the seventeenth-century crosses such as the crowing cock, the spear and the sponge, and the hammer and nails.

His secular work continued for a while under the influence of Picasso and Henry Moore, but over the years drifted back to more realistic imagery. Movement has always been a central theme in his work. He produced dancers, fish, birds, horses, footballers and hurlers with all their energies captured in strong athletic gestures.

His largest public work is the *Children of Lir* [4.27] in the Garden of Remembrance in Parnell Square, Dublin. He worked on this project for many years. He chose the Children of Lir to symbolise the fundamental change in Ireland brought about by the Rising in Dublin in 1916 and the subsequent War of Independence. The change that was immortalised in the poetry of Yeats: 'All changed, changed utterly.' Perhaps a more abstract form would have suited the notion of children turning into swans which is, after

▲ *4.28 Two Working Men (Oisín Kelly) County Hall, Cork*
These working men were conceived as typical Dublin characters to stand outside a trade union building. The bronze figures, however, treated in a realistic but simplified manner fit just as easily into Cork where they were readily accepted by the citizens who recognised something of Cork's dry, humorous wit in the two who appear not at all impressed by the height of the glass and concrete structure of the County Hall.

all, a very abstract subject. It was originally intended this way by Kelly, but he decided against it, fearing the public might find it too difficult to accept. The complex sculpture group was cast in bronze in Italy in 1970.

Two Working Men [4.28] stands outside the County Hall in Cork. In contrast to the *Children of Lir*, realistic treatment is particularly suited to this pair. They were intended to stand outside Dublin's Liberty Hall but Dublin Corporation, fearing a distraction to traffic, refused permission to place them there. Now they stand gazing at the County Hall, adding a touch of humour and charm to this crudely designed building. Also in Cork is one of his many Irish dancers. The bronze figure of the *Little Dancer* [4.29] is in Fitgerald's Park.

◀ *4.27 Children of Lir (Oisín Kelly) Garden of Remembrance, Parnell Square, Dublin*

This dramatic and impressive national monument strongly contrasts the nineteenth-century type of monumental sculpture which largely centred on the figure of a hero. Kelly, in preparation for the work, made numerous drawings of swans and studied the bone structure from a dead swan he acquired from the Dublin Cats' and Dogs' Home.

▲ *4.29 Little Dancer (Oisín Kelly) Fitzgerald's Park, Cork*

The little dancer in bronze is one of Kelly's famous series based on the theme of movement. The movement and rhythm of Irish dancing, with the arms held at the sides and all concentration on the elaborate footwork, is conveyed in the simplicity of the form. The girl, with her hair blowing in the wind, looks as if she might dance off into the woodland behind her at any moment.

Birds and their movement in flight have always interested Kelly. He has produced a whole range of birds including hawks and his delightful terns. He became permanent artist in residence at Kilkenny Design Workshops when it was established in 1964 which allowed him to give up his teaching job. Here he produced a very popular series of terracotta birds.

Kelly's contribution to Irish sculpture is now considered invaluable for two reasons. The first is his treatment of Irish subjects to which he brings a sympathetic but unsentimental understanding. The second, for bringing back the ancient modes of Irish art with a remarkable insight into how important these forms are to expressive art of the present day.

VIVIENNE ROCHE

Vivienne Roche likes to work in steel, often contrasting it with the rich and more seductive bronze. Her work is abstract, but there is always an original source from which it is abstracted. Her kind of abstraction has more to do with expressing her sense of the world in a non-literal way. It is a search for a more complete kind of image.

Vivienne was born and educated in Cork. Her father was an engineer who designed many bridges in the 1960s and 1970s. It was this family background which led to a natural interest in structural form.

She never had any doubt that sculpture was her medium and for four years in Crawford College of Art she worked mainly with steel in an abstract form. Her work has responded to different situations and experiences in her life. For this reason various themes have occupied her at different stages.

Her first major theme was architecture which she explored while she was studying in America. Since her move to the coast, where she now lives, she has become much more aware of nature and the powerful presence of the sea. This awareness has resulted in a freedom of line in her work which was no longer bound by the geometric restrictions of architecture. Wind and sea quickly established themselves as sources for her work.

Waves were the source for her first big public commission in 1983 when she was commissioned to create the *National Memorial to President Cearbhall Ó Dálaigh* [4.30] at Sneem, Co. Kerry. The sea as a theme has also resulted in installations in sailcloth and other nautical motifs.

▲ *4.30 Memorial to Cearbhall Ó Dálaigh (Vivienne Roche) Sneem, Co. Kerry*
This memorial sculpture to the late President of Ireland is made of painted steel with three connecting sections. The shell-like structure is suggestive of wave action, of mountains and of megalithic structures. It integrates a dark, almost mysterious interior with clean outward-looking forms. The structure itself is 2 m high and 5 m long. This scale allows it to retain a certain privacy, making it a fitting monument for Cearbhall Ó Dálaigh.

The fusion of man-made objects and nature has manifested itself in her work since her first visit to Scandinavia in 1986 and her encounter with Viking culture and Nordic mythology. These sources, linking armour, landscape and the human body, have proved a rich inspiration for her.

An interest in sound led her to create works in the early 1980s which related to the forms of musical instruments. In the process she became interested in bells. At first she was interested only in the form, but then she began to think about the sound of the bell. She made a series of bells including two large commissions for St Patrick's Park in Dublin and for Trim Fire Station, Co. Meath. All her bells make a sound, but she never knows what that sound is going to be like until the bell is made.

Vivienne Roche has recently completed a large work for Cork Harbour Commissioners at Ringaskiddy Ferryport called *The Sea Garden*. It is a large area of mounded grass with steel insets (paths, seats etc.) and four upright bronze and steel forms. These uprights, some of which incorporate bells, refer to the skyline of Cork harbour, with the spire of Cobh Cathedral, cranes at the shipyards, electricity pylons and water towers.

At present she is working on a series loosely based on plumb-lines. Suspended weights, usually bronze cones, hang within narrow steel frames from ceilings, wall mounts or, as in a commission for Dublin Castle, from the roof structure in a void through four floors of the recently renovated Ship Street buildings.

4.31 Liberty Bell (Vivienne Roche)
St Patrick's Park, Dublin
Based on the bronze bell of St Patrick in the National Museum in Dublin, this structure is made of bronze and is suspended in a painted steel frame. The work combines ancient and new materials in a contemporary sculptural form.

More recently (1994) another work has been placed at the entrance to the park. This work, two upright bronze forms 4 m and 2.5 m high with cast iron insets in the path, refers to both the Liberty Bell and to the architecture of St Patrick's Cathedral.

CONTEMPORARY ARCHITECTURE

SAM STEPHENSON (1933–)

The look of late twentieth-century Dublin has been shaped by Sam Stephenson more than any other architect. In doing that there are those who would say that he brutalised it. Indeed his name has been linked to controversy in Dublin from the mid-1960s to the present day, but his impact on the city is huge and he has been involved with many of Dublin's most important buildings.

He was born in Dublin in 1933. Being the youngest by far of five brothers, he perhaps spent a good deal of his time with his father. It was his father who influenced his interest in building design because of his great knowledge and interest in old Dublin. His father wrote for the *Dublin Historical Record* and frequently gave lectures on some aspects of this subject. The Stephenson family lived in Cabra which is quite close to the Phoenix Park where the obelisk shape of the Wellington Monument was one of the first architectural shapes to influence him. He considers it one of the finest monuments there is.

Stephenson saw his buildings as strong simple shapes which echoed his interest in classical music. He greatly admired Margaret Thatcher under whose building boom he moved to London in 1984. He also admired Albert Speer, Hitler's architect. He said: 'Great architects require strong clients and architecture positively thrives under autocrats.' He believed that buildings should reflect the age we live in.

He has been widely praised for his interior designs. He designed the interior of many prominent Dublin offices, one of his finest early contracts being the Horseshoe Bar at the Shelbourne Hotel. His exteriors, however, have not met with such widespread approval.

The Dublin of Sam Stephenson's youth was poor and, as he said, had been decaying for 150 years. He began in private practice in 1957, but it was in the 1960s that he got the full opportunity to make his mark on old Dublin.

The Hume St and Fitzwilliam St projects attracted a great deal of attention. This allowed for the demolition of these streets and their replacement with modern designs. Lovers of Georgian Dublin were outraged at the proposed destruction of these fine old houses. Fitzwilliam St was the longest Georgian street in Europe, but Dublin Corporation Planning Department at the time was not impressed by this; neither was the ESB which ran an international competition for the design of its new offices. Sam Stephenson has carried the blame for this building ever since, but he did win the contract without using any influence. The plain modern block façade in stone and glass will remain none the less a blight on this red-bricked, terraced, elegant and graceful eighteenth-century Dublin street.

To his frustration to the present day Stephenson never got to complete one of his most controversial buildings. Constructed on the site of one of Dublin's most important archaeological sites, that of the old Viking city, its erection was met with storms of protest both for its design and for the site which was desecrated for its construction.

Once again he was the winner of an architectural competition. Several designs were submitted to Dublin Corporation for their new Civic Offices. All were tall modern block buildings. Sam's design, however, used the concept of four smaller buildings with connecting walkways. His design included paths and terraced parks leading down to the river.

Only two of these buildings were completed and were slated by public reaction. The square granite shapes were compared to tank traps, bunkers and grain silos. These blockhouse-type buildings with parallel lines of horizontal narrow windows were considered an insult to the surrounding architecture and especially in their effect of dwarfing the nearby Christ Church Cathedral.

With hindsight it is possible to see that Sam Stephenson was a man of his time when dealing with modern buildings. He followed the notion that 'form follows function'. Architectural thinking during the 1960s rejected the traditional idea of building and went for 'objects in space'. It was the era when the city, as it then was, was being downgraded, and it was felt that building needed to make a clean sweep. The people, however, did not respond well to the stripped-down look of this type of building, without threshold or entrance or any kind of architectural language, and in effect said 'enough of disaster' in the city. Sam Stephenson's glass box building of the Bord na Mona headquarters in Baggot Street might look well in Dallas, where its inspiration could have come from, but even with the softening effect of greenery it still looks out of place in Dublin. But Dublin as an American city was very much in vogue as a way of thinking at the time.

The Civic Offices were left unfinished after 1978 and remained so for over a decade when a competition was held for their completion. Sam Stephenson was shocked at not even being asked to submit a design. The buildings were designed by Scott Tallon Walker and completed in 1994.

4.32 The Central Bank (Sam Stephenson) Dame Street, Dublin ▶

Each of the seven floors of the Central Bank was completed at ground-floor level and raised slowly to its position where it was jacked or fixed into its own level. Each floor, with its fittings and window bars attached, weighed 400 tons. It was nevertheless a relatively simple method of construction and the resulting building has a lightness and style despite its great size.

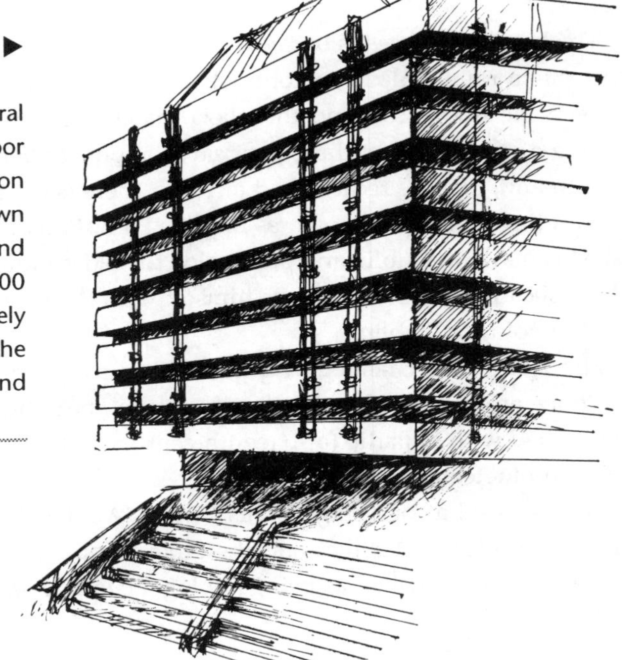

Of all of his buildings in Dublin, perhaps one will best stand the test of time. *The Central Bank* [4.32] in Dame Street has been called a monument to Sam Stephenson. He himself said: 'The doubting citizens of Dublin will come to see it', as he does, 'as a significant building. History will show it to be the best building I've ever put up.'

The building was unique in its time in that it was constructed over a twin core system. Other buildings in the world had used the idea of a hung structure over a single shaft, but none had as yet been attempted with twin cores. These shafts, rather like the trunks of a tree, were constructed using a continuous pour of concrete, starting at the bottom and finishing at the top. One took seven days to complete; the other took ten. When the shafts had reached maximum height, giant steel trusses were assembled on the roof and from these hangers were allowed to hang down.

During construction it became obvious that the building was going to exceed its permitted height. In fact it was 29 ft higher. Work halted on the building in March 1974 and did not resume again until April 1975. The three bodies involved, namely, the bank, Dublin Corporation and the Department of the Environment, came together with the architect to try to find a solution. That the architect had deliberately contravened the planning laws was typical of Stephenson's attitude to them. In effect, by implication, he was saying that planning permission did not matter.

His solution to the planning objection was to expose the structure of the roof trusses, thereby giving a visual reduction which was in fact a reduction of only six inches.

The building has elegance; its hanging bars function as decoration which have the effect of breaking the severity of the floor lines. The whole building is constructed in granite as Sam reckoned that all the best buildings in the world used only one material — marble.

The building succeeds because of the architect's desire to create a space and make the entire site a public plaza, in contrast to the great building looming overhead. The space between the undercroft and the plaza matches the height of the terraces and therefore walking along the street there is a real relationship between the buildings, because there is depth and, like the red-bricked terraces, there is continuity on the street.

Sam Stephenson is known as Skyline Sam. Perhaps his worst fault was his desire to make his mark on Dublin and push aside the old buildings. Modern architecture appealed to him because he could express himself with freedom and boldness. He was perhaps a little too bold for Dublin.

His views have changed over the 1980s during which time he said at a lecture that he was 'once an apostle of modern architecture', but has put aside that 'religion' and now 'goes to bed with Palladio (a sixteenth-century Italian architect) and gets up with Lutyens (a British nineteenth-century architect)'.

He also said at one stage in his career: 'Apologetic self-effacement should be left to public lavatories, VD clinics and the other minutiae of society.' His buildings in Dublin could never be described as being apologetic in any way.

EXAM QUESTIONS

1990 Ordinary level

Describe in detail any twentieth-century painting, sculpture, mural or batik, on a religious theme, with which you are familiar.

1991 Ordinary level

Discuss the work of any *one* of the following artists: Walter Osborne, Harry Clark, Mainie Jellett, William Orpen, J. B. Yeats, Mary Swanzy.

or

Describe any major work by Oisín Kelly.

1992 Ordinary level

3. Discuss the work of the nineteenth-century painter Nathaniel Hone
4. Give an account of any twentieth-century artist whose work you admire.

   or

   Describe any important work by a modern Irish sculptor with which you are familiar. In your answer discuss the materials and techniques used.

1993 Ordinary level

4. Select any painting by Walter Osborne, Roderic O'Conor or Jack B. Yeats and explain why it appeals to you.

   or

   Many locations in Ireland have contemporary public sculptures commemorating historical figures and events. Write in detail about any *one* such sculpture and describe its setting.

1994 Ordinary level

4. Discuss the work of *one* of the following painters: W. J. Leech, Louis le Brocquy, Robert Ballagh, Martin Gale.

1995 Ordinary level

4. Write a critical account of the work of any *one* of the following painters/sculptors/architects:

   William Orpen, Norah McGuinness, Gerda Fromel, Edward Delaney, Michael Scott, Sam Stephenson.

1990 Higher level

3. Discuss the work of any Irish painter of the nineteenth century who was influenced by contemporary artistic developments in France. Refer in your answer to *one* or *two* paintings by the artist you have chosen.
4. Describe a portrait by a twentieth-century artist which you find particularly interesting. Indicate what qualities you would expect to find in a good portrait.

   or

   Give an account of a piece of abstract sculpture by a modern Irish sculptor. Refer in your answer to technique, materials used and such features as form, texture and colour as they apply to the piece you have selected.

1991 Higher level

Modern architecture has been greatly influenced by the use of such materials as steel, glass, reinforced concrete, plastics etc. Discuss this statement with reference to a recent Irish building you know.

or

Write an account of the work of any contemporary Irish painter whose style appeals to you. Refer in your answer to specific paintings by the artist you have chosen.

1992 Higher level

Write about the development of stained glass in the twentieth century. Refer in your answer to the work of *one* stained glass artist mentioning any significant influences on his/her art.

or

Describe and discuss *one* painting by a twentieth-century Irish artist whose work deals with distinctively Irish subject matter.

1993 Higher level

3. What were the popular themes of Irish painting in the nineteenth century? Illustrate your answer by reference to a painting by a nineteenth-century artist whose work appeals to you.
4. Your school has been awarded a substantial grant to purchase either a painting or a piece of sculpture by a living Irish artist for permanent exhibition in your school premises. If you were asked to help with the selection of the piece, what painter would you choose. Give reasons for your answer, mentioning the specific qualities of the artist's work which you find interesting.

1994 Higher level

3. Describe a work by *any* Irish landscape painter of the eighteenth or nineteenth century.
4. Write as fully as you can about a contemporary Irish painter or sculptor or architect whose work is of special interest to you.

1995 Higher level

4. Give an account of the work of a contemporary Irish figurative painter and mention the particular aspects of the artist's style that appeal to you.

CHAPTER FIVE

MEDIEVAL EUROPE

ROMANESQUE PERIOD (A.D. 1000–1200)

The period immediately preceding the emergence of Romanesque art was a troubled and destructive epoch in the history of Europe. It was threatened on three sides, by the Vikings from the north, the Muslims from the south and by the Hungarians from the east, leading to great insecurity. Coupled with these upheavals was a widespread terror of the year 1000, when many predicted the world would end, so as the years after A.D. 900 passed, poverty and misery and lack of education were seen as evils not worth worrying about. All emphasis was on saving their souls to be ready for the Last Judgment. When the world did not end people cheered up and Europe began to revive. They repelled the invaders and actually took up the offensive with the Crusades and the recapture of Spain from the Moors. With a period of peace came prosperity. New farming methods led to a population growth and gradually the development of towns and cities. A new energy poured into philosophy, organisation and technology, and in a remarkably short time stone buildings were springing up everywhere, replacing small wooden structures. The change was most remarkable in the growth of churches.

The artistic renewal of the eleventh century benefited from a vigorous feudal aristocracy but particularly from a powerful militant Church. The newly reformed Church decreed that Christian life should not be contaminated by lay interference. Intelligent men of the time joined the clergy where they could rise to a powerful and influential position, but the Church was also powerful because it was not burdened by the laws of feudalism, and with the Pope's new demand for clerical celibacy, there was no question of divided inheritance.

The Church supported the three international forces that would shape the course of eleventh-century French Romanesque art: the Crusades, pilgrimages, and monasticism. The crusade against the Arab Moors in Spain encouraged Christian knights of France and Spain to take part in what they saw as a holy war. The tomb of St James the apostle was rediscovered at Compostela in north-western Spain. St James was transformed into 'Santiago the Christian slayer of Moorish infidels' and the tomb and its new church became a pilgrimage site.

The fame of Santiago de Compostela soon saw thousands of pilgrims pouring through France towards the Pyrenees. On each of the four main pilgrim routes churches were built at intervals along the way, some of which developed as important destinations in their own right. All these large pilgrim churches were similar in design, built throughout with stone and using the high Roman-style barrel vault which gave rise to the nineteenth-century term for the style of architecture: Romanesque.

Romanesque Architecture

The style known as Romanesque was first explored at Cluny Abbey in France in the early eleventh century and became common throughout France, Spain, Italy and England. Despite many regional differences in style, its distinctive features are rounded or semicircular arches, magnificent west façades to its churches, huge barrel vaulting, complex apses (altar end of the church) radiating chapels, heavy solid walls and rounded pillars sometimes with carved capitals. Cluny's huge church, the largest in christendom in its day, was consecrated by the Pope in 1130 but was sadly destroyed during the French Revolution.

Five main churches were built on the four pilgrim routes. These large churches were very similar in design and based on the needs of the pilgrims. Wide aisles were needed for their processional walks, all of which led towards the choir, high altar and the saints' relics. A semicircular ambulatory allowed pilgrims to circulate behind the altar and view the relic.

Early Christian churches had separate rectangular basilicas and a circular mausoleum. Romanesque churches combined this long basilica and half the circular shape to form an apse with radiating chapels (each one containing a minor relic). The addition of crosswise transepts made these new churches cruciform in shape. The cross of the transept was lit by a central tower. This had the effect of leading pilgrims, from darkened nave to lighted choir, towards the relic [5.1 & 5.2].

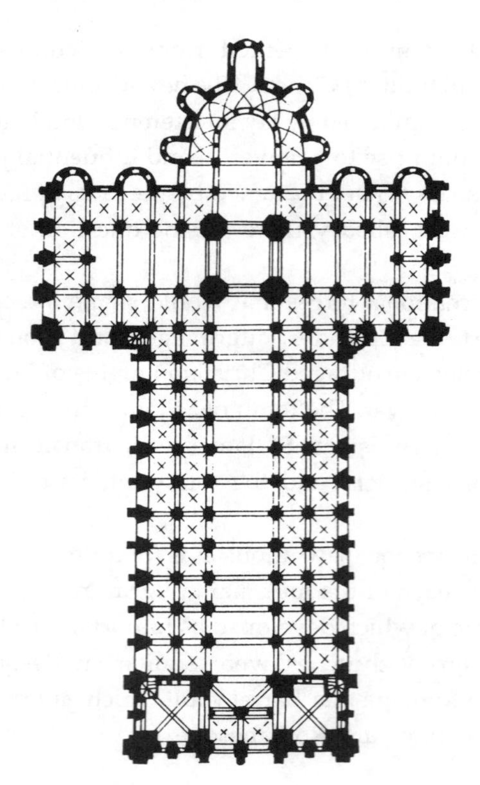

5.1 Plan of St Sernin, Toulouse

St Sernin was on one of the four main pilgrim routes. It was the first pilgrim church to be consecrated by Pope Urban II in 1095. The other main pilgrim churches are similar in design.

▲ *5.2 A typical Romanesque church*

5.3 Barrel vault ▶

Early churches had timber roofs which were not satisfactory because of the constant danger of fire. The new buildings had to have stone roofs, but stone roofs were heavy and likely to collapse. Much of the technical knowledge developed by the Romans in the art of vaulting large buildings had been lost and as a result the Romanesque architects were faced with problems that could only be solved by experimenting. A huge amount of stone was needed to construct high barrel vaults. To carry this weight, walls and pillars had to be strong and thick. Window openings would weaken these structures, and as a result, with little light in the nave, interiors had a dark and solemn look. Barrel vaulting [5.3] presented the problem of walls pushing outwards under pressure from

the heavy roof. The development of groin vaulting [5.4] improved the problem and also allowed more window space, but the problem of outward thrust was really only solved in the thirteenth century with the development of the rib vault and the buttress.

5.4 Groin vault ▶

Romanesque Sculpture

Teaching the word of God found a new and powerful medium in medieval art. The rediscovery of monumental stone sculpture in the early twelfth century was quickly absorbed into Church art by Cluny and its followers, the five great pilgim churches of the south, and particularly in Burgundy. The huge churches built towards the end of the eleventh century placed great emphasis on the east end where the main altar and relic were sited. Pilgrims coming to the church entered from the west front, often passing under richly carved tympanums dominated by the figure of Christ in judgment or surrounded by saints and evangelists. Inside, carved narrative scenes often decorated the capitals of the pillars. One of the most striking features of these carved Romanesque capitals is the way in which figures and a whole scene are adapted to the awkward shape of the capital. This bending and twisting of figures in a frame is a distinctive feature of Romanesque sculpture. Romanesque sculpture both on capitals and tympanums are to be seen at their best at the cathedrals of Vézelay and Autun in Burgundy in eastern France.

Cathedral of St Magdalen, Vézelay (early twelfth century)

Built around 1150, after the original was destroyed by fire killing 2,000 pilgrims, it is difficult to imagine how St Magdalen, Vézelay, must have looked to the crowds of pilgrims on their way to the Shrine of St James of Compostela. A Gothic pediment and buttresses were added to it in the mid-thirteenth century, and after a great deal of damage by the Revolution and the weather it was restored during the nineteenth century. The inside, however, is a perfect gem of twelfth-century Romanesque architecture.

▲ *5.5 Tympanun at St Magdalen at Vézelay (twelfth century)*

Inside the western portal we are confronted with a great doorway over which Christ sits in his great tympanum [5.5]. The scene is that of the Pentecost and a massive Christ is shown with his arms thrown open, a symbol of the glory of the Resurrection. He has a voluminous, beautifully pleated robe, a serene expression, and the flames of the Holy Spirit shoot from his large hands to the apostles, who in turn teach all races below.

The impression conveyed on entering the nave is one of balance, rhythm and light [5.6]. The sense of balance is due to the vaulting system. A series of rounded arches support the roof and between each is a system of groin vaulting. To counteract the problem of outward thrust the builders, instead of using the normal barrel vault (which loads the entire weight of the roof directly on to the walls, and is further complicated by the need to introduce daylight), used two rounded arches running the length of the nave, and another two at right angles along the arcades. In between, the four corners of the groin vaulting system meet in the centre (see diagram). The walls of the nave thus relieved of the vault load can now be pierced by the large windows allowing daylight to light up the nave completely.

The rounded arches of each bay are supported by pillars with capitals decorated at each intersection. Vézelay's particular characteristics are the pink and white stone on the arches and pillars giving a chequered effect, and the carved capitals on the pillars of the

◀ *5.6 Interior of St Magdalen at Vézelay (twelfth century)*

nave. Although it is known that Gislebertus worked in Vézelay, nothing is signed by him as it is in Autun, so the wonderful carving of biblical figures, saints, angels and devils must remain anonymous. Of particular fame is *The Mystic Mill* [5.7]. This is the church's most beautiful symbolic capital. One man pours grain into a mill while another gathers the flour. The grain represents the law given to Moses, and the mill, Christ.

Many of the capitals show demons which display the fascination of the Romanesque carvers with the grotesque. In *Lechery and Despair,* Despair is portrayed as a demon with flaming hair plunging a sword through his body.

▲ *5.7 The Mystic Mill, capital from Vézelay (twelfth century)*

Striking, however, as the beauty of Vézelay is, it must be remembered that Romanesque architecture was not built for its own beauty but as an appropriate place to hold religious services. Even the vaulting system was considered holy as it enhanced the sound of the plainchant singing. All the stories and symbols carved on doorways and capitals were neither art for art's sake nor for the amusement of the people, but were to bring alive the teachings of the Church which each person knew in his own mind.

Cathedral of St Lazare, Autun (early twelfth century)

The pilgrims entering the church of St Lazare had to pass beneath the great tympanum [5.8] on the west portal. The dramatic scene which faced them was calculated to inspire hope and fear. The west front originally faced a graveyard which perhaps accounts for the theme, that of the Last Judgment. A huge figure of an impassive Christ sits on his throne in the centre of a world filled with tiny figures of souls rising from their tombs as angels sound the last trumpet. The saved are welcomed to Paradise by Peter, and the damned are dragged in dramatic fashion to Hell by grotesque demons. The sculptor has signed his name, a rare occurrence in medieval art. *Gislebertus hoc fecit* (Gislebertus made this) is carved beneath the feet of Christ. It is known that Gislebertus trained at Cluny and probably worked as an assistant at Vézelay, but the style of the work, with its elongated figures and exaggerated expressions, at Autun is particularly unique and very distinctly his own.

▲ *5.8 Tympanun at Autun: The Last Judgment or the Weighing of Souls (twelfth century)*

The Last Judgment was a common medieval theme but Gislebertus portrays it with an intensity never before seen. The scale and drama of the imagery could not have failed to inspire awe in an impressionable pilgrim visitor, particularly in its own time when it was painted in full colour.

In the lintel below the feet of Christ the souls rise from the dead. They are divided into the saved on the right of Christ and the damned on the left. The just who look hopefully upwards are welcomed by St Peter, with a large key, to Paradise and helped by an angel into its Romanesque-style interior. Among the saved, two can be identified as having made pilgrimages to Jerusalem and to Santiago de Compostela, by the symbol of the cross signifying Jerusalem and the shell, symbol for St James, on their satchels [a]. The damned on Christ's left are driven from him, naked, with heads bowed, by an angel with a flaming sword, the miser with his heavy money bags and the adulteress gnawed by snakes as a giant pair of hands grip a tormented soul [b]. Above their heads the Archangel Michael, with souls hiding in terror beneath his robes, weighs a soul while a grotesque devil tries to weigh it down and another sits in the scales to make it heavier. The unhappy souls are then poured down the chute by a laughing demon [c]. The devils' expressions are portrayed with a taste for the grotesque which was a feature of the art of the Romanesque period. Gislebertus too seems to relish the horror and enjoy his story, reducing it to its essentials in the telling.

▲ *5.8(a) Pilgrims*

▲ *5.8(b) Hands grasp a soul*

▲ *5.8(c) Devils and Hell*

Interestingly, this amazing work survived the rigours of French history. It was hidden for many years. In later years the Church grew ashamed of the grotesque and dramatic imagery of the Romanesque period. It was considered crude and slightly vulgar and the *Last Judgment* was plastered over. During the nineteenth century this was removed revealing the scene, preserved from war and weathering. The capitals inside were all carved by Gislebertus himself and show his skill as a sculptor and story-teller. Some of the best capitals are from the now dismantled north porch. They contain some very fine ornamental foliage which is combined with the figures in expert fashion; but the key element of these works is the story itself and the simplicity of its telling. No amount of detail could better express the horror of the suicide of Judas [4.9] or the gentle wakening of the three sleeping kings by the angel who touches the hand of the king with one finger [5.10].

5.9 Suicide of Judas, Autun (twelfth century)

Judas with head lolling grotesquely hangs from a beautifully depicted ornamental tree. He is helped by two hideous devils who appear to be enjoying themselves. The three figures and the tree are skilfully composed to fit the shape of the capital.

5.10 The Three King, Autun (twelfth century)

With simple gestures the angel points to the star, and gently touches the hand of the sleeping king who opens his eyes, while the others sleep under a splendid semicircular bedcover. The story is told with the minimum of detail and yet conveys the message clearly and directly.

Gothic Period (thirteenth and fourteenth century)

As the twelfth century progressed the economy grew stronger and a new form of social contact developed in towns which grew and expanded. The country that contributed more than any other to the development of the culture of the day was France. France dominated the twelfth century with Paris the shining light in intellectual terms. Other large towns like Chartres, Tours, Orleans and Reims were also renowned centres of learning.

These amazing changes in social and intellectual activity were reflected in the frenzy of building that swept across western Europe during the twelfth and thirteenth centuries. It was a time of intense piety, a time when spirituality was expressed through the medium of art. Up to the fourteenth century when books were rare and literacy not widespread, thoughts and stories were presented in visual form. Every piece of art had a meaning behind it. Understanding medieval art means knowing something of the literature which inspired it: the Old and New Testaments of the Bible, and the legends and stories associated with the saints. The presentation of these stories was approached as a sacred science governed by fixed laws which the Church guarded and which could not be broken by the individual imagination of a sculptor or painter.

The thirteenth century was the age of the great cathedral. These were the books of the faithful who learned with their eyes all that was necessary for men to know of the sacred dogmas, from the stained glass windows or the statues in the porch. For this reason Gothic cathedrals have been called 'books of stone'. The cathedral was the most important status symbol of the towns and its great height dominated the skyline, and in many towns still does.

Gothic Architecture

It was in the Ile-de-France just north of Paris that Gothic architecture began in 1144. Here at the Abbey of St Denis the Abbot Suger devoted himself to the restoration of buildings using elements of Romanesque architecture but combining them with new and more effective methods. The main architectural features used in the restoration were pointed arches and rib vaulting [5.11 & 5.12]. Within twenty years this style known as Gothic had spread across northern France and in the next fifty years all of western Europe had adapted to a style that was to become the dominant mode for the next 300

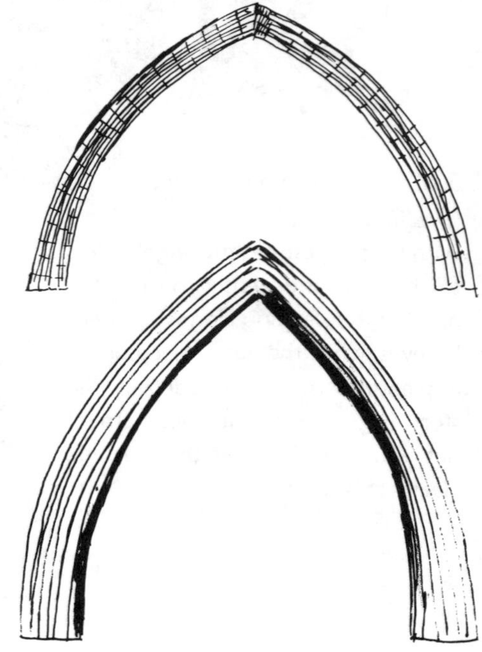

5.11 Pointed arches ▶

▲ *5.12 Ribbed vault*

years. The earliest Gothic churches were quite varied in form but a series of large cathedrals in northern France took full advantage of the new Gothic vault. It was discovered that the crosswise vaulting was a more effective system which no longer needed heavy walls to support the roof. The heavy stones used in the rounded Romanesque arch pressed down as well as out and it was discovered that the pointed arch took less stress and could therefore be built higher and stronger.

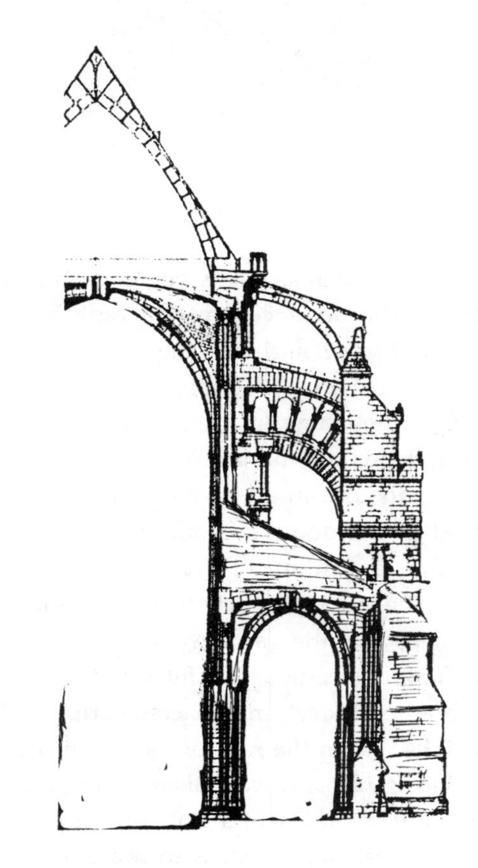

▲ *5.13 Flying buttress*

The architects of the cathedrals found that the outward thrust caused by pressure from the vaults was concentrated in small areas at the end of the ribs. Pressure was also deflected downwards by the pointed arches, but now this could easily be counteracted by narrow buttresses and external arches called flying buttresses [5.13]. The consequence of these developments was that it was now possible to replace the thick walls of Romanesque architecture

◀ *5.14 Wall of a Gothic cathedral*

with thinner walls, filled with the new art of stained glass learned from the East. The interiors reached hitherto unknown heights and were far more elegant. A revolution in building techniques had occurred.

It was at Notre Dame in Paris that flying buttresses were first fully developed. Traces of the originals may still be seen, but the present ones date from the nineteenth century.

With the structure of the church no longer needing thick heavy walls to support the roof, more attention was paid to the design of the walls [5.14]. Slender pillars divided sections of walls which were at four levels, with the tall lancet windows at the top and a gallery above the side aisle at the lower level of the nave. Greater space was now available in the walls for windows which let more light into the interior. This light was seen as God's power on high as it filtered through the many stained glass windows. The advancements in building techniques allowed the designers to build higher and higher, and with the fervent religious beliefs of the time, this was considered to be closer to God. These splendid places of worship were for the faithful, rich and poor alike, and when one considers the living conditions of many during the middle ages who lived out the winter months of darkness in fear of war, fire and disease, it is small wonder that the cathedral in all its glory must have seemed like heaven itself. With the saints gathered at the doorways offering hope and intercession to an all powerful God, the height and splendour of Chartres cathedral is as impressive now as it was when first begun in the late twelfth century. Even today as the sun streams through its magnificent stained glass, creating a transparent mosaic on the walls and a carpet of rubies and gems on the floor, the cathedral is filled with an air of richness and mystery.

The Virgin Mary's most sacred shrine at Chartres was almost completely destroyed by fire in 1194. When the relic of the gown she wore giving birth to Jesus was found in the smouldering ruins, it was taken as a sign of a miracle. A new church was immediately begun on the remains of the old one. It was the largest church ever attempted at the time and is the best preserved, with more of its original stained glass intact than any other medieval cathedral.

OUR LADY OF CHARTRES

Traces of the original Romanesque structure can be seen on the west façade of Chartres [5.15]. Over the years the style of building changed. The north tower was built nearly 300 years after the south tower and was finished in the flamboyant Gothic style. The earlier parts were respected but each period made additions in the style of its own day. Buttresses and flying buttresses support the nave. Chartres was one of the first large buildings to utilise to the full potential the flying buttress.

Inside, the cathedral is built in the shape of a cross with a central aisle and transepts forming the arms of the cross. The whole effect on entering the cathedral is one of light and space. The slender pillars soar to join the criss-crossed rib vaulting on the roof, the sheer height of the building adding to the beautiful lighting from the many stained glass windows.

▲ *5.15 Chartres Cathedral, West façade (twelfth and thirteenth century)*

Three large rose windows (so called because of their shape) adorn the cathedral, one on each transept, another over the west door facing the altar. Like the tall pointed windows which surround the church, they tell the story of Mary, Jesus and the saints.

It is easy to miss the stories contained in the glass or the sculpture. Some are taken from old stories of the life of Christ, well known to the people of that time, but long forgotten now. Around the doorway on the west front (the Royal Portal) [5.18] stands a series of column statues whose identities are not fully known. However, they appear to represent men and women from the Old Testament. They are solemn and linear forming part of the architecture, but at the same time the costume and drapery is treated in a decorative manner [5.16]. The twelfth-century artist gave no thought to the body. All life was concentrated in the face.

▲ *5.18 West or Royal portal, Chartres (thirteenth century)*
This is one of the first examples of a Gothic doorway in France. The triangular tympanums have sculptures of the Virgin Mary and the Ascension of Christ on either side. The centre is devoted to Christ in Majesty. Statues of kings and queens from the Old Testament stand around the portals. The style of the figures on the sides is inferior to those in the centre, suggesting that the master carved the centre himself and the assistant the sides.

Gothic Sculpture

Gothic sculpture was a further development of the style which began at St Denis. The abbot Suger had introduced the 'column statue' in the doorway of the façade at St Denis. These statues were almost free standing figures carved into the column, changing sculpture from a minor addition to a building to an important part of the overall design of the doorway, blending with and enhancing the architecture. This enrichment of architecture with sculpture led the way for the splendid Gothic doorways.

The Royal Portal of St Denis was the inspiration for the Royal Portal at Chartres. Using the same theme of kings and queens and figures from the Old Testament this doorway is one of the earliest at Chartres, carved in the twelfth century [5.16]. All expression is concentrated in the faces of these unknown royal figures. They are smiling and serene with beautifully pleated drapery forming thin straight lines on elongated bodies blending and yet separate from the column. Unlike the great Romanesque tympanum of Autun, with its fearful vision of Hell and grotesque demons, the theme of the three doorways is salvation. In the central door is a peaceful and calm vision of eternity, with Christ in Majesty welcoming the visitor surrounded by his apostles and symbols of the evangelists.

5.16 Kings and Queens, Chartres (twelfth century)

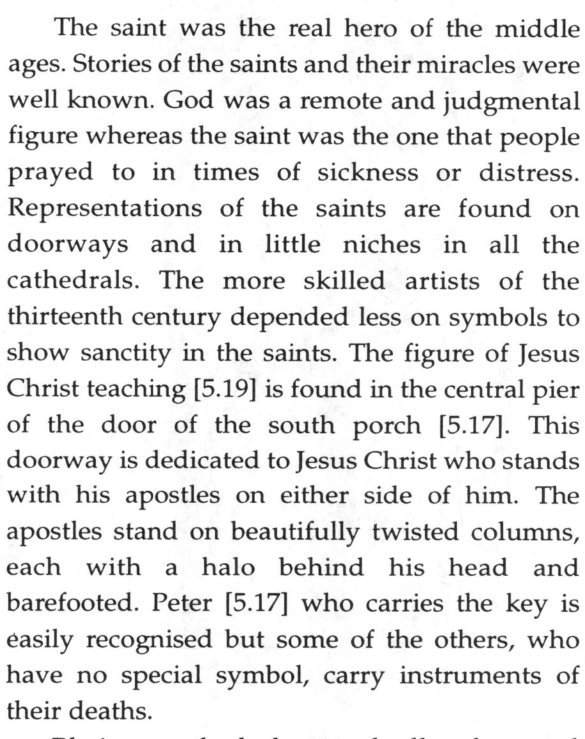

The saint was the real hero of the middle ages. Stories of the saints and their miracles were well known. God was a remote and judgmental figure whereas the saint was the one that people prayed to in times of sickness or distress. Representations of the saints are found on doorways and in little niches in all the cathedrals. The more skilled artists of the thirteenth century depended less on symbols to show sanctity in the saints. The figure of Jesus Christ teaching [5.19] is found in the central pier of the door of the south porch [5.17]. This doorway is dedicated to Jesus Christ who stands with his apostles on either side of him. The apostles stand on beautifully twisted columns, each with a halo behind his head and barefooted. Peter [5.17] who carries the key is easily recognised but some of the others, who have no special symbol, carry instruments of their deaths.

Rheims cathedral was badly damaged during World War I but much of its impressive variety of Gothic sculpture survived. The lines of the splendid west façade [5.20] soar upwards representing the union between Heaven and Earth. The façade has been greatly restored but the statues on the sides of the doorways are original. It is possible to pick out several schools of sculpture spanning over almost half a century. Devotion to Mary was very popular in the thirteenth century; her honour was above reproach in an era which valued chivalry. The central doorway at Rheims is dedicated to the Virgin. In the gable above the doorway she is crowned Queen of Heaven by her son, while on the central pier she welcomes the faithful. The four statues on the right represent the Visitation and Annunciation and show the variety of styles found at the cathedral [5.21].

▲ *5.17 St Peter, Chartres (thirteenth century)*

▲ *5.19 Jesus Christ, Chartres, south porch (thirteenth century)*

Christ is seen here as the teacher, a book in his left hand, his right hand lifted in blessing, and behind his head the cruciform nimbus. He is not Christ the Judge of sinners but the Shepherd who gave his life for and loves mankind.

◀ *5.20 West façade, Rheims cathedral (thirteenth century)*

▲ *5.21 Annunciation and Visitation, Rheims (late thirteenth century)*

The figures of Mary (*centre right*) and Elizabeth (*right*) are early thirteenth century and are clearly inspired by Roman influence. The bodies come alive, no longer resting squarely on two feet, the folds move, the faces have life-like expressions. The Virgin of the Annunciation (*centre left*) is later, with gentler movement and quieter folds in her gown. The figure of the Angel Gabriel is of the last school and has a delicate smiling face, a graceful movement and an elegantly draped body. The smiling Angel of Rheims (*left*) has become the emblem for the city.

STAINED GLASS

With the new tall building and skeleton-like structure of the Gothic cathedrals, plenty of space was left in the walls for windows. It was considered by some members of the clergy to give greater honour to God to pray in a church full of colourful beautiful light, and so for this reason glass, which shone like rubies and gold in the sunlight, became very widespread.

Coloured glass is known to have been used for small windows by the Romans but the technique was perfected during the middle ages. The coloured glass was cut into small pieces to form the pictorial shape, then details such as faces were painted on. The windows were pieced together and held in place by strips of lead. Horizontal bars gave support. Chartres cathedral was designed to have the maximum amount of space for stained glass windows, which would have been the single most expensive item in the cathedral. This suggests that the chapter of Chartres was very wealthy.

The glass in Chartres is full of stories of the saints. All the popular well-known stories of St Stephen, St James and many others are found in windows large and small. A window at each end of the cathedral depicts the Kingdom of Heaven with God, angels and saints in a large circular form known as a 'Rose Window'.

The northern rose is dedicated to the glorification of the Virgin. However, the most famous window at Chartres is known as the *Blue Virgin*. As in the sculpture of the period, she is seen here as a queen. Mary is seated and her lap forms a throne for her child. She is Queen of Heaven with angels all around, and Queen of Earth with authority over demons. Great reverence was shown to Mary in the art of the Gothic period as the image of the Mother of God.

5.22 The Blue Virgin of Chartres (twelfth century) ▶

The large figure of the Virgin of Chartres is in four panels of blue glass on a ground of ruby. This masterpiece of twelfth-century workmanship belonged to the former cathedral severely damaged by fire in 1194.

▲ *5.23 South rose, Chartres (thirteenth century)*
The south rose glorifies Christ. In the centre Christ sits enthroned surrounded by angels together with the four evangelists and in the outer circles by the twenty-four elders of the Apocalypse.

▲ *5.24 Death of the Virgin, Chartres (thirteenth century)*
This window shows the Death, Assumption and Coronation of the Virgin Mary. The central medallion (*above*) shows her surrounded by the apostles on her deathbed.

LATE GOTHIC (FOURTEENTH CENTURY)

▲ *5.25 Virgin and Child, ivory statuette (fourteenth century)*

The thirteenth century was the time of great cathedrals built in new towns. After 150 years or so these towns had grown quite large and were much more independent of the Church and the feudal lords. The nobility no longer lived shut up in fortresses in the country but now lived in the towns where they displayed their wealth in fashionable luxury.

Some of the best sculpture of the fourteenth century is small and made of metal or ivory. Little statues of the Virgin in these materials were made for the private chapels of the wealthy. Gothic artists of this time gave their figures a slight bend so the whole body seems to sway a little [5.25].

Artists and ideas travelled from one country to another and a style evolved which has become known as the 'International style'. A wonderful example of this in England, possibly painted by a French master, is called the Wilton Diptych.

It shows Richard II with his patron saints who are recommending him to the Virgin. This shows the delicacy and refinement, which was

▲ *5.26 The Wilton Diptych, International style (fourteenth century)*

fashionable at the time, in the sweet faces and gestures of the figures.

Architecture of this time was given the name 'flamboyant' because of the amount of decoration and complicated tracery [5.27].

It was the custom in the middle ages to illustrate calendars with the labours of the month. These were attached to prayer books and were called 'Books of Hours'.

The most famous of these is called *Les Très Riches Heures du Duc de Berry*. The painters here were the Limbourg brothers and one can see how much they enjoyed the pictures of dukes and courtiers and the girls in their pretty dresses. In the pictures we can see life as it was in medieval times, in the life of the peasant, the farmers and the customs of the times. The dukes' beautiful castles have now all disappeared.

WILTON DIPTYCH

For the first time a painting records real historical personages, showing a life-like portrait of Richard II. No hint of the violence which overtook this unlucky monarch and soon saw him brutally murdered is evident, as we see him kneeling in prayer, presented by his patron saints to the Virgin and her child, who leans towards him playfully. The art of the Wilton Diptych [5.26] shares with the art of the time a taste for flowing lines and delicate

▲ *5.27 Rouen cathedral, Flamboyant Gothic style (fourteenth century)*

and dainty motifs. The delicate long hands of the Virgin holding her child reminds us of earlier painting, but the foreshortening of the angel and the use of studies from nature give us the impression that the artist was now beginning to delight in a more realistic presentation of forms, particularly in the many beautiful flowers that adorn the painting.

LES TRÈS RICHES HEURES DU DUC DE BERRY

Jean de France, Duc de Berry, was the son of King Jean le Bon II, brother of Charles V and uncle of Charles VI. He was related to many other princes and queens of the Burgundy region, all of whom were collectors of books like himself.

Perhaps the Duc de Berry, more clearly than any other so far, shows that pride in ownership of art works had changed the message contained within them. The great works of the cathedrals had called out God's messages to the people for all to see and Richard II in the Wilton Diptych knelt in humility before the Virgin; but the most famous book in the collection of the Duc de Berry, *Les Très Riches Heures*, was not really for the glory of the Lord but plainly for the Duc himself.

As patron of the arts, the Duc sought out and encouraged new artists. The Limbourg brothers came from the Netherlands and probably brought with them some of the new realism which was prevalent in northern Europe. The real space and sense of action in picture after picture was a new departure for the miniature painting of France with its flat stylised backgrounds. The manuscript was obviously produced for a master who appreciated the beauty of works and delighted in the realistic portrayal of his person. The courtiers are depicted in splendid costume, his prized objects shown in precise detail and his beautiful castles can be enjoyed in all their richness. Most of these castles were destroyed after his death.

More than any manuscript or painting so far, this work illustrates the splendour and grace of the era. In May all the courtiers don leaves and garlands and go riding. In the heat of August they ride out with the falcons while the workers toil in the background, some

▲ *5.28 'August', Les Très Riches Heures du Duc de Berry (early fifteenth century)*

taking a moment to swim in the river. In September the workers on the estate gather in the grapes in front of the great chateau of Saumur. From March to December one of the great castles is shown, passing on to us what a great loss their beauty has been to Europe.

If the Duke ever worried about the plight of the tenants and workers on his estate there is no account of it and nothing in the illustration suggests that the well-dressed courtiers who rode by those sweltering workers, cutting the corn in *August* [5.28], ever showed any concern. Society was structured in an ordered fashion and everybody had their place.

WELL OF MOSES, CLAUS SLUTER (ACTIVE 1379–1404)

The sculptor Claus Sluter was one of the greatest of the many Netherlandish artists who benefited from the wealth of France. None of Sluter's work in his native town of Haarlem in Holland or in Brussels, where he was employed, survives. What we know of his work comes from the burial place of the Dukes of Burgundy, the Charterhouse of Champol, outside Dijon. This magnificent monastery was furnished with lavish care and was full of beautiful altar vessels and rich carving. Monumental stone carving was of course part of such a place and here Sluter was to receive the commission that gave him the freedom to demonstrate his genius.

A huge crucifix was commissioned to stand in the centre of the monastery giving Sluter his greatest opportunity to create a free standing piece of sculpture. The cross and the figures around it are now sadly lost, but *The Well of Moses* which was only the base of the sculpture, remains. Its hexagonal pedestal has a life-sized prophet placed against each face. These are Moses, David, Jeremiah, Zachariah, Daniel and Isaiah, all of which were originally in painted stone, with angels hovering above. Each figure has an individual character which is expressed in the facial features, stance, dress and pose.

Moses, a grand and noble figure, is dressed in a long flowing robe. His beard is divided into two long strands which reach to his breast. The paint still shows on his tablets of the ten commandments in his right hand.

▲ *5.29 The Well of Moses, Claus Sluter (fourteenth century)*

Under a wrinkled brow and god-like horns one can almost see his eyes flash. Jeremiah, wearing a turban-like head covering, holds a book. With his fingers between the pages he looks as if he is about to deliver a statement to the people. With full beard and strange hat Zachariah is one of the most commanding figures of the group.

The whole scene is a remarkable and imposing structure. These mighty figures carved in stone, with the texture of skin, hair, metal buckles, leather belts and robes with flowing folds rendered to perfection, have faces of enormous strength and character. The praying and singing angels seen above with traces still showing of their heavenly blue paint are equally impressive. The columns and capitals of the architecture behind is a perfect frame for this extraordinary work.

PAINTING IN ITALY

GIOTTO (1266–1337)

Giotto di Bondone is accepted as the first artist in European painting to have been known by name. He appeared as it were out of nowhere, bringing fresh life to the elegant, sophisticated but unreal art being painted elsewhere in Europe at the time. This Italian genius was recognised in his own time as the painter who restored art to the splendour of ancient times after years of stagnation, and the innovations he brought to painting are considered to have started a new epoch in art. Although the Renaissance did not occur for a hundred years or so after his death, Giotto has always been seen as the first old master of the Renaissance.

Previously, Giotto was considered a craftsman whose name was not well known and he rarely signed his name. However, he came to occupy a position of great respect as an artist in Florence and his name and stories about him and his life began to be spoken of far and wide.

He was born around 1266 and the story goes that he was discovered by the Florentine artist Cimabue who found the boy drawing sheep on a slate. He returned to Florence with Cimabue and learned the art of painting in his studio. Cimabue was a fine painter, but like other Italian artists of the time he was heavily influenced by Byzantine art. The Byzantine manner, with its gold backgrounds and formal rendering of light and shade, was popular in Italy before Giotto. It was based on the imagery in the icons of the Greek Byzantine Empire with whom the Italians traded. This was a stiff, rigid, two-dimensional style of art which had changed little for hundreds of years.

Giotto developed the technique of working on fresh (which meant wet) plaster, hence the name 'fresco'. This method of painting on walls was more durable as is shown by Cimabue's works on dry plaster which have all but disappeared. However, the real novelty of Giotto's work is the manner in which he rediscovered the art of creating an illusion of depth on a flat surface, not seen in art since classical times. The picture story method of the International style was completely changed in favour of real events which appeared to be taking place before the eyes of the onlooker almost like a drama on a stage. The human beings in these events had real solidity and the backgrounds had real depth.

With the use of light and shade Giotto's figures had a rounded, three-dimensional quality. His use of foreshortening allowed him to use gestures and for the first time figures had facial expressions which registered real emotion.

Giotto was employed by important families in Florence but his important patrons also included the Pope.

One of his most famous earlier works is *The Legend of St Francis* at Assisi. Here Giotto and a team of assistants covered the walls of the church with twenty-eight scenes from the life of the saint, surrounding each scene with mock architecture as a frame. These scenes are famous for his use of perspective in buildings, lively gestures and facial expressions.

Undoubtedly, however, Giotto's best-known works are in Padua. A wealthy merchant called Enrico Scrovegni commissioned him to decorate the interior of a little church next to his palace in an old Roman arena. In or about 1306, when he was about 40, he covered the walls with three tiers of frescos depicting scenes from the life of the Virgin and Christ. These frescos at the Arena chapel are considered to be some of the most important works in the history of European art.

▲ *5.30 Arrest of Christ (Giotto)*
Giotto has chosen the most dramatic moment in the story of Christ's betrayal. It is a moment of quiet intensity as Jesus stands calmly and impassively looking his betrayer in the eye. An expression of horror fills the guilty face of Judas as he realises that Christ knows. All around is a scene of chaos as soldiers with spears and torches crowd around, and Peter cuts off the ear of one of the soldiers.

▲ *5.31 Mourning of Christ (Giotto)*
Great use is made by Giotto of hands and facial expressions in this sorrowful scene. In a gesture of great tenderness Mary's hands gently enfold the lifeless head of Jesus. The two faces are again shown close together, but in sharp contrast to the tension and violence of the betrayal of Jesus, this is a scene of anguish and tenderness. The mourning women hold the mutilated hands and feet while the hands of the other mourners are clasped or outstretched in various gestures of grief.

The paintings in the Padua scenes are softer and more modelled than his earlier works. The figures are solemn but relaxed and serene. The more important figures are majestic, yet warm and human. A host of lesser characters make up each scene and their lesser dignity can be seen in their more lively facial expressions. In keeping with the tradition of the time, Giotto always depicts Christ and other sacred characters from the Bible in a dignified and serene posture.

A particularly dramatic scene is the *Kiss of Judas*. This is a scene of frenzied activity, dominated by the massive figure of Judas and the sweep of his great yellow cloak as he reaches out to embrace Christ. The beautiful dignified face of Jesus next to that of the repellent Judas is a powerful image of good versus evil.

The *Mourning of Christ* is one of the most moving and powerful scenes of the series. It is famous for its expression of intense human grief. The lifeless figure of Christ is surrounded by the apostles in despair, with the figure of St John leaning over with a foreshortened arm outstretched in a gesture of real but dignified grief. Mary, distraught with sorrow, searches her son's face for some sign of life. The group of mourners stand and sit, each showing their grief in a distinct fashion, while the angels above wring their hands and cry out in unrestrained mourning.

In his lifetime Giotto raised painting to a position of high respect among the arts, changing the course of European art dramatically. However, ten years after his death the plague or black death swept through Europe drastically reducing the population and bringing in its wake a sense of terror and pessimism. Plague was viewed as a punishment from God, and perhaps in an effort to appease his wrath, painting returned to the remote and rigid style of the Byzantine pre-Giotto style. The population of Florence was halved and it was to be another one hundred years before painters of that city again began to look at the realistic, warm human scenes and learn from them.

EXAM QUESTIONS

1990 Ordinary level

5. Describe the main doorway of a typical Romanesque church, using diagrams and sketches to illustrate its structure and decoration.

   or

   Give a brief account of the principal features of the work of Cimabue or Giotto.

1991 Ordinary level

5. Give an account of a work of Gothic sculpture that you know.

   or

   Give an account of the art of stained glass in the Gothic period.

1992 Ordinary level

5. Give an account of a major Romanesque or Gothic building with which you are familiar. Illustrate your answer with sketches and diagrams.

1993 Ordinary level

5. Discuss the architectural style, the use of sculpture and stained glass in any major church of the Gothic period.

1994 Ordinary level

5. Describe the sculpture found in an important Gothic church and discuss its relationship to the structure of the building.

1995 Ordinary level

5. Give a detailed account of the sculpture of the Gothic period, using sketches to illustrate your points.

1990 Higher level

5. Describe and discuss an example of *one* of the following from the medieval period: a piece of sculpture, a book of hours, a stained glass window, a tapestry.

1991 Higher level

5. Explain how the structure and decoration of any Gothic church or cathedral was influenced by the building techniques and religious beliefs of the time. Use sketches and diagrams to support your answer.

1992 Higher level

5. Why is Giotto regarded as one of the greatest innovators in the history of art? Refer to specific works and give their location.

1993 Higher level

5. Write as fully as you can on *one* of the following:
   (a) The Last Judgment by Gislebertus (Tympanum sculpture, Autun Cathedral twelfth century)
   (b) Madonna and Child with Angels by Cimabue (thirteenth century, Uffizi, Florence)
   (c) The Well of Moses by Claus Sluter (late fourteenth century-early fifteenth century)
   (d) A page from *Les Très Riches Heures du Duc de Berry* (early fifteenth century).

1994 Higher level

5. Give an account of the main architectural and decorative features of a Gothic cathedral and explain how the building you have described differs from an earlier church of the Romanesque period.

1995 Higher level

Write an essay on the art of stained glass in the Middle Ages. Describe how stained glass influenced:

(a) the interior of the building
(b) the devotion of the worshippers.

CHAPTER SIX

The Renaissance

The Renaissance (Fifteenth and Sixteenth Centuries)

The art of ancient Greece and Rome had lain in neglect for one thousand years, most of it destroyed. During the fifteenth century Italian artists began to look at classical Roman art which still survived in that country, and began to learn from it bringing new life or a rebirth to art.

The Renaissance is associated with fifteenth and sixteenth-century art and architecture in Italy. The word itself is French and means 'rebirth'. This intellectual movement began in the city of Florence and gradually spread to other countries in Europe during the fifteenth century.

The term *quattrocento* is the Italian for 'four hundred' and refers to the achievements of the fifteenth century or the 1400s. The term *cinquecento* or 'five hundred' refers to the 1500s or the High Renaissance in the sixteenth century.

The ideas and artistic discoveries of the Renaissance made it one of the most important movements of western Europe and was to greatly influence many artistic styles for centuries to come.

The Renaissance began from a complex set of ideas, both cultural and political, based on a movement called 'Humanism'.

Humanists studied the cultures of ancient Greece and Rome. Ideas from the literature of Rome spread to painting, the other arts and, of course, science. Objects collected from the classical period served as models for new works of art. Artists were inspired by themes from classical literature, art and architecture. With the interest in humanism the artists' own ideas were now considered important and so they achieved a new social status.

The artists of the middle ages were considered craftsmen, there to display the word of God, but the Renaissance artist was valued as an individual and helped by a group of patrons who admired the art of antiquity and bought and commissioned works of art.

The Renaissance brought ancient and pagan ideas into a Christian world. In Renaissance art mythological themes existed side by side with themes from the Bible. The Renaissance idea of beauty was based on the rules of nature with humankind as its most perfect creation. A perfect set of proportions determined the correct way for the Renaissance painters and sculptors to portray the human. Humanity was considered the centre of all things; all nature could be dominated by human will. It was considered that everything in the world could be represented according to human scale. Art was a means by which nature could be studied and represented according to human rules.

The features and expressions of the face were studied by artists, and certain aspects were considered to express ideal qualities such as honour and virtue.

The movement of the human body was also of interest to artists. Dancing was considered the language of the soul and was highly praised. Figures were often portrayed dancing by artists.

Space in Renaissance painting was realistically portrayed. The geometric problem of depicting a three-dimensional world on a flat surface was considered a problem that could be solved logically. Thus developed the skill of perspective. The rules of artificial perspective meant that the artist calculated the distances between the objects in the painting and their proportions in relation to the viewpoint of the person looking at the painting.

Art presented the new view of the world based on man and nature, replacing the medieval view which was based on God and Heaven.

Architecture

The medieval emphasis in architecture was on vertical buildings which pointed towards God and Heaven. Renaissance buildings were horizontal and hugged the ground. Antique methods of building were rediscovered which had not been used during the middle ages.

Sculpture

Sculptors of the middle ages made statues of the saints. Renaissance sculptors studied many antique statues and celebrated the human form for its own sake.

Painting

The gold backgrounds of medieval paintings were replaced during the Renaissance. Painting represented the real three-dimensional world with perfectly proportioned human figures.

Patronage

During the Renaissance the relationship between artist and patron changed. Artists had always been given financial support, but now the patron commissioned works of art to improve his own social standing and bring glory to his family. The patron commissioned artworks for religious and political reasons. In financing an artistic project the patron was finding a place for himself in history. Unlike the middle ages when patrons had appeared as small figures blending in with the scene, the Renaissance patron and his family began to appear in paintings as major characters in the story, even when the subject was religious.

The Church no longer controlled all artistic production. For aristocratic and wealthy middle-class patrons ownership of artworks was a luxury and a sign of social standing in society. With important families competing with each other in this way, artistic production increased and the more important the family, the more they wished to employ the leading artists of the day.

Fifteenth Century: Early Renaissance in Florence

Architects (early 15th century)
Filippo Brunelleschi (377–1446)
Leone Battista Alberti (1404–1472)

Sculptors (early 15th century)
Lorenzo Ghiberti (1378–1455)
Donato Donatello (1386–1466)

Painters (early 15th century)
Masaccio (1401–1428)
Paolo Uccello (1397–1475)

Painters (late 15th century)
Piero della Francesca (1415–1492)
Sandro Botticelli (1446–1510)

The Early Renaissance in Florence

Architecture

Renaissance architecture followed two basic principles. It was based on:

(a) the formal elements of Greek and Roman architecture; and
(b) the rules of perspective.

The formal classical elements derived from ancient Greece and Rome were: columns, pilasters, capitals, entablatures and arches.

Renaissance architecture with its classical elements was very different in appearance from the Gothic architecture which preceded it. Medieval buildings were considered unnatural by Renaissance architects. Walls of buildings, which during the Gothic period had been filled with stained glass, were now solid again. On the exterior, walls were either left plain (rusticated) form or covered with a coloured marble.

Two ground plans were used in the building of churches:

(a) the basilica which took the form of a Latin cross had a long nave and two shorter arms;
(b) the centralised ground plan which was considered the ideal Renaissance church. (The circle was considered the most perfect geometric shape and as such was considered to be the work of God.)

The chief architects of Florence were Filippo Brunelleschi and Leone Battista Alberti.

FILIPPO BRUNELLESCHI (1377–1446)

It was in Florence in the first quarter of the fifteenth century that the style now known as Renaissance originated. Its beginnings were largely due to the work of one man who rediscovered the antique methods of building. Filippo Brunelleschi joined together his practical learning and artistic knowledge of a great culture.

Born the son of a notary in Florence, the young Brunelleschi was destined by his father to follow in his footsteps. He was eventually allowed to follow his real interest, that of art and design, which was then taken to be the study and invention of all sorts of mechanical techniques. He began in a goldsmith's workshop where he was soon embossing and engraving in silver and casting small figures in metal.

The fifteenth century was welcomed in with a competition to build a pair of bronze doors for the baptistery of St John, an octagonal building in the centre of Florence. Brunelleschi submitted a design and was selected as one of two finalists. After heated discussions, not only among the judges but among the people of Florence, Brunelleschi's design was rejected in favour of Lorenzo Ghiberti's.

Brunelleschi soon felt the need to continue his lessons from antiquity. He departed for Rome with Donatello, his young sculptor friend, where he spent several years drawing and copying ancient buildings and statues. Brunelleschi excelled at mathematics and geometry in particular, but was also a student of literature and knew the Bible by heart. Artists at that time were expected to excel in several areas and be able to tackle a wide variety of artistic projects. Linking theory and practice together, Brunelleschi was the ideal Renaissance man: sculptor, architect, painter and scholar. Having studied the ancient buildings of Rome he returned to Florence in 1410 well equipped to take on the challenge of finishing the greatest project of Florence, the *dome of the cathedral of St Maria del Fiore* [6.1].

6.1 The dome of the Cathedral of St Maria del Fiore (Brunelleschi) Florence ▶
Brunelleschi designed the dome of the cathedral on an octagonal base with ribs and an inner and outer shell. The dome placed on a high drum dominates the skyline of Florence. It was built for external effect which was a characteristic of Renaissance architecture and was the largest dome since the Pantheon.

The cathedral in the centre of Florence had been started in the thirteenth century under the direction of Giotto, with special emphasis on the bell tower. Its building had continued slowly during the fourteenth century and its plan included a long nave and two aisles ending in an octagonal space. The width of the nave and the aisles meant that an extremely large space had to be spanned that would have been impossible with the traditional Gothic vaulting system. Knowledge of mechanics as well as the study of ancient Roman buildings enabled Brunelleschi to tackle this architectural challenge. He had studied the vaulting system of the Pantheon in Rome and, using mathematical calculations, he submitted a design for a cupola that was constructed by resting a series of concentric rings on the octagonal stone drum. These courses of brick and stone were each strong enough to support the next as the dome slanted inwards and upwards. The stones then formed eight heavy ribs resting on the corners of the octagonal-shaped drum. This meant that the huge drum was actually self-supporting during construction. Between the ribs the brickwork was laid in a herringbone pattern for added strength.

The dome itself is constructed to have an inner and outer shell, with an internal support system of chains of timber and iron. The inside shell served to solve the problem of access during building and later for maintenance. The walls are thick (5 m) and the dome is quite steep. The massive stone ribs bind the outer and inner shells together and ensure the strength and stability of this great landmark which looks as though a great umbrella was opened over the centre of Florence.

Another of Brunelleschi's designs is a little church built for the powerful Pazzi family as part of the church of St Croce in Florence. *The Pazzi Chapel* [6.2] is a rectangular shape but the domed roof places a circular form on the space. It is decorated on the interior with bright colours and classical ornaments. The decoration includes shells and cherubs and low relief sculptured medallions.

6.2 The Pazzi Chapel, St Croce (Brunelleschi) Florence

This little chapel is a brilliant example of fifteenth-century architecture. Its most noticeable feature is the way the two sides of the portico are united by a central arch which was later used as the basis for the design of the Palladian or Venetian window.

LEONE BATTISTA ALBERTI (1406–1472)

A fellow architect of Brunelleschi was Leone Battista Alberti. Alberti was a humanist but also a painter, sculptor and influential architect. He had written a book translating his artistic work into words which made him the ideal man for explaining Renaissance artistic theory.

Elaborate and beautiful villas were built in the country and in the cities during the Renaissance by middle-class families as well as the nobility. A town house was known as a palazzo. A palazzo became the symbol of the 'urban lord' in the same way as the castle had been in medieval times. Large windows looked out on to the street and large spacious rooms opened off an inner courtyard. Alberti designed the *Palazzo Rucellai* [6.2] in Florence for the rich and influential Rucellai family. It was traditional to divide the building into horizontal bands to separate each floor. The three floors are clearly defined: the bottom storey is constructed with rough stone to give a fortress-like look of rusticated stonework; the second storey has dressed well-defined stone; and the third storey is finished in smooth stone to give the maximum contrast. Alberti broke the horizontal lines of the façade with a series of vertical pilasters of classical design, creating a grid which seems to hold the façade in a tight grip. Here he used what was to become a recurrent theme in Renaissance architecture, that of reintroducing a system of superimposed orders, common in ancient Roman buildings. Superimposed order means that a different architectural style is used on each floor: Doric on the first floor, Ionic on the second, and Corinthian on the third. These classical orders were used for the first time on a palace façade.

6.3 The Palazzo Rucellai (Alberti) Florence ▶

Having had direct experience with Roman architecture, the façade of the Palazzo Rucellai designed by Alberti was probably inspired by the Colosseum. The rusticated stone and strong simple decorations expressed the power of the people who lived there. Like the Palazzo Medici designed by Michelozzo, the Palazzo Rucellai has a seat, with an elegant diamond-patterned back, which runs all around the base of the exterior where the nobility could sit in the afternoon sun and converse with other citizens or passers-by.

Church façades made up a large part of the work of Renaissance architects and sculptors. The design and style sometimes matched the interior of the church and was at other times completely different, as was the case with *St Maria Novella* [6.4] redesigned by Alberti in Florence. The design was based on the combination of a Roman temple on top and a Roman triumphal arch on the lower façade. The two sections were joined together with volutes—scroll-shaped ornaments that became very popular then and in the following centuries. The love of the Renaissance artist for geometry is clearly demonstrated in the façade of St Maria Novella. The composition is based on a square divided into two rectangles, the upper and lower storeys. These are then divided into squares giving the façade a sense of rhythm and balance.

▲ *6.4 St Maria Novella (Alberti) Florence*

The façade had been partly built when Alberti took it over. He then adapted it to Renaissance taste making its central section taller and narrower, linking the two floors of separate classical orders with large volutes.

SCULPTURE

To the Renaissance mind, like that of classical antiquity, man became 'the measure of all things', the most noble and important creature of creation. The human body had been one of the main themes of Gothic sculpture, but it was mainly shown covered in drapery and was symbolic rather than celebrating the human figure itself. The sculptors of the Renaissance were interested in man as an individual, a living creature of bone and muscle. The artists studied anatomy from life and from corpses and worked out a system of proportion following the rules of classical sculpture. Sculpture influenced painting a great deal during the *quattrocento*. Painters often began their careers in the workshops of sculptors or goldsmiths, and used sculptural models in their paintings. Sculptors were also very influenced by the great marble statues. Although subject matter varied, those most commissioned were religious, mythological or historical themes, and a wide variety of materials was used including stone, marble, wood and bronze. These materials were sculpted into statues, portrait busts and relief carving.

Sculptors like other artists of the Renaissance continued to study and explore new methods and techniques. The most significant new technique was perspective which was important to every form of art including sculpture. It enabled the sculptor to portray proportions correctly, especially when grouping figures together, allowing the artist to have the correct relationship of space between them. It was also important in low relief sculpture for the composition of backgrounds. An innovation in low relief sculpture which became common during the Renaissance was to vary the degrees of relief to suggest foreground, middle distance and background.

LORENZO GHIBERTI (1378–1455)

At the beginning of the fifteenth century the powerful guild of wool and cloth merchants organised a competition which was to be one of the most famous artistic competitions of the period. The competition was for the design of a second pair of doors for the baptistery of St John in the centre of Florence. The competition caused much controversy and bitter rivalry between the two finalists, Filippo Brunelleschi and the winner of the competition, Lorenzo Ghiberti, who at 20 was the youngest competitor. Both designs featuring the *Sacrifice of Isaac* have been preserved.

The south door, created in the fourteenth century, was the work of Andreo Pisano who was one of a family of sculptors who had worked in Florence and Pisa during the fourteenth century. The new doors were to have the New Testament as subject matter and were to complement the original doors completed in 1336 by Pisano.

The north and east doors were completed by Ghiberti in the fifteenth century who devoted fifty years, virtually his entire working life, to twenty-eight reliefs on the north door [6.5]and ten on the east [6.6]. All three are considered masterpieces.

For the the south door Pisano created twenty-eight low relief sculptured panels, most of which featured the life of John the Baptist. The panels were square and the sculptured figures were contained within a quatrefoil shape. The doors themselves were bronze and

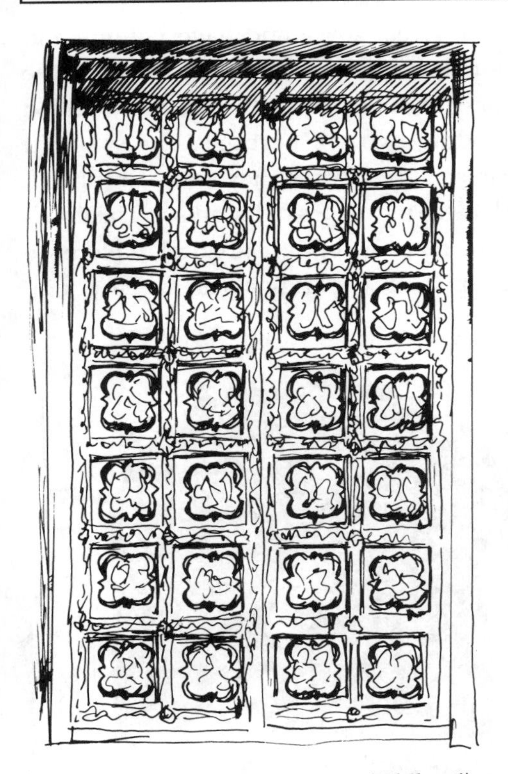

▲ *6.5 North door, baptistery (Ghiberti) Florence*

▲ *6.6 East door, baptistery (Ghiberti) Florence*

the figures in the quatrefoil and the border around the square were gilded (covered in a thin sheet of gold). Ghiberti, as instructed, decorated the north door with twenty-eight scenes from the New Testament in the same format as Pisano. The panels on Pisano's door show beautifully modelled figures with flowing robes and with rocks and trees in some. In contrast, groups of people in more contemporary clothes feature in Ghiberti's more realistic and deeper reliefs. In the earlier north door the figures are still somewhat static, but in the later east door they are almost free standing and the scenes are full of rich detail. Ghiberti fully integrated the background into the ten scenes which

▲ *6.7 The story of Jacob and Esau, panel from the east door*

depict biblical themes. The figures appear to occupy real space and have volume and depth, all of which was achieved by the pictorial methods of painting and by the sculptural techniques developed in Ghiberti's workshop of casting, chiselling and gilded bronze [6.7]. In the frames are several faces including two self portraits. The splendid golden doors were considered to be the ultimate in sculpture when they were completed, causing Michelangelo in his famous remark to call them the 'Gates of Paradise'. The doors have been recently restored and are on display in the museum of the cathedral in Florence and are a marvellous sight. Copies now occupy the place of the originals on the east door.

DONATELLO (1386–1466)

The study of the human form in art was central to the ideas of the Renaissance. It allowed the artist to express man's individuality, emotions and spirituality. The old formulas handed down by medieval artists were no longer acceptable to Florentine artists. Like the Greeks and Romans they admired, they began to study the human body and use life models. Donatello, perhaps the greatest sculptor of the fifteenth century, carved a figure which was a supreme example of this new spirit. The figure of St George [6.8] is one of his best-known and most admired sculptures. The quiet confident naturalism and inner strength of the figure are immediately apparent. This shows how much Donatello had broken with the tradition of the Gothic past. In contrast to the vague beauty of the figures which stood around the porches of the Gothic cathedrals in solemn rows of serene but unreal people, St George is a real man. The hands, facial expression and pose show the imagination Donatello used in portraying the saint in this new manner. It also shows that he used a real model. The pose is one of character and determination. He stands firmly with feet apart, his shield resting before him,

▲ *6.8 St George, Church of Orsanmichele (Donatello) Florence*

looking out, his face concentrated and full of energy, aware of what must be done, ready to step out and face the fight.

St George's fight with the dragon is depicted on the base. The statue, made for the Guild of Armourers whose patron saint was St George, was to occupy a niche outside the church of Orsanmichele in Florence. The space around and the bare simplicity of the niche adds to the feeling of intense solitude and silence that precedes a battle. The statue has remained famous as an example of youthful strength and courage.

Donatello was the first sculptor since Roman times to represent a nude human figure. The male was again revered and loved during Renaissance times and the small bronze figure of David [6.9] is the ideal of the young boy sculpted in an affectionate manner. The gentle 'S' shape is similar to the poses of Greek sculpture.

In the museum of the cathedral in Florence can be seen one of Donatello's most haunting works, the tragic figure of Mary Magdalene [6.10]. All the misery of human suffering is represented in this amazing creation in painted wood. Her sad blue eyes stare out from hollow sockets; the thin line of her partially opened lips show the broken white teeth within; bones protrude from the gaunt cheeks and neck. Her yellow-streaked hair is matted and twisted in tangled curves and the long boney fingers are held together in prayer and humility. Magdalene was famous for beauty in her youth, but now all her flesh is eaten up from fasting. However, in a pitiful gesture of grace, she bends one knee to lean slightly over the long veined feet. The figure is realistic, but Donatello's masterpiece is much more than clever realism. The figure 'lives' as she did centuries ago, with unseen energy throughout the whole body; even the spaces around the arms and legs are full of tension. The harrowing figure has the power to touch at the emotions of the viewer with a timeless presence that can be felt. Her suffering is all human suffering; her pain is all human pain.

▲ *6.9 David, Bargello museum (Donatello) Florence*

▲ *6.10 Mary Magdalene, museum of the cathedral (Donatello) Florence*

PAINTING

Story-telling was the main purpose of a Renaissance painting. The idea behind the painting was just as important as the execution of the work. Certain rules governed the expression of ideas in the same way as rules governed the techniques of painting. Renaissance painting was quite different to the painting of the middle ages. Decorative frames and architectural settings no longer constrained the painted figures who were now, instead, imaginatively composed in more realistic settings.

The discovery of linear perspective by Filippo Brunelleschi had a revolutionary effect on painting though its adoption was quite gradual. Drawing was the basis of painting in Florence (painting was considered as a painted drawing). Perspective meant that figures could be placed in a space that was clearly defined. Using perspective to create an illusion of three-dimensional space the artist placed objects on imaginary lines which met at a central point, or vanishing point. Linear perspective leads to a formal, stable kind of picture as classical art had been formal and stable. Artists delighted in their ability with perspective by arranging figures in odd foreshortened positions seen from awkward viewing angles.

Because they wished to make subjects appear more natural, early Renaissance artists wanted to paint figures which appeared solid like sculpture. Influenced by Greek and Roman sculpture, they made figures appear statuesque using the technique of shading. Artists made their subjects appear to have the solidity of statues by imagining a light source from one side and casting the other side in shadow.

Man and his surroundings was of central significance to Florentine Renaissance painting. The search continued throughout the fifteenth and sixteenth centuries for increasingly realistic methods of representing man and nature, albeit in a religious setting.

The role of paper over parchment played a part in the early Florentine Renaissance. The use of cartoons or large sheets of paper made fresco painting much easier. In previous times when paper was not available artists worked straight on to walls. Now the artist could draw the subject in the studio and transfer it to the wall by dusting the back with chalk and pressing the design through with a pointed object.

MASACCIO (1401–1428)

Renaissance painting started in Florence with a group of artists sometimes referred to as the first generation. Tomaso Cassai, nicknamed Masaccio, was one of the most important artists of this group. One hundred years earlier, Giotto had broken the tradition of Byzantine painting with its gold backgrounds and decorative figures and placed his figures in a real three-dimensional space giving them expressions and gestures. Giotto's artwork was different to the International style then popular in that it was largely undecorated, and this is probably one of the reasons why he had no heirs in the next generation. It was Masaccio who, in his short life, revived these discoveries, giving new life and realistic muscular form to his figures.

Brunelleschi the architect and Donatello the sculptor had made an enormous contribution to the early Renaissance in Florence. Brunelleschi had led the way with the discovery of perspective with mathematical calculations, while Donatello was the first to sculpt free standing realistic figures with muscular bodies derived from his studies of classical antiques. Both were well known and respected in Florence and both influenced Masaccio. From the two older men he learned the rules of perspective and anatomy and applied them to his own work.

The art of nearby Sienna, with its gold backgrounds, flat figures and decorative Gothic frames, had been the most influential form of painting until Masaccio. Leaving aside the decorative surrounds as Giotto before him had done, Masaccio developed a new humanity in his figures and a sense of space in his pictures.

▲ *6.11 The Tribute Money, the Brancacci chapel, St Maria del Carmine, Florence*

The Tribute Money is an exceptionally long painting, almost two and a half times as long as it is high. Peter is involved in three scenes but all are united against one background of fairly simple distant landscape. No great dramatic action takes place. The solemn robed figures stand gravely making gestures rather than movement. Masaccio's figures have a reality which shows his awareness of the world around him but they also suggest a sculptural feel for form and the dignified look of classical Greek art. Of the three scenes the central group is the more dominant, with Christ a little left of centre pressing forward. The tax collector in the centre stands almost on the edge of the painting linking the onlooker with the figures in the picture, having the effect of involving the audience in the story.

The painting makes use of the new element of perspective: all the heads of the figures are more or less on one line, with their feet telling us how far back they are in the painting. The building on the right shows clearly the effectiveness of perspective, with the doorway and the steps defining the space in which the men stand. Christ is cleverly if subtly set apart from the group not only by the pink and blue colouring of his robe but also because the perspective lines of the roof and steps of the porch all meet in his face.

Florence had just passed through a period of turmoil and war but was at that time enjoying a period of calm and peace under the Medici family who were establishing themselves as the first family and rulers of Florence. In this peaceful atmosphere the arts flourished. It was the Brancacci family who gave Masaccio the opportunity to work on a huge scale, giving him the space to create a monumental work of powerful realism free of any trivial or irrelevant decorative details. The Brancacci family had been patrons of a little chapel in the church of Santa Maria del Carmine in Florence for generations and it was here that Masaccio painted his splendid fresco series based on St Peter's leading role among the disciples of Jesus. The three walls of the little chapel are painted with scenes from the gospels. A fire in 1771 damaged the chapel and darkened the colours of the frescos. Recent cleaning has, however, restored the glowing colours and rediscovered some of the details lost in the smoke damage.

The most dominant scene is *The Tribute Money* [6.11] which occupies the upper half of one whole wall on the left-hand side. For more than five and a half centuries this fresco, painted by a man in his twenties, has continued to be admired as it was when it was first made. Seventy-five years later the young Michelangelo made drawings from it.

This subject has a very particular relevance to the family who commissioned it. It is based on the scene from the gospel of St Matthew and tells the story of Jesus arriving at Capernaum where it was necessary to pay tribute to enter the city. The gateman asked, 'Doth not your master pay tribute?' Peter felt this tribute to be unnecessary, but Jesus said, 'Lest we should offend them, go thou to the sea, and cast a hook, and take up the fish that cometh up and when thou hast opened his mouth, thou shalt find a piece of money; that take, and give unto them for me and thee.'

Masaccio's painting of this scene looks particularly vivid and dramatic considering this undramatic text. Like the Medici and other important Florentine families the Brancaccis were bankers, and spending money on religious artworks was considered for the greater glory of God. It was beneficial not only to the Carmelite order of monks to whom the chapel belonged, but of course also to the Brancaccis themselves. Their livelihood was money and everyone knew that; but that they should ask for the subject of *The Tribute Money* to be displayed in such a large and prominent position suggests that it was a reminder to those who believed that money was a vice, that Christ himself knew the necessity of money in some situations.

The composition of the painting is in three parts, using the old story-telling method of combining three episodes of the one story in the one painting. The central figure is Christ. He is surrounded by the twelve apostles and confronted by the taxman. Some of the figures may be members of the Brancacci family. Christ gestures towards Peter who in turn gestures towards the water and his own reappearance there. On the left, Peter has discarded his long robe and is taking the money from the fish's mouth; and on the right, he is giving the money to the taxman at the steps of the town. The taxman is dressed in the Florentine fashion of the time.

In a separate painting on the same wall as *The Tribute Money* is the *Expulsion of Adam and Eve from Paradise* [6.12]. In misery and nakedness they are cast from the Garden of

▲ *6.12 The Expulsion of Adam and Eve, the Brancacci chapel (Masaccio) St Maria del Carmine, Florence*

This scene is set on a very bare stage. The narrow gate on the left is not very dominant but has the effect of defining the space. Against the plain background are three figures. The angel who drives Adam and Eve from the garden is calm and grave in contrast to the two who gesture in despair. They are very much a pair and yet completely contrast each other, their nude figures expressing powerful human emotions. Eve howls aloud and covers her nakedness while Adam expresses his horror silently, his hands covering his face in a theatrical gesture. Eve's face is almost a mask, but its simplicity emphasises the total agony she is suffering making it one of art's most famous faces of grief. Although naked, with head bowed in despair, Adam's fine muscular figure strides out across the bare earth.

Before the recent restoration and cleaning the bright blue of the sky and the strong flesh tones of this scene were lost in a film of dirt. Also removed during the cleaning were the garlands of leaves added to hide their nakedness in the seventeenth century.

Eden (suggested by rays of light coming from a doorway behind them), creating a strong contrast with the dignified robed figures of *The Tribute Money* beside them. Their clumsy but human despair is concentrated in their faces as they stumble away. Eve cries in an expressive gesture of heart-rending grief while Adam, blind with despair, covers his face with both hands.

The Carmine frescos were unfinished when Masaccio died at 27. Some of the fresco scenes were worked on by his teacher Masolino and they were later finished by other artists. Masaccio's figures stand like the stone statues which inspired him, weathered but not faded.

PAOLO UCCELLO (1397–1475)

Some of the most original and inventive paintings of the early Renaissance comes from the hand of Paolo Uccello. An innovative and decorative use of perspective and a flair for colour set them apart from others of the time, making them unique and charming. Under the influence of Donatello, who explored perspective in low relief sculpture, Uccello was the first artist to master linear perspective in painting.

He trained as a sculptor with Lorenzo Ghiberti whose workshop in Florence was one of the liveliest and who had just won a competition to sculpt the huge bronze doors of the baptistery of St John. Following his apprenticeship as a sculptor, Uccello quickly turned to painting, settling in Florence where he established himself. Having gained a reputation as a leading painter he was soon commissioned by some of the most influential families of the time including the powerful Medici family.

Some of his best-known works are a series painted for the Medici family of a battle between the Florentines and the nearby Siennese. The battle itself was probably not very important and may have been no more than a skirmish which took place in an orange grove outside Florence, but it was painted in gay colours giving the occasion a carnival atmosphere. It was designed in three parts to hang on the walls of the Medici palace and celebrate the hero of the battle, the leader of the Florentines, Nicolo da Tolentino. One each of the three panels now hangs in the Louvre in Paris, the Uffizi in Florence and the National Gallery in London.

The Battle of San Romano [6.13, 14] in the National Gallery, London glorifies the battle fought in the orange grove in 1432. The main character in the painting, General Nicolo da Tolentino, is shown in the best possible light, idealised beyond belief in his best outfit, his parade armour rather than his battle armour. A page by his side, completely unaffected by the battle, carries his ceremonial helmet. His lovely white horse is a creature of almost geometric perfection balanced carefully on a tuft of grass. The horses look as if they were cut out of cardboard, even though their posture and proportions show that Uccello was aiming for a high degree of realism. The stiffness and wooden appearance of the horses as well as the background which has the look of a tapestry gives the painting a theatrical effect. The battle scene appears to be taking place on a stage. The painting is more a decoration than an account of a historical event. It is decorated by plumes, gold leaf, roses,

▲ *6.13 The Battle of San Romano (Uccello) the National Gallery, London*
Uccello has given the battle scene the appearance of a tournament or a joust with its gaily coloured lances fluttering in the wind and the intricate patterns of garments and horses' harnesses. He was consumed with mathematics and in this painting indulged his taste for perspective and neatness. Broken lances point inwards while others cross them at perfect right-angles forming the lines of perspective that meet at a vanishing point in the centre. The scene appears to have an artificial floor and all the linear perspective is confined to the foreground, but the backdrop is an accurate depiction of a landscape and figures in the distance continue the fight.

6.14 The Fallen Soldier, detail from the Battle of San Romano ▶
The fallen soldier is a dramatically foreshortened figure showing Uccello's grasp of technical tricks which were no doubt thought of as extremely clever in his day. It is interesting to note that there is no historical account of any casualties from the battle itself.

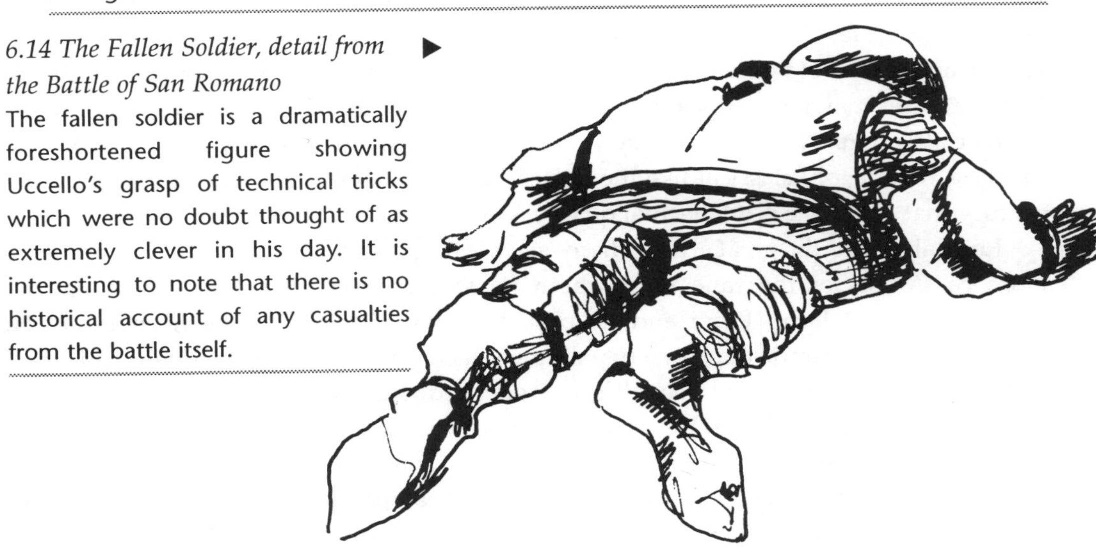

oranges and even pomegranates. The three panels commemorating the event, which over the years gained the title of a rout by the Florentines, were painted twenty-five years afterwards and obviously improved on the real thing. It probably hung in the house of Cosimo de Medici who was a great friend of General Nicolo.

Uccello's popularity declined in his later years. His eccentric solitary nature as well as his obsession with perspective caused him to lose favour as other artists emerged with fresh approaches and ideas. With his decline in popularity he left no artistic heirs and more of his work has been lost than almost any other artist of that time. However, we are left with an account of his life and work by the artist and historian Georgio Vasari who wrote *The Lives of the Artists* in the sixteenth century. Vasari recounts Uccello's passion for perspective which led him to work late into the night. To his wife, who would beg him to leave his work and come to bed, he would only reply, 'Oh what a wonderful thing perspective is!'

PIERO DELLA FRANCESCA (1415–1492)

The intellectual atmosphere created by the Medici family made Florence an outstanding centre of artistic activity. Though no other Italian city of the fifteenth century could claim such a concentration of genius in art, those closest to Florence were also administered by enlightened patrons. One of these was Federigo da Montefeltro, the Duke of Urbino. At the court of Urbino, which set a standard for good manners and accomplishment, the Duke entertained a number of painters, principal among whom was the great Piero della Francesca.

Now considered one of the greatest of all Italian painters, Piero's name was however forgotten by the end of the sixteenth century. He was an outstanding master of space, light and mathematically perfect forms; yet even before he died his art was going out of fashion and he was better known as a writer of mathematics. This neglect of his genius may have been due to the fact that he worked in small, little-known towns but also, compared to the vitality and colour of work by artists such as Uccello and the appealing grace of Botticelli, Piero's figures may have appeared stiff and austere with nothing in any way frivolous to distract attention. With his obsession with geometry, solid forms and perspective, his painting was deeply classical like the austere art of ancient Greece and it is only in this century that this austere intellectual quality seems to be once more appreciated.

Piero absorbed the great artistic discoveries of his predecessors and contemporaries in Florence. Artists of the time with whom he worked were Fra Angelico, Domenico Veneziano and Filippo Lippi and he probably learned a good deal from these. He developed his geometric approach to painting which was derived from Alberti's ideas. At that time also Donatello and Brunelleschi were producing works of outstanding renown and Masaccio had painted his fresco cycle in the Brancacci chapel just before his premature death at 27 in 1428. Masaccio's grave figures, inspired by the discoveries of Giotto and antiquity and the use of mathematical perspective, had revolutionised painting in Florence. Piero absorbed these qualities into his work but he also mingled a coloured gentle light and more subtle tones. This clear soft light and delicate pastel colouring is combined with perfect perspective in his painting, *The Baptism of Christ* [6.15].

6.15 The Baptism of Christ (Piero della Francesca) the National Gallery, London

Soon after returning to Sansepolero in 1442, Piero received his first commission. His years of study in Florence can be seen clearly from the painting, but already the clear light and delicate colouring for which his work has become famous is present. At the exact centre of the work stands a very human Christ with no halo but with a solemn and divine dignity. The dove above his head hovers in motionless space. All is calm, nothing disturbs the timeless feeling of the picture, as the water trickles over Christ and the figures are reflected in the mirror-still waters of the Jordan. The weight and solidity of the figures reflect the influence of sculpture.

In the mid-1450s he produced a superb masterpiece of perspective and mystery, *The Flagellation of Christ* [6.16]. The meaning of this strange painting has been a source of discussion among scholars for years. At one time it was thought to represent contemporary figures, but now it is felt that it may symbolise a reconciliation between the Roman Catholic Church and its eastern Orthodox counterpart. This is suggested by the costumes of the characters in the picture. The middle man of the three on the right wears a robe in the Byzantine tradition, the bearded man may be a Turkish emperor, and the man in the turban watching the flogging of Christ may represent the Muslim threat to the Church. The picture is divided into two separate scenes with a column supporting the palace and each scene having its own source of light. The understatement in the work is typical of Piero, with crystal clear light illuminating the space, creating a quiet solemn atmosphere emphasising the dignity of Christ and the brutish torturers who surround him. The fashionable blue and gold of the man on the extreme right show how Piero inherited the joy of portraying texture in rich detail from the Gothic tradition, while the painted architecture of the palace shows his delight in depicting details in mathematically perfect perspective.

▲ *6.16 The Flagellation of Christ (Piero della Francesca) Galleria Nazionale Urbino*
The timeless quality is once again present in *The Flagellation* with the sculptural immobility of the legs as smooth as the marble pillars in the painting. All the lines of depth converge at a crucial point, to which the eye is attracted, to Christ to the left of the man with the whip. Everything in the picture is decided by mathematical values with the checkerboard patterns of the floor so correct that the pattern can be completely worked out. Christ and those around him are placed at the exact centre of the left-hand section of the painting in a circle on the floor pattern.

At the same time he painted his two famous portraits of *Duke Federigo of Urbino and his wife Battista Sforza* [6.17]. The Duke had been wounded in a tournament earlier in his life which left him disfigured due to injuries to his nose and one side of his face. Piero, however, managed to show the Duke in a dignified manner, depicting him as the great soldier, scholar and ruler that he was. The landscape behind Battista is thought to be Sansepolcro, Piero's home town.

In his own time Piero was to influence later painters. His influence was particularly significant in the case of Perugino who it is said was his pupil. Perugino's own pupil was Raphael, the great master of the High Renaissance. Piero is considered the greatest painter of the *quattrocento*, the calm majestic clarity of his work having overcome time and fashion.

▲ *6.17 Federigo da Montefeltro, Duke of Urbino, and his wife Battista Sforza (Piero della Francesca) Uffizi Gallery, Florence*

The striking diptych of the Duke and his wife Battista Sforza is painted on wood with symbolic scenes of triumph on the reverse. Both paintings are the same size in these most remarkable of Renaissance portraits. The intelligent dignity of the great ruler is clearly portrayed, even though it is completely truthful showing the Duke, literally, warts and all. Piero was the first artist to attempt a landscape behind a portrait; the misty ducal lands of Urbino stretch into the distance making a sharp jump between foreground and background just as if the Duke were standing on a ledge.

Battista was a highly respected figure in her own right, possessing a strong intelligence and personality. Piero has painted her face truthfully, if not beautifully, with a fine nobility, paying particular attention to the richly embroidered clothes and the details of her head-dress and fine jewellery.

Sandro Botticelli (1444–1510)

By the mid-fifteenth century Florence was one of the wealthiest city states in Italy. Commerce and banking had brought great wealth to the city and, as always with prosperity, more attention was paid to literature, philosophy and art. More discussion led to the questioning of what had previously been considered God's will and the self-will of the individual was held in higher esteem.

Wealthy families in Florence were patrons of the arts, the most powerful for a number of years being the Medici family. In this golden age of the Florentine Renaissance one of the artists patronised by this wealthy influential family was Sandro Botticelli. Now one of the best-known painters of the early Renaissance, Botticelli fell out of favour in his own lifetime and was 'rediscovered' during the nineteenth century.

Born Allessandro di Mariano dei Filipepi, he went from a goldsmith's workshop, where he acquired the name Botticelli, to the studio of the artist Fra Filippo Lippi. Fra Filippo Lippi was a Carmelite monk under the patronage of Cosimo de Medici. Filippo Lippi painted an idealised form of female beauty in his charming religious works. His figures, with slender faces, small mouth and raised eyebrows, had a certain look of wistfulness, an expression he passed on to his pupil Botticelli.

▲ *6.18 Primavera (Botticelli) Uffizi Gallery, Florence*

The figures in this composition are set against a tapestry-like background of trees and glide weightlessly across a carpet of flowers. The painting 'reads' from right to left with the arrival of Flora spilling out flowers from her mouth. The theme is mythological which was very popular at the time with the neoplatonists, but the style of the figures and the background looks back to Gothic painting. The delicate forms of the characters stand out in dramatic fashion against the dark wood with its strange fruit. The three graces in their endless dance are some of the most appealing figures in Renaissance painting. In their tissue-thin silken gowns, flowing hair and delicate jewels, they show Botticelli's skill in creating female beauty, their wrists and entertwining fingers overhead show his understanding of anatomy and his ability to use it correctly if he so wished.

▲ 6.19 *The Birth of Venus (Botticelli) Uffizi Gallery, Florence*
The elegantly elongated Venus has one of the most beautiful faces in art. Her hair blows in the wind in long flowing lines as she holds her hands delicately in the pose of modesty associated with the Roman sculpture of Venus Pudica. She is blown ashore on her shell by two zephyrs, one male and one female. The figures are wound together with the female's body twisted at a strange angle to her head and legs, but the impossibility of this pose is accepted in the harmonious blending of the pair as they glide across the abstract Vs of the water in dream-like manner. The nymph Flora waits on the shore with a robe covered in a pattern of flowers to clothe the naked figure of Venus.

Botticelli excelled in the portrayal of grace and beauty. His facial features and expressions hold all the beauty that his teacher aimed for. His most beautiful and best-known works come from a time when he associated with a group of intellectuals at the Medici court. Botticelli's friend and patron was a cousin of Lorenzo de Medici, called Lorenzo the Magnificent, who was the ruler of Florence at the time. Lorenzo's circle of intellectuals were known as neoplatonists after the Greek philosopher Plato, whom they greatly admired. This influential group of humanists believed that there was a hidden agreement between Christianity and pagan mythology. Botticelli's painting has to be seen in the light of that thinking. *Primavera* or the *Coming of Spring* [6.18] painted for a member of the Medici family in 1477 is a complex allegorical work.

The theme of this painting has had several interpretations but most agree that the central figure is Venus who stands back a little reminding us of a madonna in a niche. The facial expression on the figure of Venus is very similar to religious paintings of madonnas painted by Botticelli. They have the same expressions of melancholy purity. The picture has layers of meaning, none of which takes from its beauty. The golden-haired goddess of love has the look of one lost in a daydream. She appears in the very centre with a blindfolded cupid above her head. She is the goddess of love, but also in her pregnant state the goddess of all nature and its blossoming forth in spring. To the left of Venus is Zephyr the wind pursuing Chloris the wood nymph who tries to avoid him. Flowers, a sign of fertility, fall from her mouth as she transforms into Flora scattering flowers. To the left of the picture the three graces perform their little ballet in a circle representing the endless circular process. On the extreme left Mercury, the messenger of the gods, holds up his staff to remove the cloud which hides the truth.

Probably Botticelli's most popular painting is *The Birth of Venus* [6.19] painted later than *Primavera* for his patron Pierfrancesco di Medici. Both paintings hung in the Medici palace but were not necessarily painted as a pair. It is an allegorical painting based on a classical poem. The legend of Venus's birth and arrival from the sea was well known at the time. It has been said of Botticelli that he was 'the greatest artist of linear design Europe ever had'. Unlike many artists of the time who used light and shade to give a three-dimensional effect, he preferred to use single lines. In *The Birth of Venus* the elegant figure of Venus with her flowing locks and the graceful lines of her body take the place of volume and sculptural monumentality found in the paintings of artists like Masaccio and Piero della Francesca. The figure is elongated and has an unnaturally long neck, sloped shoulders, and the left arm is strangely joined to her body. However, these details are overlooked in the poetic beauty and grace of the figure as she stands delicately poised on her shell. In humanist thinking Venus was the personification of beauty rather than erotic love, and to the philosopher Plato truth was identified with beauty. In this painting Botticelli was able to show the female nude, not as an object of lust or a temptress, but as a symbol of untouched beauty.

In later life Botticelli became a religious fanatic and a follower of Savonarola who preached fiery sermons against the paganism of the Medici court. The Florentines responded with a frenzy of religious intensity when Savonarola suggested they make a bonfire of their 'vanities' and Botticelli was one of them. Many of his early paintings disappeared in the flames and his reputation declined over the years. He died in 1510 neglected and forgotten.

THE HIGH RENAISSANCE

Architecture

Donato Bramante (1444–1514)

Michelangelo Buonarroti (1475–1564)

Raphael Santi (1483–1520)

Sculpture

Michelangelo Buonarroti (1475–1564)

Painting

Leonardo da Vinci (1452–1519)

Michelangelo Buonarroti (1475–1564)

Raphael Santi (1483–1520)

THE HIGH RENAISSANCE

One of the greatest periods in the history of art has come to be called the High Renaissance. This famous period of Italian art came at the beginning of the sixteenth century. The *cinquecento* or High Renaissance, the time of the great masters, began with Leonardo da Vinci who reached a new height in drawing, proportion and the study of nature, and culminated in the genius of Michelangelo.

The artist was now a master in his field, considered a genius and sought after by princes and wealthy patrons for whom it was an honour and a status symbol to have him work for them. The artists could now pick and choose their patrons, abandon commissions if it suited them and make demands on the client.

Italian cities were independent and took pride in commissioning artists to design buildings to enhance the beauty of their surroundings. Cities vied with each other to engage the most renowned artists to design their buildings, but Florence with its artistic advances and magnificent cathedral remained a leader in fame. The artistic discoveries of the fifteenth century were all but obscured by the dazzling achievements of the High Renaissance style.

During the years leading up to the fifteenth century Rome had remained a rather provincial city, with a poor economy and a papacy in exile. Around 1450 several Popes sought to revive Rome, restoring the ancient capital with churches, streets and bridges. By engaging the services of artists of high renown Rome became an artistic centre for the artists of the High Renaissance.

The epitome of Renaissance centralised building was the *Tempietto de San Pietro* [6.20] designed by Donato Bramante. The Little Temple of St Peter was constructed on the spot where St Peter was crucified. All the ideals of the Renaissance are contained in this small commemorative chapel. It is a round building (the circle was considered the most perfect shape) and it is capped by a small dome.

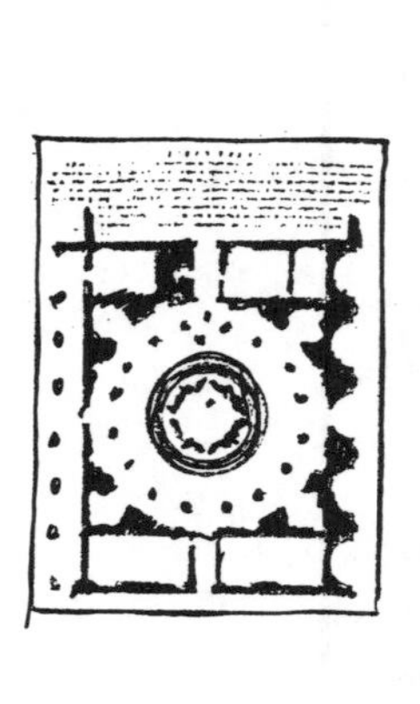

▲ *6.20 The Tempietto di San Pietro (Bramante) Rome*

This little structure represents the highest ideals of the Renaissance. Even though the dimensions are tiny the temple is a perfect model of the Roman style. The column is the module to which all other aspects including the windows relate.

Bramante was the first artist of the Renaissance to design a building in the classical style. He had studied the ruins of ancient Rome extensively and used this knowledge in his design. The idea and structure of the building are united. The circular form of the building is emphasised by the colonnades and niches, creating an overall sense of balance and volume. When Pope Julius II saw this temple he must have realised the potential of Bramante and engaged him to work on the new St Peter's and his programme of restoring the greatness of Rome.

It was Florence, however, which was once again to produce the artistic names which have come to be so well known.

LEONARDO DA VINCI (1452–1519)

Leonardo da Vinci was the oldest of these great masters. He was born in Tuscany, less than twenty miles outside Florence, in the little town of Vinci. At school he excelled at drawing and even at that time he was interested in everything to do with nature.

His life can be divided into three periods: he spent thirty years in Florence, twenty years in Milan, and ten years wandering.

He was apprenticed to the studio of Andreo del Verrocchio, a sculptor of considerable fame at the time, where he learned superb standards of craftsmanship. The earliest work attributed to him is in a painting by Verrocchio called the *Baptism of Christ*. Leonardo is said to have painted the angel in the lower left-hand side. Vasari says that when Verrocchio saw the excellence of his young student's work he never painted again.

Very few artists drew as much and painted as little. Only one fresco and fifteen paintings have survived. During his working life religious painting competed with portraiture as the main subject of Leonardo's work.

In religious painting his approach varied greatly. *The Annunciation* is his earliest known complete work. It is considered one of his first masterpieces. The carpet of flowers shows his love of botanical detail and his knowledge of nature is shown in the angel's wing which was modelled on a real bird's wing.

In 1481 Leonardo received his first major commission. However this painting, the *Adoration of the Magi*, for an altarpiece in the monastery of San Sepolcro, was never finished because he moved from Florence to Milan where he spent the next twenty years.

The crowning glory of his years in Milan is one of the most famous paintings in the history of western art, *The Last Supper* [6.21] painted on the end wall of the refectory (dining-hall) in Santa Maria del Grazie in Milan. The large fresco is in poor condition due to the experimental techniques used by Leonardo which, even in his own lifetime, had started to deteriorate. Later, inadequate restoration work only added to its troubles, but recently painstaking renovation has been carried out on what is left of the original. Even in its semi-ruined state it is majestic. The picture tells a story, the narrative suspended at the very moment after Jesus has announced that one of his disciples will betray him. It is a superb psychological study of human emotion. Jesus is seated in the centre calmly, while on both sides the apostles reel in horror at the announcement, each one reacting in a gesture of denial or disbelief.

Leonardo studied the Bible passages, as Giotto had done earlier, relating to the Last Supper and imagined what the scene must have been like when Jesus spoke these words to his followers.

The figures are arranged in four groups of three, some drawing away from him, others leaning towards him. All are connected by a communication of hands. The gestures of the faces and hands of the apostles convey a silent language as each one reacts. One lifts his hands in disbelief; another asks, 'Lord is it I?' and clasps his hands to his breast. Peter leans forward to John, who is seated at the right hand of Jesus, and whispers in his ear, a knife clutched in his hand. This action has contrived to push Judas aside and isolate him from the group, and he alone recoils from Jesus, his hand clenched, the knife held by Peter behind his back.

To Christ's left, one disciple holds up a pointed finger. This motif often occurs in Leonardo's work, but its significance only adds to the many mysteries concerning Leonardo's painting. A finger points upwards also in a drawing for *The Virgin and St Anne* and in one version of *The Virgin of the Rocks* the angel points a finger inward at St John.

Two versions of *The Virgin of the Rocks* exist, one in Paris in the Louvre [6.22], the other

▲ *6.21 The Last Supper (Leonardo da Vinci) Santa Maria delle Grazie, Milan*
Leonardo broke with the traditional method of depicting the Last Supper where the apostles all sit quietly at both sides of the table, with Jesus breaking bread in the centre. He chose instead the moment when Jesus announced his betrayal by one of the disciples and the turmoil caused by this. All the apostles are seated at the same side of the table facing the viewer who can distinguish them by their gestures of hands and face.

The picture is set at the height of the seated monks, thus giving the impression that Christ and the apostles are sitting at the high table of the community. It stretches right across the wall of the refectory and gives the impression that the dining-room has been extended further back, with daylight coming through the windows. Christ is in the exact centre of the rigidly geometrical composition which forms a triangle, with the window creating a natural halo. The architecture is composed so that all the perspective lines of the wall hangings converge on his face and the blue and red of his garments draw the eye naturally towards him.

in the National Gallery in London. The scene is set in an imaginary enchanted grotto. The group of the Virgin and child with St John is treated with great tenderness but none the less Leonardo's love of the mysterious shows through. The two versions of the painting are similar, but in the later version the figures are a little more formal with halos and the baby St John carries a cross. The gentle light and rugged shadowy background create more of an air of mystery than in the earlier version.

It was typical of Leonardo to explore in great detail whatever he worked on or whatever interested him. His genius led him to observe the anatomy of the human body and he continually sketched such subjects as the human eye, the structure and workings of bones and muscles, and the position of the baby in the womb. He also developed war machinery and of course produced his famous design for a flying machine. All these ideas and sketches are contained in his many sketchbooks where he wrote in a backward left-handed script.

6.22 The Virgin of the Rocks (Leonardo da Vinci) the Louvre, Paris

In Leonardo's work there is always an element of mystery and fantasy. In his painting *The Virgin of the Rocks* we see the 'various and strange shapes of nature' seen on his travels which he wrote about in a letter. The family group is set in an imaginary enchanted grotto. The darkness of the rock surface brings out the radiant glow of the Virgin who in a gesture of human warmth spreads her cloak over the little St John. At her left is an angel and the baby. The composition is triangular with the Virgin the largest and most dominant figure, but the baby, with his hand raised in blessing and bathed in divine light, is the very pivot of the composition.

Leonardo observed perspective and atmospheric effects like rain and dust and their effect on colour and distance. He was constantly playing with light and shade. He also developed a technique called *sfumato*. This technique softens the outlines and allows a smooth passage from light to shade. The term comes from the Italian word for smoke. *Sfumato* was particularly effective on faces both in his religious works and in his portraits.

Leonardo's portraits show the range of techniques he had mastered. *Ginevra de Benci* [6.23], an early portrait painted to mark the wedding of the daughter of a friend, is a grave and somewhat mysterious work. The gently blurred outlines of the hair and face blend imperceptibly against a skilfully darkened background. His portraits combine *sfumato* and *chiaroschuro,* the balance of light and shade, a major element in all his paintings. In many of his works, with the barest touch he creates the effect of subjects dissolving into their backgrounds. This technique is shown to perfection in his most famous work, the portrait of *Mona Lisa* [6.24]. A fleeting expression crosses the face of this placid mysterious girl which is gently brought to life with a subtle range of shadows on the flesh tones. The beautiful pose, skilful *sfumato* on the flesh tones and the strange wild landscape of the background represent Leonardo's work at the height of his artistic development. It was

6.23 Ginevra de Benci (Leonardo da Vinci) National Gallery, Washington

This was painted for the wedding of a friend's daughter. In the background is a juniper bush. Leonardo makes a pun on the Italian word for juniper which is similar to Ginevra.

6.24 Mona Lisa (Leonardo da Vinci) the Louvre, Paris

Leonardo had gained an international reputation when he painted *Mona Lisa* late in his career. Something in the sitter must have attracted him to accept the commission. This famous painting is so familiar that it is difficult to see it in a fresh light.

The genius of Leonardo lay in capturing the living quality of his sitter. This he has achieved by the use of *sfumato* or the blurring of the eyes and the corners of the mouth, making it difficult to read her mood. One is never sure if she is happy or sad. The background also contributes to this. One side is higher than the other, so she appears to be taller if we look at one side. The changing background also appears to alter her facial expression. These clever devices, combined with skilful brushwork to produce the exact rendering of living flesh and the folds of cloth, make this a work of art that will continue to fascinate viewers for many years to come.

painted around 1503–6 for the wife of a Florentine merchant, but Leonardo appears to have kept it for himself and when he left Italy for France, where he died three years later in 1516, he took the painting with him.

The painting was later bought by the King of France and is now in the Louvre in Paris. It is in poor condition, but because of the materials used in its execution, is difficult to restore.

Before going to France, Leonardo went to Rome hoping to get commissions from the Pope, but his reputation for not finishing commissions went ahead of him and, besides, the Pope considered him yesterday's man. The new young artist now impressing Pope and public alike was Michelangelo Buonarroti.

MICHELANGELO BUONARROTI (1475–1564)

The greatest name of sixteenth-century Italian art is that of Michelangelo. He was born in Florence and is one of its famous sons. A sculptor, a painter and an architect, he worked for almost a century and has given the world of art some of its richest jewels. Throughout his long life he worked incessantly and, unlike his older rival Leonardo, gained himself a reputation as one who worked fast and completed his commissions. Many changes were to happen in his lifetime. Those were the turbulent years of the Reformation, the scientific discoveries of the earth's position in the universe, and freedom of thought and independence for the individual, liberated from the medieval ways of scholasticism. Great changes also came about in the position of the artist and Michelangelo himself, with his determined character and genius, brought about much of this change.

Michelangelo's mother died when he was 6. At 13 he was apprenticed to the workshop of Ghirlandaio where he began to learn the craftsman's trade. A year later Lorenzo the Magnificent, who was ruler of Florence, invited the young boy to live at his court. In those days Lorenzo's court was filled with famous poets, philosophers and artists of the time. He had the freedom of the gardens with its collection of classical statues and more or less taught himself how to model in clay and to draw from the human form. Not satisfied with all he learned at Ghirlandaio's workshop, the young Michelangelo studied the great works of Greek and Roman art himself. He worked from the human body and drew from life, dissecting bodies in an effort to understand anatomy and movement. He went out himself and studied from the works of the great Florentine artists before him, Giotto and Donatello, and drew from Masaccio's *Tribute Money*.

He was constantly looking for challenge in drawing the nude. He had superb drawing ability and drew from difficult angles, setting the model in ever more difficult poses until as a young artist he gained a reputation as having surpassed the old masters of the classical era.

As an infant Michelangelo had been reared by a wet nurse in a family of stonecutters. He himself said that this led to his future as an artist. He had a great knowledge of stone and selected each block with care and attention, often spending weeks in the Carrara marble quarries outside Rome.

With the death of Lorenzo the Magnificent, Michelangelo returned to his father's house and had to leave Florence when it became difficult for the Medici family who had been his patrons.

SCULPTURE

At the age of 21 Michelangelo went to Rome for the first time and spent five years there. At the age of 23 he produced one of his most moving and, in the words of Vasari, a work of 'divine beauty'. In *Pieta* [6.25] he approached a subject more associated with northern art, but it was the first of the sculptor's many variations on the theme of the lamentation of the dead Christ. The youthful Madonna with downcast eyes grieves over her dead son in a manner not attempted before. He solved the problem posed by the placing of a grown man across the knees of a young woman by building up a pyramid of folded clothing as a support. The effect is one of elegance and harmonious proportions. The drama of the event is restrained in the classical manner and both figures, although realistic, are idealised, their perfection beyond mere human beauty.

▲ *6.25 Pieta (Michelangelo) St Peter's, Rome*

The elderly French cardinal who commissioned *Pieta* was promised 'the most beautiful work in marble that exists in Rome today'. The promise was fulfilled and Michelangelo produced a work of such refined delicacy and technical perfection that his reputation was established.

Michelangelo returned to Florence in 1501 when the city was declared a republic after many years of political turmoil. He was immediately given a huge block of marble and a commission to create *David*, patron saint of Florence, by the guild of wealthy wool merchants.

With *David* [6.26] Michelangelo broke away from the traditional manner of representing the saint. He did not portray him after the fight as the winner with the giant's head at his feet, but instead showed the youth before the fight. He stands, brow furrowed, deep in concentration, with the sling on his shoulder. He is represented in the manner of Greek heroes, but is in no way an imitation of any ancient sculpture. In a perfect *contraposto* position the figure's weight rests on one leg giving a feeling of muscular tension, yet relaxed. (The term *contraposto* came to be associated with the twisting poses that Michelangelo adopted in sculpture later in his career.) He looks to where the giant is coming from, reminding the citizens of Florence of the need for constant vigilance in the face of the enemy. The muscles and tendons are developed to the strongest point and clearly show Michelangelo's mastery of anatomy. David still retains

▲ *6.26 David (Michelangelo) Accademia, Florence*

This statue was planned for a buttress in the cathedral, but when it was finished its symbolic potential and brilliant sculptural excellence was quickly recognised and it was placed in a central area in Florence.

During the Renaissance the male was once again revered as it had been in classical times. This time the subjects were biblical heroes as well as Greek gods. Michelangelo sculpted the all time beautiful male body as a handsome youth who is magnificent in his nakedness.

something of the awkwardness of youth, with hands and head large in proportion to his body, but leaving no doubt as to the strength of this young man who can defeat such a strong enemy. *David* was the first large nude statue in Italy since ancient Rome. However, not only was it accepted in Florence but it was placed by a high ranking committee of citizens and artists in the main square of the town. Because *David* was a powerful symbol of strength to the free Republic of Florence surrounded by hostile states, Michelangelo was able to create a strong and symbolic but quite political work of art.

In 1505 Michelangelo accepted a commission from the Pope and went to Rome. He was to complete a tomb in five years. The tomb was to be huge and free standing with forty-five life-sized statues surrounding it. Michelangelo began the task but found his patron very difficult to deal with, as he kept postponing the work on the tomb in favour of painting the Sistine Chapel and other commissions.

The Pope died shortly after the completion of the Sistine Chapel and the plan of the tomb was reduced in size. The size of the tomb was reduced twice more after Michelangelo had completed some of the figures of slaves and Moses.

Moses [6.27] can now be seen in the central bay of the tomb of Pope Julius II in the church of St Pietro in Vincoli in Rome. This figure is a masterpiece of technique with superb carving in the deeply cut beard, the veins on his arm and the folded drapery on his knee. He sits with the tablets of stone in his hand and a look of complete authority on his face as he looks angrily on his people adoring the golden calf.

6.27 Moses (Michelangelo) St Pietro in Vincoli, Rome ▶

Moses was one of the forty or more figures planned for the tomb of Pope Julius II. He has been seen as an idealised portrait of both the Pope and Michelangelo himself. The figure is larger than life size, with a ferocious stare made all the more tense by the left hand which is entertwined in the folds of his mighty beard. One leg is pulled under the seated figure, the other as strong and tense as a tree trunk. This powerful character is ready to stand up at any moment and deal with the waywardness of his people.

The Madonna and Child is a constant theme of Michelangelo's work. He composed five such groups before starting the Sistine ceiling. Later he made others including his last Pieta called the *Rondanini* which remained unfinished on his death. The theme is possibly linked to the loss of his own mother at the age of 6.

Death became a dominant theme in Michelangelo's work in his last years. Among his last sculptures two or three pietas deal with this. Almost fifty years had passed since his first pieta in Rome. Vasari said that he intended one for his own tomb but smashed it because the marble was faulty and the leg broke as he worked. A servant collected the pieces, sold it, and the new owner constructed it according to Michelangelo's plans. It can be seen on the stairs of the cathedral museum in Florence [6.28]. It is generally accepted that the figure of Nicodemus is a self portrait.

▲ *6.28 Pieta (Michelangelo) Museum of the cathedral, Florence*

Almost half a century has passed between the execution of this Pieta and the Pieta in Rome. Nicodemus has taken the place of the Madonna and she now supports her son with Mary Magdalene on the other side. The dead Christ falls heavily and is caught halfway. The figures blend into a single piece, united in their despair and pain.

PAINTING

When Michelangelo returned to Rome, the Pope had another project in mind for him. He wanted him to paint the twelve apostles on the ceiling of the Sistine Chapel in the Vatican. Some of the walls in this famous chapel had been already decorated by other artists including Botticelli.

Michelangelo considered himself a sculptor, not a painter, but he had learned the technique of fresco painting in Ghirlandaio's workshop. Overcoming their former tense relationship, the artist and the Pope together came to an understanding and inspired each other to a grander design for the ceiling, with Michelangelo eventually having the freedom to use his own artistic imagination. Three years later, in 1512, the ceiling was complete and more than 300 figures decorated the ceiling which had previously contained a starry sky.

It is difficult to imagine how Michelangelo completed such a mammoth task in so short a time lying on his back for three years. In the triangles and semicircular shapes, called lunettes and spandels, are the giant-sized figures of the ancestors of Christ. These prophets and sybils who foretold the coming of the Messiah sit deep in thought or read, write or argue. In the four corners are scenes from the Old Testament such as David and Goliath, and in the central panels of the nine bays of the ceiling proper are other biblical scenes. The first five panels deal with the creation of the world and man. The other four deal with humanity fallen from grace [6.29].

▲ *6.29 Plan for the design of the ceiling of the Sistine Chapel (Michelangelo) Rome*

Michelangelo prepared these figures with care and precision studying from the model and making detailed drawings in his sketch-book of muscular gestures and positions of figures. Not only did he excel at anatomy in these life-sized figures, he also succeeded in creating a vision of the heavens as never before shown. The great figure who moves around the heavens, with raised arms, creating a spinning effect as he brings life to the planets, seas and plants has become the accepted image for God the Father.

One of the central panels is probably the best known. *The Creation of Adam* [6.30] is one of the finest expressions of the mystery of creation ever made. Adam lies on a rock raising himself in an effortless gesture as he stretches his hand towards his Creator. As the powerful figure of God in his whirling cloak, surrounded by angels, looks directly on man as he leans forward longingly to receive his soul, a spark of divinity passes through the pointed finger of one to the other.

▲ *6.30 The Creation of Adam (Michelangelo) Sistine Chapel, Rome*

All the interest in this depiction of the Creation of Man is concentrated on the figures; there is no landscape or details to distract from them. This is in accordance with the importance during the Renaissance of man and the study and appreciation of the human body. Michelangelo was a master of anatomy and brought the rendering of the human form to its highest degree.

In the story of the Fall, Adam and Eve are alone in the garden with nothing earthly to attract their attention except the tree. Together they make the decision to eat from the tree and share the fruit. They are bound as one in their guilt; the woman is no longer the villain and temptress of man.

The ceiling is now completely restored and years of grime have been carefully removed. For years Michelangelo's colours were thought to have been dull and subdued, indicating that he was more suited to sculpture. Now the cleaning has shown him to have also been a great colourist. The restored ceiling seen in natural light shows up vivid lemons, lime greens, pinks and brilliant blues.

▲ *6.31 Jesus Christ (detail) The Last Judgment (Michelangelo) Sistine Chapel*
Christ is a muscular athletic figure who gestures away the damned from his presence while Mary, the traditional intercessor, turns her head at his right side. A swirl of bodies float about him in a space undefined by perspective or atmosphere. When a cleric complained about the nudity, Michelangelo responded by placing the features of the priest on one of the figures in Hell. Draperies were added in later years to the figures.

Twenty years after the completion of the ceiling, Michelangelo was once again at work in the Sistine Chapel. This time he was working on a commission for Pope Paul III who forced him to a rapid execution of *The Last Judgment* on the wall behind the altar.

At the centre of this powerful composition is the figure of *Jesus Christ* [6.31] with his right hand raised, some say in blessing, others, in condemnation of the damned who are trying to ascend on his right-hand side.

ARCHITECTURE

The restoration and remodelling of St Peter's in the Vatican brought together some of the greatest architectural efforts of the Renaissance and employed the most important architects of the era. The redesign had been one of the major projects of Pope Julius II who had employed several architects including Raphael and Bramante. However, the Pope and both architects had died and the building remained incomplete. When the Pope asked Michelangelo to take the job the ageing artist protested that architecture was not his work. The Pope insisted and, as was characteristic with Michelangelo, he became deeply involved in the project. The nomination of the post of chief architect of St Peter's was undoubtedly a position of the utmost importance for him. He took over the design that Bramante had worked on and centralised the entire space with a huge dome [6.32].

He designed a cupola that rests on double columns that are set on the end of each rib. Chains within the masonry help to resist the outward thrust. The dome is formed as is Brunelleschi's in Florence with a double shell. In this case the outer shell is pointed and the inner is more rounded. There are twice as many ribs around the dome of St Peter's as there are around the dome of the cathedral of Florence. The columns around the drum at the base form a link to the ribs on the dome itself and line up with the smaller columns on the lantern which rests on top of the dome.

When Michelangelo died in 1564 only the drum with its distinctive columns was completed.

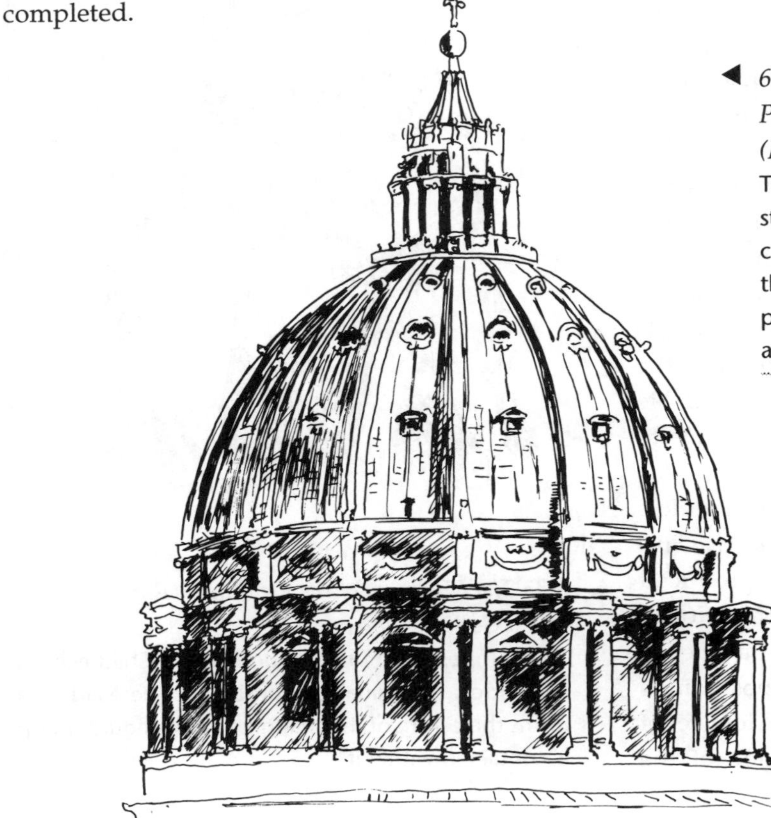

6.32 The dome of St Peter's in the Vatican (Michelangelo) Rome
The dome of St Peter's set a standard for every dome constructed afterwards. It is the most widely recognised piece of Renaissance architecture.

RAPHAEL SANTI (1483–1520)

In 1504 a young man arrived in Florence at a time when Michelangelo's great statue of David was being set in place and Leonardo's painting was known far and wide. Both these artists were setting standards never before thought possible. Many artists might have been discouraged by the two older geniuses but Raphael was eager to learn and was accustomed to learning from the work of others.

Properly called Raphaello Sanzio, he was born in Urbino in 1483 the son of a painter who was probably his first teacher. After the death of his father he was apprenticed to the artist Perugino. Perugino's style was sweet and devout and his pictures were serene and harmonious. In his workshop the young Raphael mastered and absorbed the manner of his master and also learned to copy the style of other artists.

Raphael's personality contributed to his success as an artist. He had not the deep knowledge and cleverness of Leonardo or the powerful drive of Michelangelo. But Michelangelo was a strange and prickly character and Leonardo had a reputation for leaving work unfinished and getting absorbed in his inventions and ideas instead. In contrast, Raphael was even tempered and easy to work with. He was able to complete commissions and get on with his work without getting involved in political violence or turmoil which were constant in Italy at that time.

During his years in Florence, Raphael began his series of the Madonna and Child with which his name came to be associated. Raphael had seen the use of *sfumato* by Leonardo and adopted the technique in his own work. He softened the edges of his forms to avoid sharp edges. He was also influenced by Michelangelo's figure compositions. *The Madonna of the Goldfinch* [6.33], produced shortly before he left for Rome, shows Michelangelo's influence very clearly. The composition is very similar to an early low relief sculpture by Michelangelo of the

▲ *6.33 The Madonna of the Goldfinch (Raphael) Uffizi Gallery, Florence*
The composition of the Madonna and Child echoes Leonardo's pyramidal compositions. The Madonna forms the centre of the triangle and the figure group is contained within it.

Virgin and Child with St John called the *Pitti Tondi*. In the older artist's work the children are lively and climb on their mother's knee; but in keeping with Raphael's quieter style, the child Jesus stretches gently towards the other child who offers him a goldfinch, a symbol of Christ's passion. Great tenderness is shown by the artist in the painting of the children and their poses with the mother. The child Jesus rests his foot on hers and leans on her knee. The mother herself is one of Raphael's typical Madonnas, beautiful, gentle, caring and tenderly caressing the children. The landscape behind is natural and suggests that Raphael may have been familiar with the Venetian landscape painter Giorgione.

After some years in Florence, Raphael went to Rome where Pope Julius II found work for him. Raphael was known as a great space composer and the painting done in the Vatican's Stanza della Segnatura of *The School at Athens* and the *Disputa* are two of the best examples of this. These great murals are part of a series of rooms decorated by Raphael. The style of the figures in the frescos reminds us that Michelangelo was working at the time on the Sistine Chapel and that Raphael, by all accounts, had a secret viewing, much to Michelangelo's anger.

▲ *6.34 The School at Athens (Raphael) Stanza della Segnatura, the Vatican*
The immense baths of Caracalla and Diocletian in Rome were more intact in Raphael's time than now. The artist studied these ruins and included them as a background for this painting in keeping with the traditional belief that great philosophical discussions took place in public in ancient Greece.

In *The School at Athens* [6.34] the philosophers of ancient Greece are arranged on the steps of a building which are used as a compositional device. In the centre are Plato and Aristotle framed in an archway and others are grouped in fours and fives. Plato may be a portrait of the elderly Leonardo with the gesture of the upward-pointing finger so often used in Leonardo's work. Michelangelo's features may be seen in the figure of Heraclitus who sits alone on the left of the composition, and Raphael himself is on the extreme right glancing at the viewer. The space is mathematically composed with deep perspective in the true tradition of Masaccio and Piero.

When Pope Julius II died his successor continued to work with Raphael. As was fitting for a Medici Pope he spent a great deal of money on art. In 1518 Raphael painted his portrait surrounded by his nephews. The portrait is not particularly flattering to the figure of the plump, short-sighted Pope, but the painting of the lush velvet garments and gold braid is superb [6.35].

The Renaissance was one of the rare times when a circular shape was popular. It is a difficult shape to compose in because there is no top or bottom. Raphael's *Madonna of the Chair* [6.36], one of his most popular Madonnas, shows his mastery of the tondo.

▲ *6.35 Pope Leo X (Raphael) Uffizi Gallery, Florence*
The main figure of the Pope is set in the triangular shape against the diagonal lines of the cardinals' positions. Great care has been taken with the details of the objects in the painting.

Raphael had become the leading artist in Rome receiving commissions from wealthy private citizens as well as the Church. His last years were busy ones and his last works were left unfinished when he died suddenly of a fever in the spring of 1518 at 37 years of age. He is buried in the Pantheon, a surviving building of old Rome which he greatly admired.

▲ *6.36 The Madonna of the Chair (Raphael) Pitti Palace, Florence*
Raphael was recognised as a master of composition. The colours of *The Madonna of the Chair* display an unusual combination of strong red, blue, orange and bright green.

The Early Renaissance in Northern Europe

The Renaissance was by no means confined to Italy. German and French humanists contributed to science and philosophy and major innovations took place also in the arts in northern Europe. New forms of painting appeared throughout the fifteenth century that were in no way influenced by what was going on in Italy. The techniques of *chiaroscuro* (contrast of light and shade) and linear perspective which had revolutionised Italian art were found also in the art of Flanders (part of modern day Belgium). Flemish painting of the fifteenth century developed quite independently at the time of the early Renaissance in Italy. Painting in Flanders and the Netherlands differed considerably in emphasis from that in Italy for many years. Northern painting was a development of miniature painting. It excelled in the depiction of rich detail such as flowers, jewels or fabric, while Italian artists painted in strong outlines, sharp perspective and placed enormous emphasis on the mastery of anatomy.

Flemish artists of the fifteenth century invented a new technique. They mixed the traditional paint pigment with oil instead of water and painted on wood panels. Oil was used as a medium rather than tempera due to the damp climate which tended to destroy fresco painting. Painting with oil ensured a good covering medium which avoided the problem of transparency and created a smooth, velvety, luminous surface which dried to an opaque enamel-like surface. This technique of oil painting, unknown outside Flanders, brought with it a new method of layering the paint, allowing the artist time to bring out more detailed modelling in the picture by means of a subtle grading of the colours. Jan Van Eyck and his brother Hubert are often said to have invented this technique, but in fact oil painting had been common in the paintings of fourteenth-century artists. However, the Van Eycks perfected it. With this oil technique a glow of light was achieved in the painting which was applied layer upon layer of thin paint or glazes. This allowed the artist to emphasise textures and produce effects with microscopic detail. Portraiture was particularly successful with this method, with its effect of reality and naturalistic detail. Jan Van Eyck and his brother Hubert, founders of the Flemish school, were active in their native city of Ghent, now in present day Belgium, at the time when Masaccio was working in Florence.

JAN VAN EYCK (1390–1441)

Jan Van Eyck was to change for ever the way of looking at the natural world. With his innovations he founded the Renaissance in the Netherlands and succeeded in impressing the Italians as well as his own countrymen. Jan and Hubert Van Eyck's great innovations were the development of oil painting and the discovery of atmospheric perspective.

Hubert died early in his career but Jan continued as a painter and was to surpass all others in northern Europe with his detailed life-like depiction of elaborate clothes and individual faces. He was a skilled painter of realistic landscape, interiors, hands and faces. The development of oil painting contributed to his success as a painter in that the slow drying oil paint allowed him to blend the colours and achieve detail not possible with egg tempera which was used in Italy at that time. Tempera dries quickly, making it difficult to make changes, and often results in a dry powdery look. Oil paint which is built up in layers is a more versatile medium and has a more tinted translucent look. With oil paint Van Eyck achieved a hard lustrous enamel-like finish and detail in his life-like figure painting never before seen in Northern art.

One of his earliest paintings *The Ghent Altarpiece* is the largest surviving piece created by both brothers. The closed doors of the altarpiece are quietly coloured. Van Eyck's use of atmospheric perspective, showing objects not only getting smaller in the distance but also fading into the atmosphere, is seen in one section where a fifteenth-century Flemish city is glimpsed through an archway.

Inside are twelve panels with figures splendidly coloured showing the brilliance of the young artist in the depiction of minutely detailed work. Of the twelve sections, the central area called the *Adoration of the Lamb*, painted by Hubert, amazed his contemporaries with its realistic and life-like figures.

Most of Jan Van Eyck's life was spent as a court painter in the famous and wealthy courts of the Dukes of Burgundy. At that time Belgium and some of Holland was part of the Duchy of Burgundy and Van Eyck was in much demand to paint the wealthy merchants and nobility. One of his most magnificent portraits is *Man with a Turban* [6.37]. This may be a self portrait and is the first time that a sitter is shown half turned, with the eyes looking at the viewer. The red hat (a turban) was in fact part of the elaborate head-gear of the fashion in Burgundy and makes a strong contrast between the sitter's pale complexion and the dark background.

▲ *6.37 Man with a Turban (Jan Van Eyck) National Gallery, London*
Portraits like this marked quite a remarkable change in subject matter. The early fifteenth-century artists had always painted stylised religious painting. A portrait would have been a very 'worldly' subject, but the total realism of this work must have appeared quite revolutionary in its day. The details of the face are still impressive. Every fold of skin can be seen on the intelligent face that gazes unblinkingly at the spectator. The long nose, small eyes, sensitive mouth and chin are perfectly rendered, and the dark background and red head-gear add to the dramatic impact of this super-real work.

It was very common at the time to include the patron in a prominent position in the painting. In the *Madonna with the Chancellor Rolin* [6.38] the patron's wealth and power are just as important as his piety. Nicholas Rolin became Chancellor of Burgundy in 1422 which put him in a position almost as powerful as a prime minister. He kneels before the Virgin who presents her child to him in his own splendid and wealthy home. However, the devotional atmosphere of the scene remains in spite of the sumptuous surroundings and the panoramic view seen through the arches.

6.38 Madonna with the Chancellor Rolin (Jan Van Eyck) the Louvre, Paris
The Chancellor kneels before the Virgin in deep piety. Both are dressed in splendid robes which are depicted in stunning detail. Van Eyck's mastery of perspective of space and atmosphere can be seen in the receding floor tiles and the minute details in the landscape, seen through the arches, as it stretches back past the town to the distant hills beyond.

Van Eyck's most famous work is, of course, one of the best-known paintings in the world. *Giovanni Arnolfini and his wife* [6.39] celebrates the betrothal of an Italian merchant Giovanni Arnolfini and Giovanna Cenami who were both living in Bruges. The couple are dressed in ceremonial costume, he in a large strange-looking hat and she in an elaborate green velvet gown trimmed with fur. In a solemn gesture the groom who faces the onlooker takes his wife's hand, while behind is a detailed description of a room and its contents.

The picture is full of symbolic detail. The room is one of middle-class prosperity. The shoes on the floor indicate that this is a holy place where a sacred ceremony is taking place; therefore people must walk barefoot. The dog at their feet is a symbol of fidelity in marriage, the fruit on the window a sign of man's innocence in the Garden of Eden, the crystal beads and the spotless mirror are a sign of the purity of the Virgin Mary, and the one burning candle is a sign of Christ but also signifies that an oath is taking place. With her hand resting on her stomach and her gown pulled up to suggest pregnancy, the pose of the bride symbolises future children of the marriage.

The figures are standing in the marital chamber and between them, on the wall at the back, a mirror reflects the painter who also acts as a witness to the ceremony. As a witness and painter of the portrait he has signed his name. On the wall just above the mirror is a signature in the formal decorative handwriting associated with legal documents stating 'Johannes Van Eyck fuit hic' (Jan Van Eyck was here).

▲ *6.39 Giovanni Arnolfini and his Wife (Jan Van Eyck) National Gallery, London*
An amazing amount of detail is contained in this very small painting. Giovanni Arnolfini was an Italian merchant living in Bruges. His wife was also from the same town in Tuscany in Italy. For some reason, however, neither looks particularly Italian, but extreme care has been given to the depiction of their ceremonial clothing. Giovanna Cenami wears a long and elaborate green velvet dress with particularly fine pleating under the fur-trimmed sleeve. Her lace head-dress and hairstyle are shown in exquisite detail. Giovanni himself wears a long fur-trimmed tunic and a large wide-brimmed hat. Equal care has been given to the furnishings and pattern on the oriental rug, but these details in no way take from the figures who are portrayed disproportionately large to emphasise their importance in the picture.

Apart from its realism and attention to detail, the painting is of considerable importance for a variety of reasons: it puts the portrait in a historically significant position; it was the first full-length portrait; and it involved real people in a real life event.

Van Eyck's fame continued to grow after his death, but the realism was so radical that Netherlandish painters were slow to imitate it and it was not until the seventeenth century that the full legacy of Van Eyck's work was to bear fruit.

THE HIGH RENAISSANCE IN VENICE

VENETIAN PAINTERS OF THE HIGH RENAISSANCE

Giorgione da Castelfranco (1478–1510)
Titian (Tiziano Vecelli) (1483–1576)
Paolo Veronese (1528–1588)

Considered the 'Queen of the Adriatic' Venice was a splendid city. Its commercial fleet dominated trade between Europe and the East for centuries, with its own production of glass and textiles unique and famous worldwide. The city itself was always spectacular, built on water and at the crossroads of East and West which contributed to its cosmopolitan atmosphere. The streets and squares were colourful and filled with the exotic costumes of the world. Venice was a city of luxury and power.

The art of Venice was a combination of this power with pleasure. It was in painting that Venice made its most significant contribution to art. The blue lagoons on which the city is built have the effect of blurring sharp outlines and bathing colours in a soft radiant light. This and perhaps contact with Constantinople and its craftsmen may have taught painters the use of colour, but the technical contribution and in particular the use of oil as a medium made the painters of Venice different to all other painters of Italy so far in the Renaissance.

It was in Venice that the practice of painting on canvas, which has continued to this day as a suitable ground for painting, began. The climate of the area is humid which prevented plaster from setting properly, making the art of fresco painting, so popular in Italy, impossible. Oil painting on wooden panels which developed in the Netherlands in the fifteenth century then spread to Italy where it was used by Leonardo da Vinci among others. The Venetians adapted this technique for mural painting and working on the woven material transformed the medium.

The colour and technical approach of painting in Venice made it very different to painting which was practised at the same time in Florence. The difference can be summed up in two words, drawing and colour. The Florentines, of course, used superb colour in their painting and its application was of great importance to them; but perspective and composition were the primary means by which painting in Florence drew the figures and objects together. Paint was added only when the underlying drawing was perfected. In contrast, the Venetians painted directly on to canvas or worked in colour following quite a rough sketch. For them colour was not an addition to drawing but a process which was an end in itself.

Giovanni Bellini was the first of the great Venetian painters. He is thought to have known works by Jan Van Eyck and other Northern artists from whom he certainly learned a great deal. The Venetian work is however very different. One of the first characteristics of a Bellini painting is the richness and mellowness of the paint. He ran a large workshop in Venice, as did Verrocchio and Ghirlandaio who were working in Florence at the same time. Like those masters he was destined to become better known by his successful pupils.

GIORGIONE

It was Giorgione, one of Bellini's more successful pupils, who brought about the transformation of the technique of oil painting in Venice. It was he who, according to Vasari, abolished drawing from the painting process and applied paint directly to the canvas. The dream-like and mysterious quality of his paintings brought a new word to the language of Renaissance art, *poésie* or poetic painting.

In the year 1500 Leonardo was in Venice, having escaped from Milan which had just been overrun by the French. Here he was introduced to the Venetian artistic world of painters, scholars, philosophers, poets and musicians of noble birth. Among these was a young painter called Giorgio Castelfranco, better known as Giorgione. Very little is known about the relationship between Leonardo and Giorgione, but Vasari in his *Lives of the Artists* mentions Giorgione as having followed in Leonardo's footsteps and shaded his pictures 'giving them tremendous motion'. Vasari was of course referring to Leonardo's famous *sfumato* technique. Giorgione was the first artist to use Leonardo's technique in his own work. His pictures were halfway between dream and reality and, like Leonardo's, were full of mysterious overtones.

Giorgione's own life is something of a mystery in that very little is known of him, but he is said to have been charming and good looking and played the lute. Leonardo and Giorgione would have had much in common in that Leonardo played the lyre and both were sought after by scholars and the nobility. In fact both were regarded as a new type of artist, a gentleman artist.

One of Giorgione's typically mysterious pictures is *The Tempest* [6.40]. It is a landscape with a seated figure suckling a baby while a shepherd stands near by. Many explanations have been put forward suggesting it as linked to a novel or based on a mythological theme. The atmosphere is somewhat melancholy with no real contact between the figures who are part of the composition of the landscape. Behind the buildings in the distance a flash of lightning dramatically lights up a lurid green sky. This is an extremely innovative element in painting of this time.

Titian is thought to have painted some of Giorgione's other mysterious paintings, which is possible as both painters were working in close contact at the time. *The Concert Champêtre* [6.41] is a romantic scene set in the pastoral surroundings of grass and trees. Once again it is poetic and dream-like with no particular theme. Three figures are seated on the grass in a warm balmy light. Two men, one lazily plucking a lute, who are dressed in the costume of the time and turned towards each other appear quite detached from the women. The women are nude and have the perfected rounded shapes associated with classical Greek figures. One holds a flute but does not play; the other, the standing figure, dips a jug into a water trough suggesting the need to cool off on a hot afternoon. The scene is in no way erotic; the figures are far too dream-like and self-absorbed to be just an ordinary group of people on an afternoon picnic. The picture suggests rather an atmosphere of nymphs and shepherds.

6.40 The Tempest (Giorgione) Accademia, Venice

6.41 Concert Champêtre (Giorgione) the Louvre, Paris

▲ *6.42 The Sleeping Venus (Giorgione) Gemäldegalerie, Dresden*

In the same way that the nude male figure of David is considered the symbol of Florence and its art, the reclining nude female is associated with the art of Venice. Giorgione established this subject with his most influential of pictures, *The Sleeping Venus* [6.42]. The pose of Venus is derived from antique statues which Giorgione exploited in a gentle intuitive manner rather than a formal study. Venus lies sleeping peacefully with one hand behind her head, the other covering herself modestly. She lies on her white folded sheet and red coverlet in the silence of the landscape, creating a mysterious bond between woman and idyllic countryside. Giorgione's style is romantic and very unique, but the warmth and colour of this smooth rounded figure of Venus is typically Venetian.

Giorgione's life was tragically cut short when he fell victim to the plague which swept through Venice in 1510. In his short career he had created a highly distinctive and influential style, one which was taken up and continued by the young Titian, the painter who had worked at his side and is said to have worked on many of his paintings.

TITIAN (1485–1576)

Titian, who was to have a long and successful career, was one of the most versatile of Italian artists. He began his career in the workshop of Giovanni Bellini and on completion of his apprenticeship he won his first commission working with Giorgione. Giorgione's romantic style was to affect Titian so deeply that for a while the work of the two artists could hardly be distinguished. In his painting *Noli Me Tangere* [6.43] Titian's colours are

6.43 Noli me Tangere (Titian) National Gallery, London
The picture relates the story of Christ's meeting with Mary Magdalene when he had risen from the dead and she failed to recognise him. She leans out to touch his garment, but Christ pulls away from her gently, asking her not to touch or '*Noli me tangere.*' The gown that Magdalene is wearing is of the strong shade of red that became known as 'Titian red'.

stronger and richer than Giorgione's and his figures have more drama and energy. The background, with the building in the distance, is however almost identical to the landscape in Giorgione's *Sleeping Venus*, thus giving rise to the suggestion that Titian painted it.

Titian also continued Giorgione's practice of painting straight on to canvas without preliminary drawings, the technique which more than any other was to characterise Venetian painting. After Giorgione's death Titian quickly became the leading artist in Venice creating masterpieces for patrons in the Church, nobility and state.

One of Titian's first great portraits was the *Man with a Blue Sleeve* [6.44]. This assured and confident work may be a self portrait of the twenty-year-old artist. The composition is triangular, with the man's great sleeve spilling over the window sill which forms a strong horizontal line across the base. The blue of the sleeve is echoed in the blue background. The strong light of the face and neck is framed by the dark of the hair and beard. The real strength of the painting lies in the skilful rendering of the magnificent sleeve. The range of colour in the blue satin of the cloth includes whites, purples, mauves and pinks which ripple through the shiny surface.

▲ *6.44 The Man with the Blue Sleeve (Titian) National Gallery, London*
Following this very accomplished portrait, where Titian excelled in the painting of the face and the glorious but muted colours in the sleeve, he established a name as a brilliantly versatile artist. His initials are signed along the horizontal bar of the window sill.

Titian was the first artist to fully explore the possibilities of oil painting and capture the range and splendour that was to make Venetian painting famous for its triumph of colour. A glowing example of his skill with colour is found in the altarpiece of the church of Santa Maria Gloriosa dei Frari, the largest altarpiece painted in the city at the time. *The Assumption of Mary* [6.45], with its dynamic vigour, drama and range of colours, was the painting that was effectively to bring about the High Renaissance in Venice. The composition is in three parts. United by colour and light, it conveys a dramatic upward motion reaching from the human to the divine. The apostles stand in various poses forming a firm base as they stretch out their arms following the assumption of the mother of Christ. She ascends on a cloud supported by angels to God the Father, where a glowing, golden yellow pool of light forms a halo behind her head. Her blue cloak fills and knots in the wind and her magnificent red tunic swirls with the motion of her ascent. The figure of God, foreshortened to the point of being just a head, is surrounded by a host of little angels painted in various tones of golden light and golden shadow bringing the painting to a final point.

Titian's brushwork had a beauty of its own, with a fluffy texture which was very suitable to the handling of delicate flesh tones. He had worked with Giorgione on the *Sleeping Venus* and recognised in the subject an opportunity to explore and display the potential of oil paint in the rendering of the nude female body. *Venus of Urbino* [6.46] is one of his most famous paintings whose title is somewhat misleading, in that the figure may

◀ *6.45 The Assumption (Titian) Santa Maria Gloriosa dei Frari, Venice*

not be Venus but an ordinary girl, and there appears to be no connection with Urbino. Whereas Giorgione's Venus was an innocent image of a goddess peacefully asleep in idyllic countryside, Titian's painting has a more sensuous appeal. Venus lies in her boudoir gazing quietly and invitingly at the viewer. Neither is she fully naked; in her hand she holds a bouquet of flowers and wears a bracelet, headband and earring. In painting an image of ideal love and beauty Titian has not ignored the baser, more erotic instincts of love.

In his last years Titian returned to religious subjects. He continued to paint, but allowed his assistants in his large workshop to do much of the work. He died in 1476 rich and famous, not only in

◀ *6.46 Venus of Urbino (Titian) Uffizi Gallery, Florence*

Like Giorgione this was intended as a marriage picture with the goddess of love blessing the union. The flowers in the hand of Venus and the plant on the window suggest the permanence of marital affection, the little dog curled up on the end of the bed is a symbol of fidelity, and the maids in the background open the marriage chest.

Titian has obviously delighted in the painting, not only of the flesh and the soft warmth of the sunset outside the window but also in the splendid green drape behind the figure. The red of the cushion on which she lies is echoed in the gown of the maid in the background.

his native Venice but throughout Europe. He was one of the most respected artists ever, whose patrons included the Dukes of Mantua, Ferrara and Urbino, Pope Paul III and the Emperors Charles V and Philip II.

VERONESE (1528–1588)

Pageantry, which had all but disappeared since the time of Botticelli, made its return to the art of Venice with the decorative work of Paolo Veronese. He was the last of the great High Renaissance artists. His painting is famous for its magnificent architecture and fine costumes. These splendid settings and lavish figures have become part of the image of Venice ever since. Veronese had seen the solid forms and architectural settings in the work of Michelangelo and Raphael in Rome. He also greatly admired the vibrant, glowing colour in Titian's work and combined the influence of these masters in his own work. Colour in Veronese's painting can be described as having a cool silvery light, rather than the warm glow of the work of Titian, but he is best known for his huge canvases, containing many figures and representing feasts held in sumptuous architectural settings. He had established a reputation creating a series of paintings of feasts for the refectories of wealthy monasteries. Following the success of one of these, *The Marriage Feast at Cana*, he produced a similar painting for a Dominican monastery, *The Last Supper*. The grandeur and the worldliness of the painting were, however, to bring him into conflict with the

▲ *6.47 The Feast in the House of Levi (Veronese) Accademia, Venice*

Italian Inquisition, newly revived to counteract the effects of the Reformation. He defended himself before the tribunal agreeing only to change the name to *The Feast in the House of Levi* [6.47]. Christ in the central area of the painting, influenced by Leonardo's *Last Supper*, is calm and dignified, but all around are a great number of 'worldly' people in the elaborate costume of sixteenth-century Venice who have no part in the sacred story. Three great arches act as a stage set with all the characters lined across. In the distance the city stretches away in a strange thundery green light.

Veronese is one of the three giants of the Venetian High Renaissance whose painting was to influence the following generations of artists, when painting in the 'Venetian mode' came into vogue in the eighteenth century. He died suddenly at the age of 60. The great paintings and magnificent ceilings in the grand buildings of Venice remain as a reminder of the splendour and glamour of Renaissance Venice.

EXAM QUESTIONS

1990 Ordinary level

6. Donatello was an important and influential sculptor of the early Renaissance in Florence. Discuss any *one* of these major works:
   (1) David, (2) St George, (3) Mary Magdalene.
   or
   Raphael, whose work includes religious subjects, figurative compositions and portraits, was a major painter of the High Renaissance. Discuss in detail any *one* of his paintings.

1991 Ordinary level

6. Describe any major building of the Renaissance period, referring in your answer to its structure and decoration.
   or
   The Last Supper and *The Virgin of the Rocks* are two major works by Leonardo da Vinci. Describe *one* of these paintings and discuss the grouping of figures within it.

1992 Ordinary level

6. Discuss the treatment of the human figure in any major sculpture by Michelangelo.
   or
   Describe a typical work by *one* of the following Venetian painters:
   Giorgione (1477–1510); Titian (1487–1576); Tintoretto (1518–1594);
   Veronese (1528–1588).

1993 Ordinary level

6. The architect Brunelleschi, the sculptor Ghiberti and the painter Uccello each contributed to the artistic achievements of the early Renaissance in Florence. Write as fully as you can about any of these artists.
   or
   The Madonna and Child was a popular subject with Renaissance painters. Select a painting on this theme by any major artist of the period and describe its composition in detail.

1994 Ordinary level

6. Botticelli was a distinctive and individual figure among the artists of the early Renaissance. Discuss the characteristic features of his painting.

   or

   How did Leonardo da Vinci arrange the figures of Christ and the Twelve Apostles in his painting of *The Last Supper*? Give a description of the work and use sketches and diagrams to illustrate your answer.

1995 Ordinary level

6. Jan van Eyck (1385–1441) was a major Flemish painter of the northern Renaissance. Discuss the technique he used and features characteristic of his work.

   or

   Discuss the sculpture of Michelangelo. Refer in your answer to *one* of his major works.

1990 Higher level

6. Jan van Eyck created 'the illusion of nature by patiently adding detail upon detail till his whole picture became like a mirror of the visible world'. Discuss this statement with reference to *one* or *two* of van Eyck's works with which you are familiar.

   or

   What features characterise the work of the Venetian painters of the sixteenth century? Refer in your answer to the paintings of at least *one* major artist who worked in Venice at the time.

1991 Higher level

6. Discuss the development of either painting or sculpture in Florence during the early Renaissance (first half of the fifteenth century). Refer in your answer to specific works of painters or sculptors of the period.

   Give an account of Michelangelo's decoration of the Sistine Chapel, referring in your answer to the scheme of the decoration and to Michelangelo's approach to the human figure.

1992 Higher level

6. Write as fully as you can on *two* of the following:

   a) *The Battle of San Romano* by Uccello;
   b) *The Tribute Money* by Masaccio;
   c) *The Baptism* by Piero della Francesca;
   d) *The Birth of Venus* by Botticelli;
   e) *The Virgin of the Rocks* by Leonardo da Vinci;
   f) *The School of Athens* by Raphael;
   g) *The Tempest* by Giorgione;
   h) *Bacchus and Ariadne* by Titian.

   or

   How did the architects of the Italian Renaissance make use of classical elements in the design and decoration of churches, palaces and other prominent buildings of the period?

1993 Higher level

6. Give an account of the development of sculpture in Florence during the first half of the fifteenth century, making reference in your answer to the work of at least *two* specific sculptors.

   or

   Discuss in detail the treatment of a biblical or mythological theme by a painter of the High Renaissance.

1994 Higher level

6. What characteristics do you attribute to *either*:

   (i) The architecture of the early Renaissance in Florence; or

   (ii) The art of the Venetian painters of the sixteenth century.

   or

   Discuss the treatment of the human figure in the sculpture of Michelangelo and contrast his work with that of any twentieth-century sculptor whose approach to the human form is significantly different.

1995 Higher level

6. While the painters Jan van Eyck and Masaccio were contemporaries, their individual approaches to painting were fundamentally different. Discuss this statement with reference to *one* work by each of these artists.

   or

   Who were the major patrons of the arts in Italy in the Renaissance period, and how did patronage influence the art of the time? In your answer mention specific works and the artists who created them.

CHAPTER SEVEN

IMPRESSIONISM AND EARLY TWENTIETH-CENTURY ART MOVEMENTS

IMPRESSIONISM

Impressionist paintings are some of the most popular in museums and art galleries today. Yet at the first Impressionist exhibition not much more than one hundred years ago, people came more to laugh at what was considered a bad joke and the works on display were slated by the critics.

It is hard to imagine why these paintings should have caused such controversy. The subjects chosen by the artists were for the most part simple, everyday scenes and were colourful, cheerful in mood, and easy to understand. They had no moral or political overtones which might have offended spectators and were completely uncontroversial in intention. To understand the strong reaction and public outcry against these works and the painters it is therefore necessary to look at the background of art and society in France at that time.

Late nineteenth-century France was going through an economic and social transformation. On the political side the country had just been declared a Republic after the defeat in the Franco-Prussian War of 1870–71 and the disappearance of the second Empire under Louis Napoleon virtually overnight.

Society too was changing radically. The Industrial Revolution had brought wealth to the middle classes who grew rich and powerful, while the working classes began to resent the apalling conditions under which they lived and worked. These discontented workers organised a revolutionary government, the Commune, in Paris at the end of the Franco-Prussian War, which was bloodily suppressed by the army.

A deep fear of revolution in France and a distrust of social unrest or protest of any kind were the moulding factors in society's attitudes to art.

The middle classes were now the main 'public' for art. Living in a climate of confusion and political uncertainty, they lacked any cultural background in art and depended on the 'experts'. These experts were governed by an organisation called the Institute de France, part of which was the Academy of Fine Arts, responsible for painting and sculpture. The Academy was a group of elite artists who elected their own members and in this way kept a tight hold on the École des Beaux Arts (the school of art) and the Salon which displayed the work of aspiring artists. A great exhibition was held at the Salon every year and any artists wishing to succeed had to be seen regularly at these exhibitions. The paintings were selected by a jury who were all members of the Academy and who encouraged the 'noble' and the 'ideal' in the classical style of painting. This kind of classical painting had developed into a hard set of formulas governed by what was acceptable politically, socially and artistically. Success and respectability were guaranteed for any artist who was technically accomplished and comformist in style and subject matter. Anyone who tried to take another approach was treated as an outsider and threatened with mediocrity.

The establishment was able to continue under this regime due to the level of influence it exercised over public opinion. Any group therefore wishing to express life around them in more realistic terms came up against the solid wall of the Academy and public prejudice which preferred fantasy, sentimental or moral 'stories' in art, and shied away from anything sexual or connected with the less glamorous side of life.

European painting had developed under the shadow of the great Renaissance painters. However, by the late nineteenth century the possibilities of the Renaissance and the eighteenth-century Baroque which followed were more or less exhausted. Heroes and idealised beauty were becoming out of place in a new climate of scientific, rational explanations and changes in social structure.

The middle class buyers of art were conservative and so the traditional forms of art continued to fill the Salon every year. However, some critics began to recognise the fresh approach in landscape painting. The three great masters of landscape painting were the English painters Constable and Turner and the French painter Camille Corot. Each of these painters in his own way had come up against the problem of combining the spontaneity and freshness of nature with the 'finish' which the public had come to expect in a painting.

Landscape was a subject full of possibilities and it was in this area that the Impressionists chose to make their mark. At first they were no more than a group of friends working together, but by about 1870 they had established a style of painting that set them apart from all other schools of painting. The were not, however, accepted by the Academy and, believing that somehow they might have more success with the public, they took the unusual step of organising their own exhibition. But instead of success they were ridiculed by the public and treated to witty insults by journalists.

The public were suspicious and nervous of new styles. They were as conservative and sometimes as hysterical about art as they were about moral issues. The Impressionists were branded as filthy and low and any nude in their work was automatically branded a prostitute. The loosely painted and boldly composed landscapes were quickly attacked by the critics and the word 'Impressionism' was coined as a dismissive term by a journalist, Louis Leroy. In a review of the first exhibition in the spring of 1874, he took a work by Claude Monet named *Impression Sunrise* and described the work as an 'impression' of nature, nothing more, and named the group 'Impressionists'. The group of artists did not all share the same ideals. In fact thirty exhibited and only eight of them, Monet, Renoir, Pissarro, Sisley, Berthe Morisot, Guillaumin, Degas and Cézanne, were to become famous as Impressionists.

Largely due to the persistence of Camille Pissarro, an older member, the group continued to have seven more exhibitions and gradually the public became used to the new style. In 1884 a new salon was opened which was not connected to the Salon of the

Academy or the Impressionists. The Salon des Indépendants was to accommodate a wide range of diverse styles by which time the Impressionists had broken as a group, with each member going his own way.

By 1900 the style was internationally recognised and had many followers in other countries. The success of the artists owed much to the art dealer, Durand Ruel, who passionately believed in the movement and its artists. He often came near to bankruptcy in his efforts to acquire their work and worked tirelessly promoting them.

Some artists, and in particular Cézanne, worked in an Impressionist manner for some time, but finding it too limited developed beyond it. This in time led to further developments and some of the modern movements. Impressionism, the first movement in modern art, began in the 1860s and can only be said to have ended with the death of Claude Monet in 1926.

Impressionist Artists

Edouard Manet (1832–1883)
Claude Monet (1840–1926)
Camille Pissarro (1830–1903)
Edgar Degas (1834–1917)
Auguste Renoir (1841–1919)
Berthe Morisot (1841–1895)

EDOUARD MANET (1832–1883)

Manet never set out to be a rebellious character, but his name is forever linked with the controversial painting which shocked the art-loving public in Paris of the 1860s. He was a well-off gentleman from an upper-class background whose ambition was to achieve success and respectability from his painting. Year after year he pinned his hopes on the Salon exhibition and the bourgeois public who attended it. Rejection and hurtful criticism did not shake his belief that the Salon was the real battleground in his struggle for success in his career, even though his young friends urged him to break with the system and exhibit with them. He did not deliberately go out to shock in his painting, but his work simply led him in the direction that it did.

Manet was born into an aristocratic family in Paris in 1832. His father reluctantly agreed to let him study painting after he failed an entrance examination for the navy.

He attended the École des Beaux Arts for six years where he learned the traditional methods of painting from a teacher who scorned the new Realism movement.

Manet had some success with his early works in the Salon and his work was then accepted by private galleries. It was at this gallery of Louis Martinet that the young artist Claude Monet first saw his work and admired it. The critics, however, were less than impressed with Manet's bold colouring, and when he submitted his work for the Salon of

▲ *7.1 Le Déjeuner sur L'Herbe, Edouard Manet, Musée d'Orsay, Paris.*
When Giorgione painted *Concert Champêtre* he showed two nude women next to two clothed men, but these figures were idealised, their faces overshadowed and demure. The painting was covered in a glow of twilight creating a melancholy and poetic atmosphere. Manet, however, has refused to idealise his subject and has depicted his figures in modern dress. But he was more interested in the painting itself than the subject. When he wanted to add a light patch he painted a nude and when he wanted to contrast this with a dark patch he added a man in a dark jacket. For Manet, painting which had up to this been a means of showing a subject now became an end in itself. This innovation was lost on the public whose attitudes were traditional and ingrained.

1863 all three were rejected. This was the year that the Emperor Napoleon III intervened to decree a Salon des Refusés. So many paintings had been refused that year that he felt the public should have a chance to see and judge the work for themselves.

Spurred on by the newspapers, thousands of people came to the exhibition to laugh and jeer at work rejected by the 'experts'. One of the paintings they jeered at most relentlessly was Manet's *Déjeuner sur l'Herbe* [7.1]. The story goes that the Emperor himself was offended by its daring and the Empress had turned away pretending not to see such a shocking picture. What made the *Déjeuner* so shocking was the inclusion of a nude woman with fully dressed men, all sitting at a picnic in the woods. These were no idealised gods and goddesses but young men one might expect to meet on the streets of Paris; and the woman who looks with mild interest at the viewer was described by one critic as a commonplace woman of 'questionable morals'. The source for the painting was Giorgione's *Fete Champêtre* [6.41] in which the men were dressed in what was then contemporary Venetian clothing. But the poetic atmosphere and unreal quality of the figures made the work acceptable. An English journalist reviewing the exibition wrote, referring to Giorgione's picture: ' The doubtful morality of the picture is pardoned for the sake of its fine colour; now some wretched Frenchman has translated this into modern French Realism on a much larger scale and with horrible French costume instead of graceful Venetian ones.' He concluded: 'The nude when painted by vulgar men is inevitably indecent.'

Though Manet was extremely upset by this reaction against his work, he was at least free from money worries as his father had died and had left him a substantial sum. He had made himself even more respectable by marrying his former mistress.

Having been successful in the Salon again, Manet submitted *Olympia* [7.2] for the 1865 showing. The source for this work was once more Venetian. The painting is an item by item comparison with Titian's *Venus of Urbino* [6.46], but Manet's young woman is in modern dress and is sitting up looking at the viewer. The jury, more lenient following the Salon des Refusés scandal, accepted the painting. Its reception by the public was, however, one of real hatred. All the critics were harsh in their condemnation both of the subject matter and the paint handling which was considered to have been rendered with a 'childish ignorance of drawing'. Manet was criticised for his arrangement of forms with little or no depth and which ignored the time-honoured conventions of perspective, detail and illusionistic modelling. The subject was even more disturbing. One of the critics remarked: 'The model is puny, the bed covered with cat's footprints, the general effect ugly, but that could be forgiven if it were truthful; even the least beautiful woman has bones, muscles, skin and some sort of colour, whereas on this woman the flesh colour is dirty and the modelling non-existent.' The critics failed to notice the splendid harmonies of colours and tones in the simplification of the masses of light against shade. The jury ordered that *Olympia* be moved to the top corner where it would be less noticeable. Manet, hurt and upset, went to Spain.

His work had now become notorious and the Salon continued to reject it. All the same by the late 1860s he had built up a circle of admirers among literary friends and young artists. He enjoyed spending evenings at the Café Guerbois. After the *Olympia* scandal young artists gathered around and his table was the place where Degas, Monet, Renoir, Pissarro, Cézanne and others met to discuss art and to argue about the need to stand firm against the mediocre majority. Manet had by now become the revered elder of the group and was looked upon as their leader, even if he never sought this position himself. The young painters admired his attitude towards official painting more than his painting itself.

The 1870s began well for Manet with the sale of his large painting *Concert in the Tuileries*. Although he had steadfastly refused to exhibit with the Impressionists, his name

▲ *7.2 Olympia, Edouard Manet, Musée d'Orsay, Paris.*
This painting caused an even bigger scandal than *Déjeuner*. Like *Déjeuner*, *Olympia* had sexual overtones. Instead of a demure classical nude, Manet painted a young woman in a neck ribbon and bracelet, a ribbon in her hair, and with one satin slipper on, the other casually off. These items of dress only serves to emphasise her nakedness as she gazes without shame at the spectator. The girl is confident, her gaze cool, neither inviting nor provocative but simply neutral. The model was Victorine Meurent who had posed for Manet in the *Déjeuner* and other paintings. To contrast the mass of light area of the figure and the bed, he has added a negress who presents a bouquet of flowers to the girl and at the foot of the bed is a black cat with its back arched taking the place of the gently sleeping little dog in Titian's *Venus of Urbino*.

was linked with them and he received the same hostile reviews as they did. By 1874 Berthe Morisot, who had become his sister-in-law, brought him closer to their way of painting, with the use of brighter colours and observations of light on water. He never really was an Impressionist, however, and all through the 1870s he suffered the rejection of the Salon jury painfully and depressingly.

At last in 1880 came the recognition he had been waiting for with a one-man show, Salon acceptances and medals of honour. He was by now a sick man but still painting. The *Bar at the Folies-Bergère* [7.3] was shown at the Salon of 1882, but by the time he painted it he was so ill that he had to work sitting down. In the spring of 1883 his condition was so

▲ *7.3 The Bar at the Folies-Bergère, Edouard Manet, Courtauld Institute, London.*
When Manet chose to work in the Impressionist manner he did not give up his use of strong greys and black which he had used before 1874 with dramatic effect. *The Bar at the Folies-Bergère* was created by combining the skills of Impressionism with what he had learned from the great art of the museums. Here he has united novelty and tradition. The blurred, fleeting effect of the moment blends with the solid, strong and stable in a picture. The painting was done in his studio with a real barmaid as a model, standing behind a table covered with bottles, fruit and glasses. A huge mirror in the background reflects what appears to be a great crowd of people gathered together talking and drinking. Every detail in the painting has been rendered with meticulous realism from the labels on the bottles to the buttons on the barmaid's dress. This picture, rich in detail and strong in composition, was Manet's last and one of his greatest paintings.

bad that his left leg was amputated and he never recovered. He died in April aged 51.

After his death his work was exhibited at the École des Beaux Arts and five years later at the International Exhibition held in Paris his works were greatly admired. In 1890 Claude Monet raised a subscription to buy *Olympia* and have it installed in the Musée de Luxembourg which was the stepping stone to the Louvre. Finally, in 1907 *Olympia* was tranferred to the Louvre.

CLAUDE MONET (1840–1926)

Claude Monet represents the Impressionists better than any other. He was the one who pushed to the limit the possibilities opened up by *plein air* painting and the use of pure colour. He was one of the most dedicated members of the group, obsessed with capturing the fleeting moment in time on canvas, the moment which is created by the effect of light and atmosphere. Other painters wavered from this goal or changed direction, feeling that the subject needed more structure and that the solid forms of the old masters should not be abandoned completely. Monet continued steadily in his pursuit of these momentary sensations. This was eventually to lead him to the verge of abstraction so that the subjects of his paintings were almost lost, melting into the swirling shapes of colour dissolved in light. His dedication to his chosen method of painting made him completely independent of the other young painters he met in Paris in the 1860s.

Monet was born in Paris and grew up in the French port of Le Havre. He began his career making and selling caricatures, but the painter Eugène Boudin introduced him to painting out of doors.

He went to Paris to study at the Academie Suisse where the atmosphere was free and easy. Here he met Camille Pissarro, a painter ten years older and, like himself, interested in landscape painting. Through his association with Pissarro, he came to an appreciation of the artist Camille Corot. Corot had acquired a certain place in the world of art in the 1860s with his landscapes. He painted out of doors but finished the paintings in his studio and sometimes included figures suitable to the tastes of the Salon in his work. Monet and Pissarro spent much time in discussion as to how to go beyond Corot and made many expeditions to the country.

He spent two years in Algeria when his father withdrew financial support and insisted he joined the army. After a serious illness he returned to Le Harve where once again he took up sketching out of doors and met with an older artist Johan Jongkind from whom he realised he had a lot to learn.

His father insisted that he take his career more seriously and have proper tuition, so he returned to Paris and enrolled at the studio of the Swiss painter Marc Gleyre. He found that there was little for him to learn there, but at the studio he met Bazille, Sisley and Auguste Renoir. After Gleyre's studio closed these artists worked together on landscapes and seascapes. Some of Monet's seascapes were shown at the Salon, but life was to prove very difficult for him in these years of the late 1860s. His family withdrew support, his mistress Camille gave birth to a son and he could not be with her. He was working on a large canvas of his own *Dejeuner sur l'Herbe* for the 1866 Salon, but he had to give it to one of his many creditors who kept it wrapped up in a cellar and by the time he recovered it, it was irreparably damaged. He had worked hard on a large canvas of women in a garden, but the Salon of 1867 rejected it. By 1869 his financial affairs were in a bad way and the Salon still rejected his work. To the jury he was increasingly identified as the subversive of the new generation. In spite of all these difficulties, throughout the summer of 1869 Monet and Renoir were painting some wonderful riverside pictures that were to mark the real beginning of Impressionism.

The history of Impressionism is bound up in Monet's progress in the next decade. 1869 was the summer that Monet and Renoir painted their famous scenes at La Grenouillère (the Frog Pond) on an arm of the Seine just outside Paris. This was a place where the people of Paris came to swim and enjoy boating. It became a favourite place for both artists to work and in later years they were hardly able to distinguish their work. Both were extremely hard up financially but as Renoir later recalled, it was Monet who never lost heart and gave Renoir the incentive to go on. He was also the more adventurous painter of the two, leading the way as the friendship turned into a full working relationship. The paintings done at this time mark a turning point for Impressionism. The subject of people enjoying themselves in the sunshine was to dominate the Impressionist mood of the 1870s. Their technique was developing in the study of colour. They discovered in studies of snow scenes in winter that there was no such thing as a black shadow, nor indeed such a thing as white snow. Light and shade alike were influenced by all the surrounding colours and atmosphere of that moment. One important effect of this was to unify the picture in a new way. Instead of being divided into dark and light areas, the picture became a continuous expanse of colour, demonstrating the possibilities for the use of bright colours. Another discovery of Impressionism was optical mixing. This is the manner in which the spectator sees the separate colours on the canvas and mixes them mentally to form one colour. Monet and Renoir developed this technique and began applying small brush strokes of vivid colour on to the canvas instead of mixing them on the palette. The study of water was one of Monet's favourite themes. No longer content to sit on the river bank, he devised a floating studio, painting both from his boat and the boat itself.

Monet missed the drama of the Franco-Prussian War by going to England where he made some paintings of the Thames and the Houses of Parliament. This was a theme that he returned to in later life, being fascinated by London, then a city of thick fog. After he met Pissarro the two artists painted together occasionally. Good fortune also led him to meet the art dealer Durand Ruel who took a keen interest in his work and bought as much as he could in the following years.

During the early 1870s Monet's life was bound up in the struggle to survive as well as the struggles with his painting and the organisation of the Impressionist group. He was at this time painting his splendid *Argenteuil* and *Gare St Lazare* series. After his return from England he settled at Argenteuil where he was enthralled with the beauty of the countryside. He painted some of his best-known works here at this time, after using his wife as his model [7.4]. *Regatta at Argenteuil* [7.5] is a splendid study of reflections. The artist uses slabs of pure colour to suggest the shimmering effect of the reflections of sails and the buildings on the water.

He produced a whole series of paintings of the railway station at St Lazare, where his interest was in capturing the effect of the steam shooting from the engines and the light filtering through the grimy glass roof.

In 1879 the first Impressionist exhibition created a scandal, but Monet persisted. His financial situation did not improve. His second son Michel was born in 1878 and his wife remained seriously ill after the birth and died in 1879.

It was in the early 1880s that Monet's fortunes improved and he became very successful. He moved to Giverny, a small village on the Seine, with Alice Hochedé who stayed with him after Camille died. She brought her own family of six children with her.

During the years at Giverny Monet travelled in Normandy, painting the coastline. His work now took the form of a series of paintings of the one subject painted under different light conditions. The series included studies of haystacks, poplar trees and Rouen Cathedral. He travelled to Rouen where he rented a room opposite the cathedral and painted many canvases simultaneously, each one at a different time of day [7.6].

In his later years he devoted himself to creating a beautiful garden at Giverny where he painted continuously. He developed his magnificent water garden by diverting a stream from the local small river. He painted the water and the Japanese bridge which crossed the water lily pond [7.7]. After his second wife died he became very depressed but managed to recover and in 1915 began work on his final project. He built a huge studio and worked on a large-scale series of water lilies. He eventually presented these paintings to the French state but could not bear to be parted from them during his lifetime.

After Monet's death in 1926 *The Water Lilies* were transferred to the Musée d'Orangerie in Paris where one year later they were placed on permanent exhibition. The large canvases are placed around the curved walls of two rooms designed specially for them in the manner specified by Monet himself.

◀ *7.4 Woman with an Umbrella*
Monet painted his wife in the open air with the sunlight behind her. In this way a long shadow spread across the grass which the artist painted in glowing contrasting colours. The figure is viewed from a lower angle, as the wind blows her clothing and scarf which are painted in broken sketchy brush strokes, giving a lightness to the fleeting moment captured in paint.

▲ *7.5 Regatta at Argenteuil*
Reflections of objects in water was one of Monet's favourite subjects. The scene at Argenteuil was intended as a sketch and is simple in form. The scene is one of glowing colour. The strong white triangles of the boat sails on the left are balanced by the deep reds and oranges of the buildings on the right. These colours are reflected in the blue water in bold slabs of pure colour, skilfully capturing the movement of the water.

CAMILLE PISSARRO (1830–1903)

When Monet met Pissarro he was influenced by the landscape painter Corot, but it was Monet who was to guide the older artist and lead him towards Impressionism.

Pissarro liked to paint subjects like river banks or the corner of a road. Sometimes he would set up his easel opposite a farm gate or where a peasant was coming through the fields or pushing a wheelbarrow. One of his favourite subjects was a group of houses half hidden by trees which he loved because of their green touches on the red roofs and because the branches formed a design all over the canvas. Despite his Impressionism he retained a belief in solid structure in his work and it was this quality which later on inspired Cézanne.

During the 1870s Pissarro's stature grew and he became a father figure to the Impressionist group. He was able to combine his own work with organising exhibitions and patching up disagreements and personality clashes among the other members of the group. Liked by all, he had a capacity to get on with even the most spiky of characters. His teaching skills were recognised by Paul Cézanne who was a difficult and touchy

7.6 Rouen Cathedral

Monet wrote to his wife while he was working on the series of Rouen Cathedral. 'Everyday I discover something I haven't seen before.' In all he painted twenty-nine paintings from five different angles recording the effect of the changing light on the colours of the stonework. The architecture often appears to dissolve under the effect of the light which turns the grey stone golden and renders the shadows in deep purple and red.

7.7 The Water Lily Pond—Harmony in Green

Monet designed a footbridge over his water lily pond in Japanese style. He had a huge collection of Japanese prints and this painting was probably inspired by one of these. Some of the plants in his garden were flowers that he saw in these prints. The weeping willows in the background are reflected in the water between the lilies. Although Monet loved plants and flowers and collected rare species, he was not interested in distinguishing them in a painting. It was their reflections in the water which interested him. The surface of the painting is a rich carpet of colour, with brush strokes of yellow, pink and lavendar woven in with the shimmering green of the plants. The colours reflect a brilliant sunshine with the flowers indicated by blobs of white tinged with yellow and pink. He painted this view of the bridge from a small boat he kept moored for painting the water.

member of the group. It was his ability to learn from his pupil that gave Pissarro this unique quality and allowed him to have a relationship with artists younger and completely different to himself. Mary Cassatt was a young member of the Impressionist group who came to know Pissarro through her friendship with Edgar Degas. She later painted beside him and said he could teach the stones to draw. His role as exhibition organiser was most important in the 1879–1882 shows, but he was in fact the only Impressionist who exhibited at all eight shows.

Pissarro's work was selling quite well during the 1880s, but he was dissatisfied with it himself and a meeting with two young artists Paul Signac and Georges Seurat led him in the direction of Neoimpressionism. This was the format developed by Seurat of placing dots of colour in tiny brush strokes side by side thus allowing the colours to mix in the eye of the spectator. He eventually found this method too laborious and abandoned it in the early 1890s, which was just as well because the reputation of his Impressionist work had begun to rise. In 1892 fifty of his works sold at a major retrospective exhibition and Pissarro was in a position to offer his wife the security she had always yearned for and bought a house at Eragny. This was to be his home for the next twenty years and though he travelled in Normandy and to London to paint, he produced some of his finest works from the countryside near his home. *Landscape at Eragny* [7.8] is a study of warm diffused

▲ *7.8 Landscape at Eragny, Camille Pissarro, Musée d'Orsay, Paris.*
Pissarro spent long periods away from his home when he felt he had exhausted its painting possibilities. Despite the Impressionism of this painting and the freer style compared to his earlier works, the buildings are strong and well structured even though the colours are warmer and the light more dissolved. Pissarro was the one who remained faithful to the realistic origins of Impressionism.

sunlight and the effect on the colours of the landscape.

Due to a serious eye infection he could no longer work out of doors and rented hotel rooms from where he painted splendid boulevard scenes. He died at the age of 73 in 1903 from a badly treated abscess which turned to blood poisoning.

EDGAR DEGAS (1834–1917)

Edgar Degas exhibited at nearly all the Impressionist exhibitions and was a member of the group. Despite this he had very little in common with Monet and Renoir and had no interest in working out of doors or in landscape painting. He frequented the Café Guerbois with the other Impressionists where, cultivating the image of a dandy and a snob, he delighted in provoking contoversial arguments and lapsing into irony when the discussion grew too serious. Being the difficult personality he was, he ended up quarrelling with all the other members of the group with the exception of Pissarro.

It has often been said that he was not really an Impressionist at all and certainly as an artist he was out of step with the rest of the group. He was first and foremost a draughtsman, whereas the other Impressionists drew very little. He was a great admirer of Ingres, a leading artist of the Academy, but Degas was one of the most vigorous organisers of the Impressionist group shows of the 1870s.

He drew from an early age and had some advanced ideas very early on in his career. Horse racing was one of the first themes he explored from contemporary life. Although he began working with horses as early as 1862, it was not until 1873 that he revealed what was to be one of the chief characteristics of his work, an unexpected layout. No European painter before Degas had ever thought of presenting the carriage pushed into a corner, cutting off the bottom of it and eliminating part of the horse's legs. The inspiration for this came not only from Japanese prints, which had become very popular at that time in France and influenced many of the other Impressionists, but also from photography. Degas' painting possessed many of the qualities of a snapshot.

Fascinated by movement, he studied the action of the human body by observing the dancers of the *Opéra* [7.9]. He studied them backstage and in the practice room and many of his paintings concentrate on this aspect of the dance when the figures adopted less graceful and more unusual attitudes. Degas said: 'No art is more spontaneous than mine.' Many of his later works cultivated this air of spontaneity in his oil paintings where he carefully imitated the marks of a charcoal pencil with a brush and simulated the matt finish of pastels by taking the shine off the oil paint. In this manner his backstage paintings give the impression that the colours have been applied hastily at the scene while the dancers are waiting to go on stage.

During his lifetime he produced about fifteen hundred drawings, prints, pastels and oil paintings, all on the theme of ballet dancers.

He was interested in other aspects of the theatre. Some of his works show the orchestra in the pit with a portion of an instrument visible and the feet of the dancers. His interests included the circus. Like most Parisians of the time he was captivated by the daring acts. He liked to visit the famous circus in Paris, the Cirque Fernando, and made a drawing of the acrobat *Miss La La* [7.10]. Sometimes he portrayed singers, concentrating on the unusual light in the theatre or café entertainment, and he experimented using light to widen or deepen a space and shadow to narrow it.

His method of working is illustrated very well in *Absinthe* [7.11]. It gives the impression of a scene taken directly from life, but in fact this was a carefully planned painting. Composition plays an important part in the work, its impact coming largely from the contrast of the dark tones of the background with the woman's light shirt and the table tops. The figures are placed in the right-hand corner and the composition has a zig zag effect, drawing the viewer into the scene.

Always anxious to discover new aspects of reality, Degas drew figures trying on hats at the milliners and made studies of women ironing. He made many studies of women washing. These always appeared to be taken at a moment when the woman was unaware she was being studied. There is always the feeling that the washing will only last for seconds and that the woman will cover up again in a moment.

In later years Degas developed a condition in his eyes that made work very difficult for him. He worked in a dimly lit studio away from the daylight which irritated this condition. He became more and more of a recluse and died a lonely old man at 83. After his death several wax sculptures of dancers in various positions were found in the artist's studio. Degas' sculpture had been unknown before this except for one bronze statuette, *Little dancer aged 14*, which had been shown in an Impressionist exhibition in 1881.

7.9 The Dancing Class, Edgar Degas, Musée d'Orsay, Paris.
Degas met one of the greatest male dancers, Jules Perrot, who by now was a renowned dance teacher. He made numerous studies of his new friend. He drew detailed studies of the dancers in every conceivable pose and from these he created several imaginary paintings of the master's class. The dance master stands in characteristic pose, standing legs apart, with a long stick in his outstretched hand directing the young dancers.

One dancer, with her back to the spectator, holds a red fan and wears a green ribbon on her skirt. This adds colour to the scene which is echoed by the blue ribbon on the dancer on the upper right-hand side.

7.10 Miss La La, Edgar Degas, National Gallery, London.
Degas has chosen to view the young acrobat from below as she is hoisted aloft by the strength of her jaws, moving her arms and legs rhythmically as she rises. The warm colour of the circus building suggests danger which spills on to Miss La La's satin costume. The position of the figure left of centre and the angles of her arms, lower legs and feet all echo the line of the roof beams, giving the effect of tremendous height and making the painting as tense and exciting for the viewer as it was for the audience at the original Cirque Fernando.

AUGUSTE RENOIR (1841–1919)

Renoir was a painter of humanity, particularly of women. Open air painting was a part of, but by no means the whole of his art. While he shared Monet's fascination for the effects of light, Renoir was also interested in his human subjects. He painted scenes of human gaiety, smiling faces and people dancing and enjoying themselves. His admiration of the old masters created a conflict in himself, between tradition and innovation, which led to an irregular development during the 1860s. His works are considered to be among the masterpieces of Impressionism, but even in the early 1880s after a visit to Italy, he considered that he knew nothing about drawing and painting and began to concentrate more on draughtsmanship. For a while his painting grew a little stiff and hard edged as a result, but gradually he came through the crisis and his work was rejuvenated with a new firmness in his forms.

Renoir was the only member of the Impressionists who came from a working-class background. He worked for many years in a porcelain factory in Paris decorating the china with little flowers. He left this work to attend the École des Beaux Arts and went from there to Gleyre's studio. It was here that he met the artists who were to remain his friends and become part of the Impressionist group.

Renoir always had ambition to succeed as an artist, but even with early success at the

Salon he did not get enough commissions to make a living as an artist.

In the summer of 1869 Renoir was so hard up that he and his mistress were living with his parents who had retired to Bougival outside Paris. There he was living near Monet who was even more hard up. Despite this the two artists painted out of doors together

◀ *7.11 Absinthe, Edgar Degas, Musée d'Orsay, Paris.*
Degas worked hard on the composition of space in this picture. The light falling on the figures creates a play of light and shade and adds to the feeling of gloom in the work. The colours were carefully chosen, browns and whites, with a yellow-brown floor. The slumped figure of the young woman who stares ahead without expression, her hands lifelessly by her side and her feet outstretched on the floor ahead, looks so lifelike that it is hard to remember that she was in fact an actress who modelled for the painting. Her companion makes no contact with her and stares away, a fixed expression on his face. The model was a friend of Degas, a painter called Marcellin Desboutins.

whenever they could afford paint and began a partnership that was to form a cornerstone in the development of Impressionism.

Renoir was totally involved in the Impressionist movement from its earliest days and was one of the chief organisers of the 1874 exhibition. His close relationship with Monet in the summer of 1869 at La Grenouillère was crucial to the development of *plein air* techniques. He continued to be involved with the second and third shows, but he was the first of the Impressionists to return to painting for the Salon, and also the first to break with the new technique.

Renoir's work was at its most Impressionistic during the decade between 1872 and 1882. He spent a great deal of time with Monet and painted him and his wife Camille in many of these scenes. His famous pictures of the *Swing* and the *Moulin de la Galette* were from this period. Around 1882 both artists appeared to hit a crisis. Monet remained true to the ideals of Impressionism, but Renoir and Pissarro changed course. The *Luncheon of the Boating Party* [7.12] marks the end of his Impressionist phase. These years were undoubtedly happy ones for him, but they were also years of poverty.

For some years after, Renoir made his living from portraiture. This occupation suited him because with his pleasant manner he got on well with people. He got to know middle-class influential clients. At this time he produced some splendid portraits and made numerous studies of two young girls sometimes wearing hats. His mistress was 20-year-old Aline Charigot and at 40 he married her. As his model she featured in many of his scenes, as in *Dancing in the Country* [7.13] and later breastfeeding their first born. In later years after his wife died he made a small bronze sculpture of this happy scene.

His dissatisfaction with his painting arose after a trip to Italy where he was impressed by Raphael's work. He felt he still had a lot to learn. He changed his approach to painting making it more formal and solid. Different styles are noticeable in *The Umbrellas* [7.14] as he tried to emphasise draughtsmanship more.

When he realised that an over-emphasis on drawing and composition was spoiling the quality of his work, Renoir returned to a softer approach. His light was no longer rigid, but it did not regain the flickering quality of his earlier works. Some of his most beautiful paintings are of young women with pearly flesh tones, mature in body but still childlike in face.

▲ *7.12 Luncheon of the Boating Party, Auguste Renoir, Phillips Collection, Washington.*
The scene is set in a restaurant at the riverside. This was a favourite spot for boating enthusiasts and their girlfriends. It is the end of the lunch and the remains of the food and drink are on the table. All appear to be enjoying themselves after the boating expedition.

The composition of the picture is linked together by the interchange of glances among the members of the group. The girl in the centre leaning on the rail leads the eye to the three on the right. A relationship of some kind seems to be suggested by the artist. Among the group is the actress Ellen Andrée who posed in *Absinthe* for Degas. The woman on the left-hand side with the dog is Aline Charigot, Renoir's future wife and favourite model.

The figures are posed in a natural manner and the composition is open, so the spectator feels part of the group.

7.13 Dancing in the Country, Auguste Renoir, Musée d'Orsay, Paris. ▶

This painting and its companion, *Dancing in the City,* were painted for Durand Ruel the art collector who was the main supporter of the Impressionists. The model is once again his mistress, Aline Charigot, and Renoir's friend, a painter named Paul Lhote.

Aline's plump figure sways merrily with her partner as she smiles in response to the dance. The strong colour combinations of the couple's clothes are set off against the ochre and green background of the countryside, the deep blue of the man's suit contrasting with the white dress and the red of the girl's hat and fan.

Although similar in mood to the gaiety found in the earlier *Moulin de la Galette* where Renoir also showed couples dancing, this painting shows the artist's increasing concern with solidly modelled forms.

Renoir lived in the south of France in his last years. His reason for moving was arthritis which had afflicted him from his late 50s on and eventually crippled him and confined him to a wheelchair. Even when his fingers were contorted by the illness he continued to paint, the brush placed in his hand by his nurse.

He lived long enough to see his paintings hang in the Louvre, but also to see his two elder sons fight and get wounded in the First World War. It was a great tragedy to him when his wife died in 1915. By 1919 he was a world-renowned figure. He went to Paris to see his painting of *Madame Charpentier* exhibited in the Louvre, but died shortly after his return to the south.

7.14 The Umbrellas, Auguste Renoir, National Gallery, London.
This is one of Renoir's most famous works but one which clearly marks the transition between one style and another. The mixture of styles somewhat upsets the balance of the painting. The little girls on the right are painted in a soft and feathery style which is in marked contrast to the more solid forms of the other figures and, above all, the sharp outlines of the umbrellas.

BERTHE MORISOT (1841–1895)

The Impressionists were the most abused group of painters in the nineteenth century. It seems unusual that a well-bred woman of the time should be part of this group, which was so unaccepable socially, and yet Berthe Morisot was such a woman. Not only did she suffer the abuse the other painters got for their painting, she also had to battle against the prejudice against women at that time. One of her teachers warned her mother that she was in danger of becoming too passionately involved in painting and that professional painters were not suitable company for a young lady. Her mother, however, was not put off and was a constant support and source of encouragement to her daughter. Throughout her life Morisot was to be undermined again and again as a professional artist because she was a woman, and although she continued on regardless she was nevertheless hurt at being constantly considered an amateur.

Berthe Morisot was born into a well to do family and was brought up in ease and comfort and never in her life experienced any money worries. She would never have had to earn a living from whatever she did. She grew up in the town of Bourges, but in 1855 the family moved to Paris which gave her the opportunity to study painting. She and her sister Edma both showed considerable talent and the girls were constant companions until Edma married and gave up painting for good.

Berthe and her sister learned a great deal from Camille Corot who was charmed by the two girls and though he rarely accepted pupils he allowed them to work with him. Then while she was copying in the Louvre she was introduced to Edouard Manet and they quickly became close friends. She modelled for several of his paintings, including the *Balcony*, and although she was never a pupil of Manet's he did influence her a lot in the beginning.

Despite some early success with the Salon, she became one of the staunchest of the Impressionists in their developmental years. She exhibited *The Cradle* [7.15] at the first exhibition of 1874, despite all Manet's attempts to dissuade her, and exhibited in all the shows after that except 1879 when she was pregnant. In 1874 she married Eugène Manet, Edouard's brother. She was ridiculed in the same way as all the others. One critic wrote 'five or six lunatics—one of them a woman. There is a woman in the group—as in all notorious gangs.' This made her husband so furious he had to be talked out of challenging the writer to a duel.

Many of Berthe Morisot's paintings featured women and children. Her sister and her children frequently featured in her work. Although she was part of a radical painting group, she accepted the limitations of her class and time and her painting had a noticeably feminine touch. Morisot's painting celebrates woman's life in all its stages of middle-class

7.15 The Cradle, Berthe Morisot, Musée d'Orsay, Paris.
The model for this subject was the artist's sister Edma and her child. The boldness of the composition owes much to the influence of Manet.

7.16 In the Dining Room, Berthe Morisot, Gallery of Art, Washington D.C.
The pearly quivering light in this intimately domestic interior, painted with the freedom typical of Morisot's later work, could not have been produced by any of the other Impressionists.

prosperity. She represents women from pregnancy to the early months of motherhood and through the years of caring. Women at work were often the subject of her work, with the servant in the home sewing, nursing and looking after the children. She rarely painted men except for the few occasions when she painted her husband, sometimes with their daughter when she was little. Her daughter became her constant model, the paintings forming a record of her development.

After Manet's death in 1883 Morisot came under the influence of Renoir. This seemed like a natural path for her since she and Renoir were the only two Impressionists interested in portraying humanity with warmth of feeling and intimacy. Her later painting has a lightness and freedom in its brush strokes which suited the largely intimate subjects, such as a woman with an apron standing in the house with a little dog at her feet [7.16], or sitting before a mirror arranging her hair. In these later works there is something of the pearly glow found in Renoir's work.

Her friendship with Renoir was so strong that during her last illness Berthe Morisot asked Renoir to look after her daughter Julie. She died at the age of 50, four years after her husband Eugène.

NINETEENTH CENTURY SCULPTURE

AUGUSTE RODIN (1840–1917)

Auguste Rodin was the greatest thinker in stone of modern times. He could be considered the greatest sculptor since Michelangelo. He was passionate and demanding and his whole personality went into his work. His sculpture broke new barriers as he charged his strongly realistic figures with emotion and sexuality in a way never expressed before. His *Burghers of Calais* [7.15] is no mere group of men marching off to their execution. Each figure is alive with a character, meaning and significance for those who can follow his line of thinking. Rodin was aware that his deep thinking was often beyond all but the select few and to counter-balance this, he left all his work to the nation with a view to helping others who wished to be educated in art.

Rodin was born in Paris and grew up in a working-class area. He was the younger of two children. His sister became a nun but died at 24 years of age. Her death affected him deeply for many years and he himself entered a religious order at the age of 23. He remained only a few months, however, and very shortly afterwards began a relationship with Rose Beuret who remained with him until her death shortly before his.

Rodin's drawing ability was apparent from his schooldays and in response to this he was sent to a school for mathematics and drawing. This was the kind of school intended for young artisans going into the artistic industries. No higher future was thought of for the boy at the time. He learned a drawing method here that was to last him all his life. As his talent became obvious he consulted a sculptor who advised him to apply to the École des Beaux Arts. He was rejected three times. However, these years were very useful to him. He earned money working in various crafts not too far removed from sculpture, such as a goldsmith and ornamenter, which gave him valuable experience in his later career.

In 1864 he began to take lessons with a sculptor and for the next six years worked as an assistant, working on the large public sculptures in Paris. During the years that Rodin worked for other sculptors he also produced work on his own account. Under the influence of Donatello he produced a work that was immediately to make him famous but also to cause a remarkable scandal, the first of many to affect the life of the sculptor. The statue known as the *Age of Bronze* was first called *Man Awakening to Nature*. In this work Rodin was accused of taking a mould directly from the model. He was defended by a number of painters and sculptors. Shortly afterwards the damage to his reputation was repaired when the state acquired the bronze piece and he was awarded a third-class medal.

Rodin was asked to execute a door for the future Museum of Decorate Arts and, inspired by Dante, chose as his subject the *Gates of Hell*. He began this enormous task in 1880 and it was to occupy him for the next twenty years although it was never actually finished. It allowed him to use his various talents and as with his other work its chief feature is the life and movement. The famous statue *The Thinker* [7.17] was central to the gate. The figure was designed to command and contemplate all the other scenes.

Rodin was given the use of a studio free of charge by the government. During these years a number of his works were shown in the Salon and he came to know many leading literary figures. Nearly all of Rodin's works led to intense or bitter controversies and in several cases the work was refused on completion. In 1885 he won a competition for a monument in the town of Calais. The monument was to commemorate the the hero of the town, St Pierre. Eustace St Pierre delivered the keys of the town to the English King and sacrificed his life, saving further hardship, after the English had surrounded and laid siege to the town. Rodin discovered by reading chronicles of the time that there was not one hero, but several. Six of the town's most prominent citizens had sacrificed their lives. Fascinated by the account, he decided to represent them all. The idea appealed to him enormously and for ten years he laboured and studied for *The Burghers of Calais* [7.18], but when it was complete it was again the subject of controversy and criticism. When the committee was shown the second model of the final piece, they protested that this was not how they imagined their glorious citizens. However, Rodin was given enough support by the mayor of the town and other influential figures to continue the work. After the unveiling in 1886 Rodin was upset that his contemporaries did not understand his group.

7.17 The Thinker (Bronze), Musée Rodin, Paris. ▶
Rodin originally wanted this piece called *The Poet* as it represented the poet Dante whose work he passionately loved at the time. As the work progressed his conception of the work changed and *The Thinker* came to represent a universal symbol. The figure sits silently, deep in contemplation, with all his strength bound up in thought.

▲ *7.18 The Burghers of Calais, Musée Rodin, Paris.*
This work was inspired by one of the great masters of medieval sculpture, Claus Sluter. The different characters of the group can be seen by studying the work. The central figure is Eustace St Pierre whose head with long hair is bowed, but who walks without fear or hesitation. The one who said, 'we must', the figure behind, is tense with fear and holds the key. Following is the figure known as *The Weeping Burgess* whose face is covered by both hands. One man looks back at the town and passes his hand before his eyes. Then come the two who may be brothers, one with hasty steps to get the deed over, the younger of the two hesitating at leaving life behind. The magnitude of the act they are about to perform is all pervasive in the atmosphere of the group. They move with great simplicity and a complete absence of gesture, a movement which is one of great sadness as their feet are heavy but their wills urge them on.

He showed six bare headed, bare footed men summoned to the market place of the town where conditions of mercy were to be made known to the citizens. They came with heads bowed, ropes around their necks and the keys of the town and the castle in their hands. He said, 'I intended to show my burghers sacrificing themselves as people did in those days without proclaiming their names.'

Rodin met Camille Claudel at a class for young women in 1883. He was immediately captivated by her and they began a long affair. She was a sculptor of considerable talent

ony until Camille left in 1893. She had long hoped
o give up his relationship with Rose Beuret. During
haunted his work. She was the inspiration behind
e movement of the modelled bodies produced
passion, ecstasy and suffering. *The Kiss* [7.19] is
he embrace of a man and a woman in a gesture

st was much sought after, was awarded many
n lifetime. 1889, the centenary of the French
but the artistic event of the year was a joint
Monet held in Paris. Monet sent seventy-two paintings
plaster casts. These two artists, each one an innovator in his own
ned friends all their lives.

▲ *7.19 The Kiss (Marble), Tate Gallery, London.*

This kiss is considered to be one of Rodin's most important classical works. The work is filled with an extraordinary magic. The figures seem to twist in perfect unison. A tension flows through both bodies from the nape of the neck to the soles of the feet. A shiver is almost perceptible as the man's leg brushes against that of his lover and the woman's feet barely touch the ground as her whole being is uplifted in this most graceful of gestures. The kiss itself is only barely suggested in a gentle meeting of the lips.

The one great passion which filled the life of this man of genius was his work. He worked without interruption except on his occasional visits abroad, until illness struck him in 1916 and though he recovered he had to give up work completely. In his later years he lived at the Hotel Biron near the Sacre Coeur in Paris, where he and other artists occupied the ground floor. The hotel was owned by a religious community and when the tenants were asked to vacate the premises Rodin proposed an exchange. He left all his works and his collection to the state, on condition it would remain in the Hotel Biron which would become the Musée Rodin, and that he would remain living there until he died. Two weeks before her death he married Rose who had been his constant companion for fifty-two years in spite of his relationship with other women. His wife died in February 1917 and, never recovering from the blow, he himself died in November. He is buried in the garden of his villa in Meudon and a replica of the thinker watches over his grave.

POST IMPRESSIONISM

PAUL CÉZANNE (1839–1906)

Paul Cézanne had moved in the same circle as the Impressionists since 1861. He exhibited with them in some of their shows and, although exactly the same age as Renoir, he was never really an Impressionist. He had a vision in art beyond those working around him, but it was to be many years before his painting was recognised and his genius appreciated. Many of the leading Impressionists did admire his work but only in later years, after rejection and ridicule had caused his highly sensitive personality to become embittered.

He was first introduced to Manet, Degas and their friends at the Café Guerbois by Pissarro. He was known even at that time to be neurotic and suspicious, traits which were to remain part of his character all his life. His early painting mirrors the inner turmoil in his life. Subjects such as rapes, murders and orgies were all executed in a rather clumsy style. When he married, these rather morbid scenes were largely replaced by landscapes. Real strength in his work only began to appear when he settled at Auvers sur Oise in 1872, a village in the countryside near Paris, and listened to Pissarro's advice. For the next two years the two men worked side by side. Pissarro's emphasis on meticulous observation of nature influenced Cézanne's work in a profound way and led to a transformation in his painting.

Cézanne was born the son of a wealthy but domineering banker in the south of France at Aix en Provence. He studied law and for a time worked in his father's bank. His ability as a banker was so bad that his father agreed to let him study in Paris. He enrolled at the Académie Suisse where he came in contact with the other Impressionists and, most importantly, Pissarro.

▲ *7.20 The Bay at Marseilles, Metropolitan Museum of Art, New York.*
Cézanne applied paint with strong brush strokes which emphasised the solid structure of his subject. His concern was with the three-dimensional form in complete contrast to the Impressionists who used small dappled brush strokes to portray the effect of light dissolving form.

While in Paris, Cézanne studied the paintings at the Louvre. He greatly admired these masters from the past, particularly Poussin and Delacroix, whose paintings influenced his early work and led to the paintings which so shocked the public and made his thinking remote and isolated from the other Impressionists.

Under the influence of Pissarro he worked directly from nature and abandoned the old mythological scenes, but he never forgot the great artists of the past. His lifelong struggle in painting was 'to make of Impressionism something solid and enduring like the art in the museums'. He alone saw art in danger of disintegration and felt he must find a way to address this problem. The way the Impressionists discarded form concerned him greatly. In his opinion their obsession with colour and light was leading only to a collapse of structure in art. He felt that this kind of painting would eventually lead to a brightly coloured, blurred haze.

For Cézanne to fulfil himself he had to leave Paris and go to his native south where the dry and transparent air shows nature at its clearest. From 1878 he lived and worked around his birthplace, Aix en Provence, until his death in 1906.

His work is strikingly original. This originality is particularly obvious in his landscapes and his seascapes at Marseilles. *The Bay at Marseilles* [7.20] seen from l'Estaque is one of a series in which the sea is a stable mass with very few reflections or shimmering light as in Monet's work. The sea and sky are in their natural places but are surrounded by a strong framework of land in the foreground and horizon. His colours are less concentrated on the fleeting moment and are more muted than the Impressionists' work. The effect of the painting is less superficial as if the artist drew the colour out of the objects themselves.

Throughout his career Cézanne battled with two contradictory forces which caused his painting to be slow and painful. He wanted to preserve the freshness of nature but go beyond the fleeting moment and the 'disorder' associated with Impressionism. All his working life he complained of his difficulty in transferring on to canvas his keen sensations of nature without losing any of its freshness or intensity and his conscious desire to present these sensations in an intelligent, clear and orderly fashion. In the end his desire for order in his work became the dominant objective and, ignoring the perishable aspect of his subjects, pushed their forms towards the regularity and perfection of geometric shapes. His work concentrated on organising shapes and colours on a painted surface, with an emphasis on structure and composition. The subject itself was of lesser importance. His efforts rarely satisfied him and he only signed a painting if they did. When he died, many paintings were found rolled up in his studio which had failed to meet the exacting standards he had set for himself.

Cézanne did paint nudes, but flesh did not interest him. He used bodies only to build up the structure in a painting. When he depicted fruit he ignored the pulp or the flavour, concentrating instead on their shape and richness of colour. He abstracted some of the natural appearance of the fruit and added life to the subject with rich colour and strong shapes. The rules of perspective accepted in Western art since the time of Uccello were challenged by Cézanne when he bypassed these in his search for the basic foundations of art. In *Still life with Apples and Oranges* [7.21] he has tilted the table in the interests of composition. His awareness of volume and form in his solid, round and three-dimensional fruit was such that he felt no need to use the time-honoured rule of perspective. In his famous remark he said: 'Treat nature as a cylinder, sphere or cone.' He preferred to work with inanimate objects such as fruit. Fruit did not need to move or talk. He painted portraits of his wife and son, some of the workers on the estate he inherited from his father, and several self-portraits, but these figures in no way convey the inner life or feelings of his sitter. The art dealer Ambroise Vollard sat for him over one hundred times, but in the end the artist abandoned the picture declaring himself satisfied only with the front of the shirt. Portaits like this have some of the qualities of a still life, yet their very stiffness or their quiet appearance and grave colours make them very moving in a solemn and majestic manner. The sculptural three-dimensional quality of the figures and the organisation of geometric shapes in the setting is apparent in the *Card Players* [7.22] which emphasises solid reality and appeals in a mathematical manner to the mind as well as to the sensations of the eye.

Cézanne's favourite landscape subject was *Mont St Victoire* [7.23] of which he painted over sixty versions. He painted the mountain from more or less the same viewpoint, but it gradually loomed nearer and larger in his pictures of later years. The strong and

▲ *7.21 Still Life with Apples and Oranges, Musée d'Orsay, Paris.*
This painting, like most of the artist's other works of his later years, emphasises many points of vision at one time. The fruit, table and chair are shown from different viewpoints which emphasises their structure and form. The fruit that spills from the plate on to the folds of the white cloth is painted in vibrant glowing colour and the arm of the carved wooden chair and velvet cushion are particularly richly depicted. The whole composition is set against a background of loudly patterned cloth, painted with dramatic energy in its deep twists and folds.

permanent shape of this solid limestone mass rising out of the surrounding countryside continued to fascinate him from the 1870s to his death. In the early paintings the mountain is often framed by trees and details such as viaducts and houses are included. Towards the end of his life he painted it with a complete feedom in oil painting seen only before in his water colours. He continued to emphasise the solidity and structure, but in a less obvious way and no longer with lines. He concentrated on a strong pattern of brush strokes, using dense and vibrant blocks of colour to build up the structure of the mountain, sky and houses in the foreground.

Cézanne's moods swung between a humble recognition of his debt of gratitude to painters like Poussin for whom he never lost reverence and a complete lack of modesty in remarks such as, 'There is only one real painter in France and I am he.' He recognised that he was responsible for a new era beginning in art. He said: 'I have blazed a trail; others will follow.' Others did follow. He inspired many of the vital movements of the first half of the twentieth century, in particular the Nabis, the Fauves and the Cubists. His painting emphasised solid structured forms as the old masters did, but the importance of

▲ *7.22 Card Players, Musée d'Orsay, Paris.*
Cézanne has used richly contrasting colours in the white cards, the yellows and greens of the jackets, the orange of the table and the green of the bottle. The two men concentrating on their game are depicted with complete reality, but the table is slightly tilted and the legs appear to be seen from several different viewpoints, a device which was later picked up by the Cubists.

▲ *7.23 Le Mont St Victoire, Philadelphia Museum of Art.*
In these later versions of the Mont St Victoire the brush strokes are arranged in slabs of vibrant colour forming an almost abstract composition. The mountain, however, never loses its form or sense of grandeur.

Cézanne's work is the way he used these solid forms on a new and intellectually stronger basis. Although he can be considered the forerunner of modern art, his work is much more important than merely that of a trendsetter. It is the result of an individual struggle outside any intellectual movement, something much more permanent and unlikely to ever fall out of favour again.

Paul Gauguin (1848–1903)

Paul Gauguin was a stockbroker with a wife and five children. At the age of 34 he gave up this comfortable life in order to paint every day and took on a life of poverty, bitterness and suffering. The only thing that kept him going was the knowledge that he had followed his destiny, but if this may have consoled him, it also served to frustrate him.

Gauguin had spent some time in Peru as a young child, which may explain his interest in exotic places later in his life. His father died on the voyage out, but his mother spent five years there before returning to France. After a short time in the navy, his guardian found him a job in a stockbroker's office in Paris, a job at which he showed a surprising ability in spite of his reserved, unsociable personality. He marrried a Danish governess and the couple had five children. All this time in Paris, however, he was haunted by his desire to paint.

As an amateur 'Sunday painter' he came in contact with Corot and spent many weekends in the country painting. In 1877 he met with Pissarro and became involved with the Impressionists. This was to be a turning point in his life. For the next six years or so he spent his holidays working with Pissarro at Pontoise. Under the influence of Pissarro he abandoned the sombre colours of Corot and turned to primary colours. Years later Gauguin, who was not always generous to his fellow artists, admitted that Pissarro was his master from whom he had learned a great deal.

He exhibited with the Impressionists at five of their shows, though these artists did not all accept him. Monet and Renoir, in particular, disapproved of their shows being open to 'any dauber', but Degas seems to have admired and bought some of his work. His membership of the group was tolerated because of his friendship with Pissarro and also perhaps because of his wealth. In the early 1880s he built up quite a collection of Impressionist paintings. He particularly admired the work of Degas and Cézanne in spite of Cézanne's acute dislike of him. This advanced taste was a pointer to his future career even if at that time there was no sign of it in his work.

In 1883 he resigned his job on the stock exchange and took his family to his wife's home in Copenhagen. Her family disapproved of him and his wife had no sympathy with his desire to paint, resenting the loss of her comfortable middle-class life. He returned to Paris without them and, significantly, his career as a painter began to advance as he became more determined. Poverty and illness did not shake his resolve but hardened him. All he was lacking was opportunity.

In 1886 he made his first visit to Pont Aven in Brittany where he gathered a considerable following about him and was at last in the role of a master. Here, his eccentric dress, moodiness and self-centredness were seen as signs of genius [7.24]. Pont Aven was for him an escape from Paris and civilisation. He felt that rural life was making him young again. In 1888 he spent some time with Van Gogh in the south of France at Arles. This period turned out to be disastrous for both artists and Gauguin returned to Paris where he was becoming quite well known in some circles.

He 'escaped' again to travel to Panama and Martinique, but returned disappointed to Pont Aven where his painting acquired a new and personal stamp thanks to the influence of Japanese prints and the work of Cézanne. He felt that it was important not to paint too closely from nature, but to draw it out, to dream about it and think more of the creation that resulted from this. As a consequence, he reduced his shapes to flat areas surrounded by strong outlines and used only the most dominating of nature's colours. He more or less did away with shadows, made very little use of linear perspective and suggested depth in his pictures mainly by the use of colour. His work was inspired by the spirit of the world around him. Everything from the sound of the peasant clogs on the granite soil to the rough sculpture of the Calvaries which dot the Breton countryside served as a source for his imagination.

7.24 Bonjour Monsieur Gauguin, Armand Hammer Foundation, Los Angeles.
Set in Brittany, this painting takes its name from one by Courbet seen by Gauguin a year earlier in Montpellier. Gauguin uses the title to symbolise the depression he was feeling about his artistic life.

In the end a desire for a more primitive life led him to abandon Brittany and in 1891 he set sail for Tahiti. He returned to France ill and penniless in 1893, only to set off again in 1895, this time never to return.

Gauguin's work in Tahiti is the finest he produced. He used the Tahitian people as a vehicle for his sense of the mystery of human existence. His works, whilst they have an exotic character, are never merely picturesque but express his deep feeling of life. He regarded the primitive life with nostalgia, but he was always aware that he could never be innocent enough to become part of this 'lost paradise'. This explains an element of the unsatisfied and melancholy in his work. The strangeness of titles such as *Where do we come from? Who are we? Where are we going* [7.25] underlines this. The mystery was more in Gauguin's mind than in the reality of the Tahitian people's life. His paintings show men and women [7.26] removed from the influence of Europeans, but in fact Europeans were everywhere and Gauguin himself suffered seriously from the disease of syphilis brought to the island by Europeans. His dealer in France, Ambroise Vollard, sent him a regular allowance, but friends and buyers proved unreliable and he was so deeply in debt that at one time he even tried to poison himself. He constantly fell foul of the colonial authorities and suffered a broken leg in a fight with French sailors, which left him with a bad foot to

▲ *7.25 Where do we come from? Who are we? Where are we going to? Boston Museum of Fine Art.*

Painted at a time when he was suffering from deep depression after the death of his daughter in Denmark, and suffering from recurrent bouts of fever and an eye infection, Gauguin poured all his energy into this large canvas before he attempted suicide by taking arsenic.

Several of his previous paintings are built into this complex composition which includes Tahitian idols and wildlife. Very little connection is found between the figures who symbolically ask the questions, 'Where are we going?' in the form of an old woman on the left, and 'Where do we come from?' in the form of a newborn baby on the right. The tree and two figures in dark coloured garments suggest the tree of good and evil in the Garden of Eden and the Paradise which Gauguin hoped to find in Tahiti. The central figure stretches to pick the fruit from the tree, symbolising the pleasures of life. The happiness of life is however threatened by the figure of the idol which stands behind with arms outstretched, a reminder of the menace which always lurks around humanity.

▲ *7.26 Tahitian Girls with Mango Blossoms, Metropolitan Museum of Art, New York.*
The women of Tahiti, with their gentle classic beauty, fascinated Gauguin. He compared their behaviour and manner to that of the women of ancient Greece. He painted many works depicting Tahitian society, but this is one of the most beautiful. The two young women, dressed in South Sea island manner, represent Gauguin's dream of an idyllic society. They carry a basket of mango blossoms, the most typical flower of the tropics, like an offering of their innocence and purity of spirit. Gauguin's works represent a view of the islands as a serene and peaceful haven, though in reality he never found the heaven on earth that he sought there. The innocent and unspoiled paradise discovered by Captain Cook and his crew in the mid-eighteenth century had long ago vanished. This vision of a gentle, content primitive society was, however, readily accepted by the public in France.

add to his troubles. His life in Tahiti was in many ways more difficult than the life in France from which he sought to escape. The amazing thing is that none of this turbulence shows in his cool, timeless and mysterious paintings.

Gauguin's words as well as his paintings were to influence twentieth-century painting. He said he wished to 'bring painting back to its sources and to establish the right to try anything'.

Suffering from eczema and awaiting an appeal against a three month jail sentence for libel, he died suddenly of a heart attack in May 1903.

VINCENT VAN GOGH (1853–1890)

Van Gogh's painting career was one of the shortest but most intense in the history of art. He died by his own hand at 37 years of age, only four years after he discovered his style and eight years after he began painting.

It was despair that drove him to paint, his life up to then being one failure after another. The son of a Dutch minister, he set out to be a preacher. Deeply affected by all the poverty around him, he gave away all his clothes and slept in an outhouse, eating almost nothing. He condemned the drawing that he had done all his life as a distraction to his real work. It was a severe blow to him when his licence to preach was withdrawn under the pretext that he was not a good speaker, but also for his exaggerated practice of Christianity.

It was when everyone considered him worthless and good for nothing that he turned to painting, and from then on art became his mission. He became a painter of peasants and these early works show a deep concern and respect for the working life and its hardships.

During his time in Holland, Van Gogh worked hard to master drawing, lithography and painting. It was only when he came to Paris in 1885 that he began to work in the manner that was later to influence some of the great movements of the twentieth century. Here he saw the final Impressionist show, met Pissarro and had the Impressionist techniques explained to him. Later he met Paul Gauguin whom he admired intensely and with whom he shared a love of strong colour and the linear strength of Japanese prints. Under the influence of Gauguin and others his painting lost its heaviness and sentimentality. His colours were transformed and his brush strokes broken into fragments as he painted still life, views of Paris and portraits. Life in Paris however did not satisfy him. With the intellectual discussions of his fellow artists getting on his nerves and the daily struggle to find money to buy canvas, paints and brushes, not to mention food, contributing to the mental conflict of his intense and highly charged nervous personality, he became restless. The self portraits of this time are evidence of this [7.27]. These early portraits were quite Impressionistic in technique, but the mood points the way to more expressionist work.

It was time for him to find a change in his life and this he did by travelling south to Arles in Provence, just two years after his arrival in Paris. He had been brought up in rural Holland, but rural France was not familiar to him and like most notherners he was thrilled with the sun and its brightness. The reality of life in southern France hardly touched him. He saw it as 'being as beautiful as Japan' which of course he could only imagine, never having been there. For him the architecture, landscape and people fed his own imagination which was influenced by Japanese prints and the paintings of seventeenth-century Holland.

7.27 Self Portrait, Rijksmuseum Kröller Müller.
Van Gogh wrote that the best way to improve as a painter was to study the human figure. Not able to afford a model, he frequently painted himself. There are thirty-five self portraits in existence. The tortured nature of the artist can be clearly charted in these intensely honest self-examinations.

Working at a frenzied pace his strokes broadened, his drawing became more confident and his colours stronger and brighter. He spent nine months alone supported by an allowance from his brother Theo, to whom he wrote regularly outlining his struggles with his painting and with whom he shared his thoughts.

In his painting he was not satisfied to record just what he saw. In pure colours, he tried to express the emotion of his whole being as he exaggerated what he considered important and dismissed that which he considered trivial or insignificant. He used contrasting colours of red and green in his attempt to express the frightful passions of human beings or a mixture of complementary colours to portray the passion of two lovers.

He dreamed of starting an artists' colony in Arles and begged Gauguin to join him. His brother Theo encouraged him to share his rented house and gave him money to furnish it. The outside walls of the house were his favourite colour (yellow) which delighted him and in the 'Yellow House' he did a series of paintings of his room, hoping to impress Gauguin. *Van Gogh's Room* [7.28] is painted in the simplest manner with pure colour and strongly outlined shapes. In a harmony of yellows, browns and pale blue, he painted two of everthing, two pictures on the wall, two pillows on the bed and two chairs to celebrate the arrival of a friend and the end of his months of solitude.

Gauguin's stay was however a disaster. Two more incompatible people could hardly have been found. Van Gogh's naive, demanding but sensitive nature clashed with the self-protective, cynical and almost brutal personality of Gauguin, and after the first few weeks the two artists began to quarrel. In one of these quarrels Van Gogh attacked Gauguin and later that evening cut off a piece of his own ear.

Gauguin left but Van Gogh, suffering an increased number of breakdowns and regarded by the townspeople as a dangerous lunatic, signed himself into a mental asylum

▲ *7.28 Van Gogh's Room, Van Gogh Museum, Amsterdam.*
Van Gogh wrote to his brother Theo: '. . . here the colour must do the work . . . that is to suggest rest or sleep in general . . . The squareness of the furniture should express uninterruptable rest.'

at St Remy, a town not far from Arles, in April 1899. He continued to paint while at St Remy. In *Starry Night* [7.29] he includes a cypress tree so characteristic of Provence and the rocky landscape of the countryside around St Remy, with a village greatly resembling a Dutch village with its distinctive church spire.

After spending some time in this institution, he moved back to Paris where he was settled in a café at Auvers under the watchful eye of Dr Gachet, a friend and patron of the arts. At Auvers he worked as intensely as ever, though his colours were less brilliant. Now his canvases were filled with wild, swirling lines. Yellow cornfields wave and swell under a cloud of crows, houses buckle in spite of their strongly drawn lines, trees weave dramatically against whirling skies of intense sun, moon or stars. His painting of this period remains full of vigour, control and careful composition in spite of the deep black despair from which he was suffering. This depression led to his suicide. On 27 July 1890 he shot himself in a cornfield while working at his easel. He died two days later, attended by his brother Theo and Dr Gachet.

Van Gogh, who became one of the most admired of all modern masters, sold only one painting in his lifetime.

▲ *7.29 Starry Night, Museum of Modern Art, New York.*
This picture painted at the St Remy asylum in June 1889 shows Van Gogh's private world of symbols. The sun appears as a friendly element, but the moon and the stars represent the turbulent forces of the night that threaten the peaceful life of the village. The stars grow ever larger in the swirling sky and seem destined to crash into the earth.

Twentieth-Century Art Movements

Fauvism

In one of his letters to his brother, Van Gogh wrote: 'Painting, as it is now, promises to become more subtle, more like music and less like sculpture. At last it promises colour.' At the beginning of the twentieth century these words were borne out in the work of one group of artists whose paintings of glaring reds, startling blue outlines and shadows were seen by the French public as an attack on the senses. This was a turn around of the whole order in painting that had long been held dear to the French tradition.

The name was given to the group by an art critic who came to the exhibition of 1905. Remarking on a piece by Matisse, he declared it to be a 'Donatello among the wild beasts (*Fauves*)'. So it was that they became known as *Les Fauves*. Colour with its sense of well-being, gaiety and energy was the dominant force that bound the group together. There was no strong philosophy or theory forming a basis and it was not a movement in art as such, more a group of painters inspired by the vision of Henri Matisse and the landscape of the south of France.

The artists' approach varied quite considerably. Although one member of the group, Maurice de Vlaminck, was deeply impressed by Van Gogh and painted in strong bright colours, particularly red, the real influence on the Fauves was Gauguin. André Derain used pure colour outlining, as Gauguin had done, in blue, and sectioned the colours into separate compartments in a method known as cloisonnisme. The south of France was not the only inspiration on the group. Derain painted some landscapes in London which were even more highly coloured than those he did on the Mediterranean coast at Collioure when he worked with Matisse. Vlaminck too painted some fiery coloured trees set along the banks of the Seine. The Fauves, including Vlaminck and Derain but particularly Matisse, transferred the bright violent colours of their landscapes to the human figure and especially the portrait.

The Fauves intensified colour, but like Van Gogh and Gauguin they did not limit themselves to that. They worked with much more freedom, discarding the rules of painting laid down by their predecessors. They used strong colour to indicate shadow, using reds or purples as well as the cold colours. They looked for unusual colour harmonies and rejected the traditional method of light and shade in favour of shapes constructed only with line and colour. The line was generally coloured and tended not to define the object very precisely. They viewed the painting as first and foremost a flat surface to be covered with colours assembled in a certain order. The colours were not, however, only for decorative purposes. The Fauves, like Van Gogh and Gauguin, aimed to bring out feelings and sensations. For Matisse the expression of these feelings was the arrangement of figures, objects and the space around them, all of which had a function in the picture.

Only three years after its first colourful, joyous appearance, the movement suddenly ended. Matisse, who had largely shaped the movement, became dissatisfied with its crudeness and lack of discipline. In 1908 the artists of the Fauve movement went their separate ways, but Matisse embarked on a highly productive career which was to earn him a place in twentieth-century art history, second only to Picassso, his great rival.

HENRI MATISSE (1869–1954)

Matisse was a master of colour. During his career he constantly explored its potential, experimenting ceaselessly and discovering the potential of pure colour. Captivated by the sculpture of Africa and Islamic art, he developed a style characterised by vivid colour and bold patterns in his own expression of an ideal world.

In 1890, while recovering from appendicitis, Matisse was given a box of paints. This seems to have led to a desire to continue and eventually to a passion to be an artist. In his early career he was introduced to the work of the Impressionists and Van Gogh, but it was Cézanne who made the greatest impression on him. He saw Cézanne's work at Vollard's gallery in 1895 and bought *The Three Bathers* although far from wealthy himself. To support himself and his wife he opened a small school. He considered giving up painting, but gradually sales of his work improved with the influential art dealer Ambroise Vollard.

In 1905 an exhibition of works by Matisse, Vlaminck and others opened in Paris. It was at this show that the group acquired the name Fauves, a title which Matisse never liked. He more than the other artists realised the complex problems inherent in the movement. He knew that the random application of bright colours was not the essential point. His aim was to establish that colour alone could interpret the world without any need for modelling, perspective or the traditional light and shade method (chiaroscuro). Pure colour, for him, could suggest volume and space and not take in any way from the richness of the picture.

The south was a source of great inspiration to Matisse. In 1905 he went to Collioure to work with André Derain and it was here that colour developed into the strong and vibrant tones that were to shock the viewers of the autumn exhibition. It was the human figure more than any other subject in these strange hues that the viewers found so difficult. Matisse used his wife as his model: in one, wearing her best hat; in another, as a portrait of a woman, better known as *Woman with the Green Stripe* [7.30]; but these paintings caused a furore. Matisse was somewhat taken aback by the hostility of this reaction, but came to accept that any publicity was welcome.

He inevitably came under the influence of Cubism, which was one of the most dominant modern movements of the twentieth century, and for a short time his works acquired a geometric stiffness and his compositions became more severe.

He loved pattern in the form of tapestries, embroideries, silks and striped awnings. He visited a large Islamic art exhibition in Munich in 1911. In Islamic art the human figure is prohibited and he was intrigued by their use of elaborate patterns and flattened out two-dimensional forms.

7.30 Woman with a Green Stripe, Museum of Art, Copenhagen.
The use of strong unnatural colours may have been acceptable at the time in a landscape or in a still life, but there had been nothing to prepare viewers for the shock of seeing a portrait in these startling colours, with an immense green stripe running down the face of the model. The subject, Matisse's wife, was painted during the summer of 1905 and displayed in the autumn exhibition. He bypassed the traditional chiaroscuro, replacing it with areas of flat colour in strong contrasting tones. In spite of the broad brush strokes and bright colours, the work retains a strong feeling of solidity.

In all of Matisse's work there is no hint at all that he lived through some of the greatest upheavals and turmoil of European history. None of his paintings reflects any of these; nor was he involved in any political movements. In the enclosure of his studio he produced images of comfort and refuge. However, in 1917 he moved more or less permanently to the south of France. He found a huge apartment in the Hotel Regina, situated above the town of Nice. Here he painted many scenes, the same elements appearing in many of them, such as the window with the wrought iron balcony, the shutters, the curtains, the chair, and always the strip of blue Mediterranean sea. These paintings have one overriding element in common: all exude a view of the outside world from a position of comfort and security.

He had a natural interest in textiles and pattern, having come from an area where weaving was traditional, and after his move to the south this combined with his interest in the Oriental, leading to the two recurring themes in his art. The brilliant colours of the south were reflected in some of his most sensual works of harems and slave girls in elaborate interiors.

Matisse became very successful in the 1930s, receiving large commissions to paint murals for American millionaire, Dr Barnes. In his early career life had been made comfortable by the recognition of foreigners rather than his native countrymen. His first big patrons were the Russians before the Revolution and the American Gertrude Stein.

In 1941, after an operation for cancer, he was confined to a wheelchair but continued to expand his work. Rather than maintain the styles that had made him famous, he began to experiment more with line drawing, illustrating poems and creating designs for murals on the walls of the Church of the Rosary in Venice in gratitude to the nuns who had nursed him through his illness. In a further departure he relied greatly on cut-out shapes which he applied directly on to the canvas or pinned to the wall. In simple bright colours he was able to recapture the simplicity and joy of childhood imagination [7.31]. For these last thirteen years of his life he also continued to paint and when he died in 1954 he had acquired fame and fortune, his work having been the subject of a large retrospective exhibition in the Museum of Modern Art in New York.

▲ *7.31 The Sorrow of the King, National Museum of Modern Art, Paris.*
Some of Matisse's late works in paper cut-outs are purely abstract, but in *The Sorrow of the King* a king-like figure holds a guitar and the subject may echo a biblical painting by Rembrandt. The youthful vision of the ageing artist is quite amazing. Some of his colours were so bright that his doctor suggested he should wear glasses. He worked on many cut-out works in his later years when he was confined to a wheelchair and was reliant on assistants who pasted the colours in the order he directed.

CUBISM

Les Demoiselles d'Avignon, painted by Picasso in 1907, was the painting more than any other that made Cubism possible. It is considered the single most famous modern picture. The faces are distorted like African masks as one feature is wrenched out of line with the other and the figures stylised with limbs almost dislocated in an attempt by Picasso to fuse several viewpoints at once. The source for the strange faces of the women was Picasso's collection of African masks and the energy and freedom to distort in African art greatly appealed to him.

The picture also broke new ground in its brutal sexual frankness. Picasso worked on many preparatory sketches which included a male, but eventually left only the five nudes. The women are prostitutes on show and even now *Les Demoiselles*, with its strange distorted angles and the staring eyes of the five women turned directly on the viewer, is disturbing. The viewer is placed in the position of the client and faced with the anxiety provoked by the expressions which are far from attractive or inviting. Picasso himself at the time of painting was in fear and dread of venereal disease. Threat is everywhere in the painting, from the stony gazes to the melon in the foreground which has the appearance of a sharp weapon. The flattening out of space and the breaking up of the shallow background were to become the characteristic features of Cubism.

The founders of the movement were Pablo Picasso, who left Spain in 1900, and the young son of a house painter from Normandy, Georges Braque.

As a movement, Cubism was one of the most influential of all in the early twentieth century and left a strong and lasting mark, not only on the young artists working in Paris at the time, but also on the very foundations of modern art.

Georges Braque was a Fauve artist who changed direction. He admired Cézanne in an almost obsessive way. He began by painting directly in the manner of Cézanne, but gradually began to see if the solidity which so obsessed Cézanne could be pushed a little further.

Braque developed his ideas into Cubism, but he did not do this alone. In 1907 he worked with Picasso, an artist hardly known outside his own small circle at the time. Together they fragmented everyday objects in their paintings, bringing them almost to the point where they no longer existed as recognisable objects, in other words, abstract art, but did not quite cross that threshold. Subjects included a bottle, a glass, a pipe, a newspaper, a guitar or a violin. When they painted the human figure their approach was the same, with the figure stripped of all human feeling and broken up in the same way. By painting subjects 'as one thinks them, not as one sees them' (Picasso) Cubism placed the thought process or 'conception' in artwork before imitation or the representation of reality. The work of art itself became a reality or a 'pictorial fact' (Braque) and as a consequence painting became about art for art's sake and less about what it represented.

Between 1907 and 1914 Picasso and Braque broke with the Renaissance system of perspective and under the influence of Cézanne introduced a new way of representing form in space. Braque and Picasso were influenced by Cézanne's way of breaking up space into interwoven planes of colour; but while Cézanne's work was directed towards the solidity and sheer reality of nature, the younger artists based their efforts on a famous remark made by Cézanne in which he said that one must detect in nature the sphere, the cone and the cylinder. It is not certain what Cézanne may have meant by this, but what is certain is that he would not have followed the path of Cubist abstraction. The geometric representation of the human figure in primitive art was also a strong influence on the young artists, particularly that in African masks.

Braque was the earliest to adapt what he had learned from Picasso's manner of dislocating and Cézanne's innovations into the first easily recognisable Cubist paintings. *Violin and Jug* [7.32] painted in 1910 is an example of this early style. The volume of the objects is fragmented into separate components and then reassembled in a complex manner.

7.32 *Violin and Jug, Georges Braque, Basle Kuntsmuseum.*

The subject has been almost completely obscured and only gradually as one looks at the picture can the jug and violin be detected in the shadowy surface. Braque tended to use tones of one colour and the effect is one of a soft, silvery, transparent light.

When in 1912 Picasso placed a piece of oilcloth in *Nature Morte a la Chaise Cannée* to imitate the caning of a chair, he was the first artist to use collage or something other than paint applied to the surface of the canvas. A few months later Braque made his first *papier collé* by directly attaching a piece of paper painted to resemble wood to a charcoal drawing. Braque continued to develop his interest in the surface of the painting, adding pieces of cloth and textured paper to his work. His father's trade as a house painter and furniture restorer undoubtedly influenced this development. His work also included flattened letters or musical notes, painted nails, and surfaces sometimes painted to resemble wooden surfaces. Picasso was to develop the idea of collage even further, adding a greater variety of more complex materials to the surface of the painting. In his *Bottle of Vieux Marc* he used letters of the alphabet, newspaper headlines and objects never before associated with painting in its traditional manner.

Cubism was never, as is sometimes supposed, a rejection of reality. In fact the painting of Braque and Picasso's Cubist period can be said to have remained very close to the idea of concrete reality. The artists were trying to gain a closer knowledge of nature, not ingore it. According to Cubist theory a closer knowledge of nature required new methods of representing it. Their theory was that we are always moving in the presence of reality and that as we move the eye takes in many images which are then assimilated by the brain. The eye is always moving and constantly changing, shifting its range of vision to reconstruct distances, surfaces and volumes.

The influence of Cubism was considerable and painters were found everywhere who were affected by it. Neither was its activities limited to painting but included stage design, posters, sculpture and architecture. Braque and Picasso were supported in their revolutionary ideas by Edouard Delaunay and Ferdinand Leger who were influential artists in their own right, but it is Picasso's name more than any other which has remained associated with Cubism.

PABLO PICASSO (1881–1973)

In the eyes of the average lay person Picasso is *the* artist who represents modern art. Although he is not in fact the most revolutionary artist of the twentieth century (several other artists were far more opposed to tradition than he was) his name stood for everything that was daring, aggressive and extravagant. But Picasso was the artist who turned convention upside down, bewildering the public with unexpected and sensational innovations, and it was this ability to outrage that gained him his reputation as a modern artist.

Picasso first came to Paris in 1900 and up to his death in 1973 he painted, sculpted and experimented unceasingly. After a year in Paris a cold blue began to dominate his palette. He painted young, sad, bloodless women, sickly children and old and emaciated beggars. Three years later this 'Blue period' was followed by a 'Rose period' which showed harlequins, acrobats and itinerant circus folk. The figures were still solemn and unsmiling but not as mournful and depressed looking as in the previous period.

In 1907 Picasso began to work with Georges Braque, developing the first ideas of Cubism. No other artist was to influence him as much as Cézanne. He painted *Les Demoiselles d'Avignon*, one of the most powerful paintings of the century, which led the two artists to develop Cubism. The painting started out as a variation of Cézanne's *Bathers*, but during its long creation it changed and developed its own style.

▲ *7.33 Les Demoiselles d'Avignon, Museum of Modern Art, New York.*

From 1907 to 1914 Cubism went through several stages. These were later categorised as *Analytical* up to 1912, *Synthetic*, and finally *Rococco*, at which time colour returned to what had been monochromatic paintings. During these years Picasso and Braque were working so close together that their work blended to make one almost undistinguishable from the other. The two artists were however completely different. Braque's progress was slow and deliberate, whereas Picasso was always in a hurry and advanced in fits and starts. When Braque was seriously wounded in the First World War, Picasso was once more on his own. In 1917 he went to Rome to design sets for the famous Russian ballet company. Here he was introduced to a new and more glamorous social world and shortly afterwards one of the dancers, Olga Khokova, was to become his wife.

Inspired by his Italian visit he began to paint female nudes in the neoclassical tradition of Ingres, the great nineteenth-century artist. His neoclassical figures are large exaggerated female nudes. He was interested above all in the weightiness of the body and he painted the figure using little classical strokes and sombre tones of grey, grey-blue and pink. This did not mean that he had abandoned Cubist achievements. For several years he alternated between the two styles; in fact the years 1920 to 1924 have been called the 'Great Cubist period', the period of masked musicians and still lifes of musical instruments. His last Cubist works were two great compositions entitled *Three Musicians* [7.34].

◀ *7.34 Three Musicians, Philadelphia Museum of Art.*
The two paintings of the *Three Musicians* mark the end of the period of Great Cubism. The figures are all from the *commedia dell' arte* and were inspired by his ballet and theatre set and costume designs. With flat and brilliant colours they feature one of Picasso's favourite figures—Harlequin. The monk sits on the right, Pierrot in his white costume in the centre, and Harlequin on the left. The harlequin costume with its geometric possibilities fitted the style of Cubism perfectly and Picasso used it in many different styles of painting including a portrait of his son Paul.

Picasso's work changed as he searched continuously for a way to express himself with complete freedom. From the mid-1920s he showed an awareness of the Surrealist movement. He always denied being a Surrealist painter, but there is no doubt that contact with the movement led to a deeper expression of the subconscious in his work with line and colour during the period between the mid-1920s and 1933. It was also a difficult period in his life as he and his wife were finding it more and more difficult to get on. The female figure was now represented in a way that had been unknown before in Picasso's work. She was shown in a disturbing, tormented and tortured form in paintings with an aggressive sexual content.

When he returned to Spain in 1934 his enthusiasm for things Spanish returned. Now the power and strength that had led to the production of *Les Demoiselles d'Avignon* filled him and he painted fighting cocks, horses wounded in the bull ring and bulls run through with the sword. Picasso as an artist watched the oncoming tide of the war with anguish and his work was characterised by violence and emotion which reached its pinnacle in his huge work *Guernica* [7.35]. From 1937 come several versions of *Weeping Women* crying over Spain torn apart by civil war.

▲ *7.35 Guernica, Prado Museum, Madrid.*

This picture is without doubt one of the milestones in twentieth-century art. It is more than art or painting. It stands as a symbol of defenders of freedom against all forms of violence and tyranny. It was shown first in Paris at the World Fair of 1937 before it went on a world tour, then remained in New York until 1976. It was returned to Spain after the death of Franco and installed in the Prado with great ceremony. It hangs behind bullet proof glass, bearing witness to the political response its explosive power can still evoke.

Picasso worked out several versions of this work, but from the beginning seems to have felt that only black, white and grey could express the sadness of the event. The press was always important to him and the painting has the appearance of a collage cut out of newspaper, referring to the reporting of the event. London and Paris newspapers carried graphic pictures of the charred aftermath of the bombing, which killed men, women and children on market day, and eyewitness accounts were published from correspondents in Bilbao.

The most important largest and most expressive figure at the centre of the painting is the wounded horse. The bull contrasts the horse and represents brute force. The five figures in the huge canvas express surprise, horror, grief, anger and despair. The fallen warrior lies between the horse's hooves; in his hand is a broken sword with a flower growing from his clenched fist. On the right a figure throws her arms to the sky; she and the house are in flames. Another figure, reduced to the simplicity of a face and arm, stretches out of the window to light the scene with the lamp of freedom and discovers with dazed horror the spectacle of death and destruction. Below her is a kneeling figure who directs our attention to the screaming horse, the electric light which takes the place of the sun and finally to the figure of a woman who cries out in pain over her dead child. The voices of the figures lament not only the tragedy of the town, but cry out in fear for all humanity.

The Spanish Civil War moved him from his preoccupation with his own artistic and personal problems. The fate of the little Basque town of Guernica, razed to the ground by German fascist supporters, caused him to paint one of his most poignant works that an act of brutality ever inspired. The painting includes weeping women, a dead soldier, a horse in agony and the fragmented form of a bull. Its message is a unique documentation of, and the most powerful denunciation of the horror, despair and brutality of war ever depicted in modern art. The perpetrators of this violent act are not shown, but their presence is everywhere. The action of the painting involves what is shown and what is not shown. Picasso painted this work in just over a month for the Spanish Pavilion in the World Fair in 1937. With its combination of Surrealist and earlier Cubist imagery in figures and beasts, the painting hit just the right note for the mood of the time. The painting called forth the deepest responses of the civilised world and touched the consciences of the viewing public, educated and uneducated alike. It was received with praise and unreserved enthusiasm. Picasso was now a world famous artist. He refused to release the painting to Spain and instead asked that it be held in New York, where it became the centrepiece of the collection in the Museum of Modern Art.

Picasso remained in Paris during the German occupation. Although they regarded his work as degenerate, they gave him little or no trouble. After the occupation he moved to the south of France. By this time he enjoyed huge popular acclaim with almost the stature of a film star. He became involved with pottery, but continued to paint and sculpt, mixing a great deal with the world of cinema.

Picasso painted many portraits of women. Each time he saw a woman who appealed to him he painted her. He painted these women in the style that suited each one best. Throughout his life Picasso had many women. He said himself, 'My work is autobiographical.' Each period of his artistic life represents an image of the woman who was the source of his inspiration at the time. His last works were for the most part devoted to a wide exploration of one of his recurring themes, the female nude.

Picasso's entire career shows the amazing range and diversity of an artist unrivalled in this century.

EXPRESSIONISM

It is difficult to give a precise definition of the Expressionist movement. It was more a cultural mood that spread throughout Europe at the beginning of the twentieth century. The movement as a whole represents a whole variety of innovation and research and was by no means limited to fine art. The style was to influence literature, drama, stage design, dance, film and architecture. During the period 1900 to 1910 it spread throughout the German speaking world where it first began, but gradually other Western countries fell under its influence.

The formation of the group *Die Brücke* (the Bridge) in Dresden in 1905 is generally regarded as the foundation stone of Expressionism and its end coincided with the revolutionary unrest of the postwar 1920s period in Germany. This is not to say that

Expressionism came abruptly to an end at this time, but the period between 1905 and 1920 marks a time when a mood, inspired by political events and a changing social structure, found its outlet through the style of art.

The artists involved in the movement vary greatly in style. The differences for instance are quite obvious in the work of Kirchner, Kandinsky, Kokoska and Dix. The common thread, however, between the artists of that younger generation was an awareness of life and a rejection of the dominant social and political structures. The artists tended to come from respectable middle-class backgrounds, the kind of families who would have been the staunchest supporters of the political system then in place. These artists rejected the way society was being shaped by industrialisation. Their objective was to create an alternative ideal world shaped by art. They shared one fundamental aim. They tried to express what they felt in the depths of their being and they usually distorted realistic form more for the purpose of giving strength to these feelings, rather than enhancing the look of the painting. The works had one other common thread: they tended towards harsh emotional statements and were often filled with anguish.

The first signs of Expessionism did not originate in Germany but with the Dutchman Van Gogh, the Belgian James Ensor and the Norwegian Edvard Munch.

EDVARD MUNCH (1863–1944)

Munch had great admiration for Van Gogh and Gauguin, among others, and this admiration took him to Paris for some time. The first exhibition which established his reputation was, however, held in Berlin. It also caused a considerable scandal, but he was soon in a position of profound influence over young artists. This restless, morbid, pessimistic character expressed his feelings of anguish at the solitude of the human being amid the crowds of the city and before the vastness of nature in his strange moody paintings. Women were a source of attraction but he was also profoundly frightened of them. For him the happiness of love with a woman brought in its wake, regret, sorrow, rejection, conflict, bitterness and pain. These sentiments were powerfully expressed in his paintings, with long melancholy lines which stretched and curved into the distance and with colours which remained nostalgic even when he used quite bright tones. Munch is probably best known for his painting, *The Scream* [7.36], one of the most famous images of neurosis in Western art.

7.36 The Scream
This painting may represent Munch himself who, according to his own account, was strolling on the road with two friends: 'I was tired and ill . . . I stood looking out across the fjord . . . the sun was setting . . . the clouds were coloured red . . . like blood . . . I felt as though a scream went through nature . . . I thought I heard a scream . . . I painted this picture . . . painted the clouds like real blood. The colours were screaming.'

Die Brücke

In June 1905 four young students of architecture from Dresden came together and formed a group which was to launch German Expressionism. They were Fritz Bleyl, Ernst Ludwig Kirchner, Erich Heckel and Karl Schmidt-Rottluff, some of whom had been friends for several years. They were later joined by Max Pechstein, Otto Müller and for a short time Emil Nolde. It was Kirchner's idea to form the group and it was Schmidt-Rottluff who chose the name which may have been inspired by the bridges in the beautiful city of Dresden or perhaps to signify a step towards the new shores of art. The group had a common interest in art and were only studying a practical subject to please their parents. Their aim was to live and work with like minded people. They lived in exotically decorated apartments with walls covered with their own batik prints and the home-made furniture painted with colourful themes.

The friends met here every day to discuss poetry, philosophy and to paint. This led to a unified style in their work which lasted until they took their work to Berlin where, in the anonymous climate of the big city, each artist had to develop his own personal style.

The influences on the *Die Brücke* group were the post-Impressionist artists, Van Gogh,

Gauguin and Edvard Munch, but they also admired the old German woodcuts and were particularly attracted to the unspoilt simplicity of Pacific and African art. The myth of the 'noble savage' led them to develop a lifestyle of their own with self-expression and a desire to return to a state of primitive innocence going hand in hand. The founders of the movement used strong bright colours to show their affinity with the *Fauves* in France. They particularly favoured the work of Vlaminck. However, they did not strive to achieve harmony in colour but strove instead for strident, piercing strength.

One artist who represented German Expressionism at its most outrageous was Emil Nolde. His work always aimed to shock, whether he was painting the degenerate clients of Berlin's nightclubs or painting the apostles as grotesque louts in his many religious works. Even in his landscapes no colour was too strident or too coarse. He applied his paint thickly with his fingers or with scraps of card, achieving a dramatic expressive brilliance. These 'tempests of colour' thrilled the young members of the *Brücke* group and they invited Nolde to join them. He stayed with them for a year and a half before going on to develop portaiture, figure painting and religious subjects.

Ernst Ludwig Kirchner (1880–1938)

The dominant personality of the *Brücke* group was Kirchner whose nervous, restless personality can be seen in his nudes, landscapes and in particular his city streets often filled with street walkers. The shallow space associated with Cubism was for him an extremely effective manner of conveying the atmosphere of claustrophobia in the crowded city streets.

When he took his final examinations in 1905 he felt free to devote himself entirely to artistic creation and the company of friends. He took his subjects from the world around him, painting views of the city, landscapes and portraits of himself [7.37] and his companions. The influence of post-Impressionism and Van Gogh can be clearly seen in his work. Using pure bright colours and powerful rhythmic brush strokes, he worked in flat unbroken colour surfaces. The strong colours of the *Fauves* and in particular Matisse were a strong influence on Expressionism, but that optimism and love of life which were vital elements did not transfer north. Expressionism regarded the whole of modern life as negative. German art and in particular Kirchner wanted to liberate the avant-garde from the all powerful influence of French painting. He was not interested in French restraint and sought to push strong colour to its extreme.

The studio was one of Kirchner's recurrent themes and he portrayed his friends posing or dancing naked amid the clutter of African sculpture, beds and sagging bookshelves. All are painted in gestures of defiance and revolt, but they have no particular political direction.

In 1911 he went to live in Berlin where he produced more balanced works and the violent edge disappeared from his work. One of the subjects he chose to paint was the city street. He painted the rapid jerky movement of the street until the outbreak of war in 1914. He first got his ideas on the street from Munch and gradually refined them to his own style of spiky drawing and strident colours.

Kirchner spent a few months in the army, but was discharged suffering from mental and physical breakdown. After 1917 he went to the mountains in Switzerland where he painted peaceful scenes of shepherds. From the distance of the Swiss mountains he watched with interest but growing concern the cultural activities of the new Germany under Hitler. His art was declared degenerate and this, together with his nervous disposition, must have been a contributing factor to his suicide in 1938.

7.37 Self Portrait with a Model, Kunsthalle, Hamburg.

The dramatic strong shapes and colour are typical of Kirchner's work at this time. The idea was to communicate by jolts of colour and shape and shake the onlooker. The strong yellows and blues look as if they belong together. A characteristic of Kirchner's work is the strong outline seen around his figures.

The Blaue Reiter

The *Blaue Reiter* group in Munich is often seen as being so opposite to the Dresden group that in many ways comparison is difficult. The Munich group did not express their views publicly or form a collective style. The individual artists created their own way of working.

The original group was formed by Franz Marc and Wassily Kandinsky, who took the name from a publication they had been working on together. *Der Blaue Reiter* (The Blue Rider) was dedicated to encouraging a variety of artistic styles including abstract painting.

Their first group exhibition to demonstrate their theories in the form of works of art took place in 1911, but its big achievement was the publication of a book of 200 pages in May 1912. The objective was that a variety of artists and musicians would contribute to a publication dedicated to the arts. One hundred and forty illustrations came from all of Europe's leading artists, including prints from the *Brücke* artists. Marc wrote some of the leading articles, suggesting that in art everything will be created by a truth-loving spirit. It was intended that this almanac be published every year, but the outbreak of the First World War was to put an end to the group's activities.

WASSILY KANDINSKY (1866–1944)

The most outstanding artist of the Munich group was the Russian, Wassily Kandinsky. He may have owed his expressive ability in colour and taste in the power of music to his Russian origins. He was the first in Munich between 1908 and 1911 to take the decisive step towards abstract art, with his fiery interpretations of the landscape inspired by the landscape of upper Bavaria [7.38]. As time went by Kandinsky's painting became less and less associated with reality.

▲ *7.38 Composition IV, Centre Georges Pompidou, Paris.*
Up to 1913 Kandinsky's paintings continued to be somewhat figurative. In this work it is possible to recognise several objects. A blue mountain with a castle is the central piece and three figures with spears divide the painting in half. Kandinsky said of the piece: 'The entire composition is meant to appear very light with many sweet colours which often dissolve into each other.'

He began painting at the age of 30 and invented a new language in art forms to express his ideas. He began by simplifying natural objects and later used geometric figures to give shape to his inner visions. When he rejected the natural image he turned to other means of expression. He explored the geometric forms of the circle, triangle and square and the way in which they could draw a response from the viewer. He felt that each colour had its special quality: yellow was warm, blue was tranquil, and red was hot and passionate. He wrote a series of articles and books outlining his theories on abstract painting and his training as a lawyer helped him to formulate these theories in a clear and well-developed manner.

His development towards abstraction upset many of his Munich friends and of course the critics. This caused him to break with the New Artists Association and join with Franz Marc in forming the *Blaue Reiter* group. Between 1911 and 1914 he produced a series of compositions with titles like *Impressions, Improvisations* and *Compositions* chosen expressly for their associations with music. As he saw it, the power of conveying the vibration of the world's mystery could best be done when form was viewed as a spiritual presence and colours with an inner feeling. Kandinsky was savagely attacked by the press for his work even when he was travelling regularly to exhibit in many different countries.

He had to leave Germany at the outbreak of the war, having been given twenty-four hours to go, leaving his wife behind. He made his way to Russia where the Revolution of 1917 severely disrupted his painting. Though he suffered hardship and poverty he remained in Russia until 1921. Only in 1922, when he was helped by his old friend Paul Klee, did Kandinsky return to painting prolifically when he had returned as a professor in the Bauhaus.

THE BAUHAUS (1919–1933)

The Bauhaus was the creation of Walter Gropius who founded the school in 1919 in the city of Wiemar in Germany. Gropius had been one of the country's most outstanding young architects before the war. His new task was to set up a school to bring the arts of architecture, sculpture and design together, in the manner of the old craft guilds, and teach fine art under the one roof. It was intended that it should act as an inspiration for the most experimental ideas in modern art.

Klee and Kandinsky were responsible for the basic design course. Kandinsky was reputed to have a haughty manner and to be rather dogmatic, making students wary of him, but his approach was determinedly modern.

When the Nazis closed the Bauhaus in 1933, Kandinsky moved to Paris. He continued to work in an abstract manner, but a sense of melancholy invaded his work which was overshadowed by world events. He lived long enough to see the Liberation of Paris in the summer of 1944 but died in December. He had no direct followers in France even though his reputation from the Bauhaus was considerable. In his own lifetime he was considered one of the most influential artists of the twentieth century without whose early experiments abstract art might not have developed as easily or as quickly.

FRANZ MARC (1880–1916)

Marc became involved in art at the age of 20, having studied theology with the intention of becoming a priest. Having seen the work of Van Gogh and Gauguin during a visit to Paris, he began painting highly coloured paintings in strong simplified forms. Like Gauguin, Marc tried to express innocence lost amidst the materialism of his own society, but unlike Gauguin who sought this in exotic places, Marc sought this in animals. He always loved horses and they feature in many of his works.

Marc was greatly impressed by an exhibition in Munich of the New Artists Association launched by Wassily Kandinsky, which exhibited the work of avant-garde artists and aimed at a blending of the arts of music, literature and dance as well as painting. Shortly afterwards he met Auguste Macke who became his closest friend. Marc was a shy and sensitive man and Macke was outgoing and friendly. His encouragement allowed Marc to reach his full potential. It was Macke who introduced him to a non-naturalistic approach and an Expressionist use of colour. *Horse with Landscape* [7.39] shows his mature style of bold shapes, flowing rhythms and strong colours.

Marc and Kandinsky founded the *Blaue Reiter* in 1911. The name was decided over coffee in Marc's home. For Marc the horse was a heroic figure and a symbol of change, while blue was a symbol of spirituality.

The ominous signs of war were reflected in Marc's works as early as 1913 and many pictures show scenes of destruction, while in others animals are the victims of violence. Marc volunteered for service at the outbreak of war and had no further opportunity to paint. His friend Macke was killed in action and he himself lost his life shortly afterwards at Verdun in 1916.

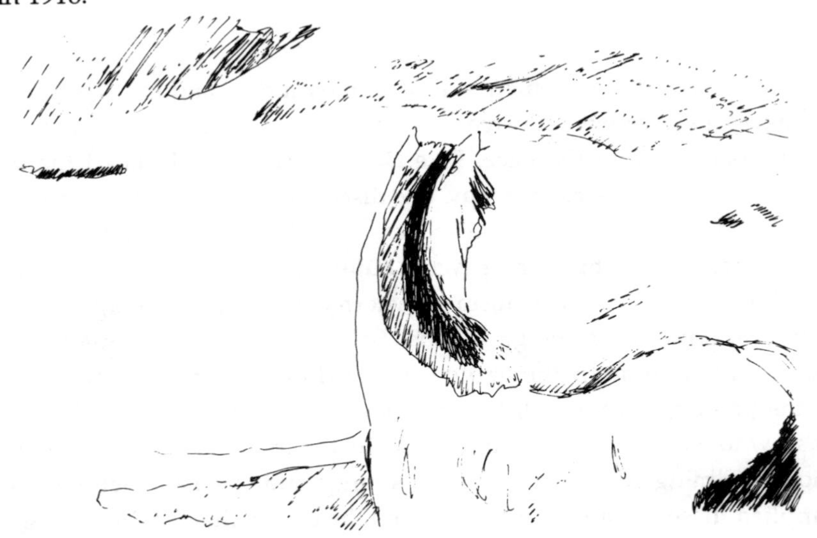

▲ *7.39 Horse with Landscape, Museum Folkwang, Essen.*
The horse is probably a subsitute for people in his art. For him they embody everthing that is pure, true and beautiful. This striking image shows the horse turning its neck to gaze into the never ending distance, suggesting a link with life everlasting

DADA AND SURREALISM

The Dada group started during the First World War. The group were not all painters but also included poets. It began in Zurich in 1916 and its principal founders were a Romanian poet and German writers, poets and sculptors. In Paris the leaders were poets but two painters, Marcel Duchamp and Francis Picardia, introduced it to New York.

Dada attacked the type of art so admired by bourgeois society. Their aim was to destroy the notion of art itself and to replace it with the idea of chance or the irrational. It appeared in different centres around Europe and everywhere it attacked established values. The exponents of Dada proclaimed that reason, logic and science had failed to prevent the disastrous war of 1914 and were indeed responsible for dragging it out.

Marcel Duchamp set out to prove that any ready-made article could reach the level of a work of art. He bought a urinal and signed it R. Mutt, the name of the manufacturer of the sanitary equipment. He called the work *The Fountain* and sent it to the Society of Independent Artists in New York.

Picardia and Duchamp had up to recently been producing very accomplished paintings but were now painting absurd mechanisms in a very precise manner with titles such as *A Compressed Air Brake* or *An Instrument for Breaking Stones*. These creations were intended to ridicule what they saw as the idols of society—the kind of art that was admired blindly—simply because it was in a famous museum or indicated technical progress. The important objective for these and the other Dada artists was not to appeal to the emotions, but to shock and cause confusion in the mind.

SURREALISM

In time of course the Dada movement's attraction dwindled and in Paris from 1922 a new movement developed known as Surrealism. Poets and painters mingled in this movement also, with the poets setting the pace. Like Dada, Surrealism declared the virtue of the irrational but in a more constructive way. The discoveries of Freud led to an interest in the subconscious and the world of Surrealism was one of the irrational, the magical and the instinctive. In many ways this pure 'psychic automation' could be described more easily with the written word, but Surrealism transferred itself to the image on canvas, with artists René Magritte from Belgium and Salvador Dali from Spain, ignoring the techniques of contemporary painting but using traditional forms of realistic painting. The details in the paintings were realistic, but they were combined in such a way that the painting as a whole was very far from realistic. Just as in dreams the fleeting images of the subconscious are mingled together to form strange and fantastic pictures, the Surrealist painters applied these to canvas and developed the possibilities of this strange imagery in a conscious manner.

One of the figures in the Surrealist movement, Juan Miro, deserves special mention. He conjured up a series of images based on psychic imagery from the depths of the subconscious. From these he created a magical world of organic forms and signs.

SALVADOR DALI (1904–1989)

For almost forty years before his death Salvador Dal
of the twentieth century. He gained a reputation as one
outrageous artists, and everything from his long waxed
imagery to his genius for self-publicity served to contri
surrealism was based on 'reasoned madness' but as he co
between me and a madman is that I am not mad.'

Dali was from the start a Spaniard turning deliberately from his
to the great Spanish tradition, preferring to study in Madrid where h
artists Velasquez, Goya and Hieronymus Bosch who all meant a great d
outrageous behaviour and eccentric dress did not impress the authorities of
Fine Arts in Madrid. He found the college extremely restrictive, and his prote
college authorities finally led to permanent suspension. His painting was se
admired by Picasso in an exhibition in Barcelona and he invited Dali to visit him in
He found the discipline of Cubism too strict but while in Paris in 1928 he was introduc
to Surrealism and was immediately captivated. The Surrealist movement had been founded in 1924 by a group led by André Breton. This romantic and deliberately outrageous movement was very influenced by Freud and the subconscious as a source for all kinds of mental visions. Returning to Spain, Dali became a devoted Surrealist. André Breton and the Surrealists disagreed with the direction his work was taking, but this did not upset Dali who was quite satisfied with his own methods. He said: 'The difference between the Surrealists and me is that I am a Surrealist.'

Under the influence of Freud, Dali developed his own theory that the artist should cultivate paranoia and the visions associated with madness, but remain sane and reasoned. His wife Gala was a moderating influence on his life and she prevented him from becoming too involved in his fantasies. Almost all his most famous works of art were painted before his 35th birthday, between 1929 and 1939. The modern view that a canvas was first and foremost a flat surface was turned around by Dali, who deliberately treated it as a transparent window. He reverted to academic realistic methods of painting, giving his extraordinary images a finish that was as smooth and polished as porcelain. This technique allowed any vision, no matter how irrational or weird, to seem convincingly real. Many of his images were of everyday objects shown in a manner which completely changed them, painting objects such as clocks in a soft, melting or liquid state or as he said himself, like Camembert cheese.

In 1936 Dali painted *Soft Construction With Boiled Beans* using grotesque tortured imagery that he said was a premonition of the Spanish Civil War, but he was not otherwise involved and lived in France producing in 1937 some of his most intriguing paintings.

One of the features Dali developed was a system of double images which had been used occasionally by artists down through the years. This method of double reading means looking at one thing and seeing another. In *The Metamorphosis of Narcissus* [7.40] the

...rned into' the mirror image of the ...s completing the metamorphosis ...ed several of these double image ... Picasso.

▲ *7.40 The Metamorphosis of Narcissus, Salvador Dali, Tate Gallery, London.*
In Greek mythology Narcissus was a beautiful youth who fell in love with his own reflection in a pool. He pined so much for himself that he died of a broken heart and was changed into a flower by the gods. In Dali's picture the Narcissus flower sprouts from the cracked shell of the egg held in the enormous hand. This idea of self-love was rediscovered by Freud and the theme of love, death and one thing changing into another (metamorphosis) opened an area of intense fascination for the Surrealist artist.

During the war years Dali went to America where his unique exhibitionism caused him to be an immediate hit. His paintings changed to an even glossier style.

Later he returned to his Catholic roots and developed religious imagery. He returned to Spain and lived without any apparent difficulty under Franco's regime. In 1974 a museum opened in his home town of Figueras. This fantastic and theatrical building displays many of his imaginative creations. Having suffered the devastating loss of his wife Gala in 1982, and the destruction by fire of his house in 1984, he was made a Marquess by King Juan Carlos before his death in 1989.

RENÉ MAGRITTE (1898–1967)

The Surrealist movement seemed to attract and provoke sexual scandals, political embroilments and self-publicity in an outrageous fashion. René Magritte was an artist associated with the movement, but he stands out from the others as a solid man living quietly in respectable Brussels with his wife. He lived in a normal house, married his childhood sweetheart at 24, and by all accounts remained faithful to her, walked the dog every day, and became even more conventional as he got older, wearing a bowler hat and dropping into the local café every day for a game of chess. He had all the appearance of a respectable middle-class citizen; indeed by the standards of Paris in the 1930s he might well have been a shopkeeper, but this artist possessed one of the most remarkable imaginations of this century.

Magritte's paintings were stories of the impossible. He was a master of puzzle-painting and he was to have a lasting influence on the formation and even more so on the interpretation of imagery in art. Central to Magritte's art was mad common sense. In 1928 he produced *The Treason of Images* [7.41], a painting of a pipe which introduced a famous catchphrase to modern art 'Ceci n'est pas une pipe' (This is not a pipe). This painting of a pipe with the phrase written below poses a question for the viewer: 'If it's not a pipe, what then is it?' The painting could reply, 'a painting of a pipe'. For the first time in art a painter has made the point that a painting is not what it represents.

▲ *7.41 The Treason of Images (Ceci n'est pas une pipe), Los Angeles County Museum of Art.*

Having attended art college in Brussels, where he was an unexceptional pupil, Magritte became interested in Surrealism and in the dream-like images of the artist Giorgio de Chirico. This gave him the incentive to develop his own unique style. As an artist he was largely self-taught. In his exhibition of 1927 in Brussels he displayed his new style which was not a great success. The exhibition did, however, feature in a review founded by Surrealist painters and this led him to Paris and contact with the leading Surrealists of the time.

Paris was not for Magritte and he returned to Brussels in 1930 and settled in a quiet suburb. His house had no separate studio. Working in the corner of a room, he produced some of his typical Surrealist works in a low key, dry, matter-of-fact style. One of his most famous pieces, *The Human Condition*, is meticulously realist and shows an easel standing in front of an open window. On the canvas is a painting of the view which directly overlaps the view itself. This play between real and painted image creates an uncertainty, asking the question, 'Is the landscape outside the window the real world we see, or is it on the canvas inside the window?'

Magritte's style changed very little over the years. For him painting technique was always secondary to the poetic idea. For the last fifteen years of his life, one image that seems to have obsessed him was that of a man in a bowler hat. He painted this man in the most absurd settings, floating in front of typical Belgian houses or with an apple or a dove in front of his face. The little man is depicted naturalistically, with his brief case and his dark overcoat, but the settings are Magritte's reminder that nothing is as normal as it is thought to be.

EXAM QUESTIONS

1990 Ordinary level

7 (a) Three prominent and influential painters of the late nineteenth century were Vincent Van Gogh, Paul Gauguin and Georges Seurat. Describe *any* painting by *one* of these artists and discuss his work.

8 Discuss any twentieth-century figurative work, painting or sculpture which interests you.

1991 Ordinary level

8 Describe in detail any still life painting by Picasso or Braque.

or

Consider the use of colour in the work of a major twentieth-century painter you admire.

1992 Ordinary level

7 (a) Rodin (1840–1917) was an important influence on the development of twentieth-century sculpture. Describe any major work by him which you find interesting.

8 Describe *one* painting by either of these two Surrealist artists: Salvador Dali or René Magritte.

or

Claude Monet (1840–1926) and Auguste Renoir (1841–1919) were two major artists of the nineteenth-century Impressionist group. Discuss the work of these *two* painters.

1993 Ordinary level

Discuss *one* figurative painting by either of these nineteenth-century artists associated with the Impressionist group: Degas; Renoir; Cézanne.

or

Pablo Picasso (1881–1973) was an innovative artist who painted in many styles during his long and productive life. Select *one* work by him from any period of his life and describe it in detail.

1994 Ordinary level

8 Describe the treatment of Nature in the paintings of *either* French artist: Henri (Le Dovanier Rousseau) (1844–1910) or Claude Monet (1840–1926).

or

Write about any twentieth-century painter whose work you admire.

1995 Ordinary level

8 Explain what is meat by the term Impressionism. Give an account of the work of either Renoir or Degas, two leading Impressionists.

1990 Higher level

8 Paul Cézanne is regarded as one of the most significant and influential painters of the last hundred years. Consider his work and state how it has influenced the art of the twentieth century.

or

Discuss the use of colour in the paintings of Picasso or Matisse or Kandinsky. Refer in your answer to specific examples of the artist's work.

1991 Higher level

7 (a) Impressionism is regarded as the most important artistic phenomenon of the nineteenth century and the first of the modern movements. Discuss this statement with reference to the work of *two* artists associated with the movement.

8 What was the Bauhaus? Describe and discuss the work of a painter or architect or designer associated with it.

or

Write about the work of a Surrealist painter or an Abstract painter whose work is of particular interest to you and refer to at least *one* painting by the artist you have chosen.

1992 Higher level

8 Write an essay on the twentieth-century art movement which most interests you and refer in your answer to the work of a representative artist of the movement.

1993 Higher level

Discuss the treatment of the human figure in a painting or sculpture by any important twentieth-century painter or sculptor. Discuss how the treatment differs from earlier examples.

1994 Higher level

7 (a) Cézanne, Gauguin and Van Gogh, often referred to as Post Impressionist, were important influences on the art of the twentieth century. Write a note on the contribution of *each* of these artists to the development of modern art.

8 Describe in some detail a painting by *one* of the following artists: Piet Mondrian; René Magritte; Paul Klee; Victor Vasserly; Joan Miro; Francis Bacon.
Explain in your answer *why* the work of the artist you have selected has a particular appeal for you.

1995 Higher level

7 (a) Describe a scene of everyday life painted by an artist of the eighteenth or nineteenth century.

CHAPTER EIGHT

General Appreciation

Appreciation questions vary considerably from year to year. However, there are certain areas which are worth preparing. These come under the general headings:

- films, video and theatre;
- architecture and local heritage;
- interior design;
- product design;
- planning and review of an exhibition.

Some of the broad areas that can be studied quite easily are:

The built environment in your own area

Find out anything you can about any building of historical interest near where you live. Look critically at the new buildings; find out who designed them and when. Consider if they fit in with the older buildings in the area. Look critically at the streets and shop-fronts; see if there is room for improvement. Compare them with other shop-fronts in a similar town or street.

Film

Film is the most modern art form and is probably the most popular. Films are entertaining and enjoyable, so much so that often we do not stop to think of them as a form of communication that is being transmitted through a unique medium. If you have seen a film you enjoyed, ask yourself: 'Did the filmmaker do a good job?' 'Did the film work?'

Film is an illusion or an artifice, and the whole point of the exercise is to suspend belief and allow the spectators to believe that the world they are looking at is realistic. A good film works if the viewer's attention is *not* drawn to the camera work or techniques involved. If attention *is* drawn to flashy camera work, the film will have failed in its creation of an illusion.

To answer a question on film:

- Tell why it impressed you.
- Reflect on the theme of the film—romantic, thriller etc. The story is important, but the important point is how the story came across, rather than a blow-by-blow account.
- What was the intention of the film?
- Refer briefly to the camera work, lighting or use of colour to suggest mood.
- Read film reviews in newspapers or magazines.
- Have confidence in your own ideas.

REVIEW OF AN EXHIBITION

Select an exhibition of your choice. With the help of a catalogue look at the works on display. Make notes of what appeals to you and why. Art is for the public as much as for the artist and your opinion is just as valid as anyone else's.

Give a general view of the exhibition, where it was, and when. Refer to the layout of the works on display and the lighting in the area.

Select some of the works and describe them in particular. If you want to say something negative, do so in a constructive way. Do not use put-down phrases like 'a heap of rubbish'.

Read reviews of exhibitions in the newspapers.

TO PLAN AN EXHIBITION

To answer a question on how you would plan an exhibition in your school, consider an exhibition that you have visited and how the items there were displayed. This will probably help you to plan the space and lighting better.

SAMPLE ANSWERS

1990 Ordinary level

12 (a) Consider any shop-front you are familiar with and discuss its lettering, colour and general design. Illustrate

▲ *8.1 The Black Bull pub*

There are approximately one hundred shop-fronts in my home town. Change of ownership has become very common in recent years. When this happened the shop-fronts were often changed and generally the emphasis was on clean, maintenance-free material like plastic.

Shop-fronts are an important part of our streetscape. They include pubs, restaurants, banks and offices as well as shops, but too often these are changed in isolation and with little or no reference to the existing street. This has led in the past to a clutter of signs without pattern in size, shape or colour. Gawdy plastic signs in red, yellow and blue have given the town a look that would be more at home in one of the worst towns in America or the Australian outback.

Happily in recent years the Urban Council have been making a great effort to make shop-owners aware of more traditional shop-fronts and quite a number of them have altered their fronts so that the look of the street has improved enormously as a result.

The most attractive shop-fronts are the traditional ones that have been handed down for many generations. The Black Bull pub was established in the mid-nineteenth century. The shop-front today is very much as it was a hundred years ago.

The front was constructed with intricate timber panelling around the doors and windows. The outside has been renovated many times, but the character of the old front has been retained. The lettering on the timber frame is traditional and is painted in white with gold highlighting and a black line, giving a three-dimensional effect. The panelling is painted in dark wine which brings out the detail on the rounded windows to perfection.

The two upper storeys are given over to offices. Though the windows are in white plastic, they have kept their traditional surround. This demonstrates that plastic can be used successfully in good shop-fronts if handled tastefully.

One of the most interesting aspects of the Black Bull is the sign which hangs above the door to the left. This sign, erected about ten years ago, was painted by a local man who has designed many excellent signs for the area in recent years. The sign is painted in green with strong gold lettering placed diagonally from left to right over a well-executed black bull with a large gold ring in his nose under a white diamond patch.

The pub is a huge tourist attraction in the town. In summer it is an attractive sight to see tables arranged out on the street and food served until late in the evening. Happily the Black Bull's attraction to tourists has inspired many of the other owners of premises in the town to look back to our own traditional fronts. The newsagent, the craft shop, the bank, and even the supermarket (for years the worst offender in gawdy plastic), have renovated their fronts. Let's hope other premises follow soon.

1991 Higher level

10. What features do you think are important in the design and layout of a modern shopping centre? Suggest how a shopping centre in (a) an urban setting, and (b) a suburban setting, should relate to its environment.

Merchants Quay Shopping Centre is an example of a recently developed urban shopping centre that has given Cork a lift in an area that had been an eysore for many years.

A good location, good anchor tenants and good off-street parking are essential for a successful shopping centre and Merchants Quay certainly has all three. The centre has three of Cork's most popular large shops, Dunnes, Roches Stores and Marks and Spencers, which create good flow patterns around the centre and up and down stairs. Some would argue that an escalator going up should be beside the one going down. This is important for elderly people in particular.

The heart of Cork city has always seemed to focus on Patrick Street rather than on the River Lee, with the quays fronted by mainly nondescript buildings. The shopping centre has gone some way towards balancing this out and has given the quays a more acceptable frontage, although the main emphasis of shopping movement is still towards the much narrower Patrick Street exit.

The long red-brick façade facing the river is three storeys high at one end and two over the shop units which have window displays but no entrances on to the quayside. All entrances are located internally from the shopping mall. To blend with Patrick Street, the block facing west on to the street is clad in polished granite and reconstructed stone panels.

The centre provides an attractive, stimulating and exciting shopping environment. Sparkle lighting, planting and water features are complemented by the natural daylight flooding from the roof windows above the mall to create the perfect shopping environment.

The focal point of the development is the plaza area containing the fountain. This forms a hub with Marks and Spencers, Dunnes, Roches Stores and the malls radiating from it. The centre is well planned to allow a free flow of shoppers without blocking any entrances.

Great emphasis is placed on the quality and durability of finishes. Columns within the plaza areas are clad in terrazzo tiling. All floors are tiled in terrazzo with a contrasting band and the logo of the centre at each entrance to the mall. This is a centre which was carefully designed to cater for large numbers of people and hard usage but to remain looking good for many years to come.

A suburban shopping centre needs to cater for much the same needs as a city centre. The centres which have a focal point like a plaza on the interior with greenery or a fountain are the most attractive to visit. It is always more interesting if there are smaller premises to contrast with the large chain stores, and stalls on the malls are of interest to people with time to spare.

Outside, car parking is the biggest problem. There is simply no way to make a large area of flat car parking look anything other than what it is. The best way to approach it is to landscape as much as possible. The design of the building has to be low but attractive and blend with the locality as much as possible. The building will always look better if it is designed to make a statement, rather than try to hide itself away with nondescript buildings with no particular architectural features. Red brick is probably the most attractive and durable of materials. Most modern suburban centres tend to focus on a strong entrance. This makes a focal point to the building, even though a centre needs to have several points of access to the car park.

Finally, in recent years large shops seem to have got the message and the signs on the sides of many of these bricked centres are strong but plain. Large intrusive neon lighting signs are happily disappearing from the later more tastefully designed suburban centres.

1990 Higher level

11. Your class has been asked to make a short video entitled 'Looking at Art'. This will be used to introduce first year students to art appreciation as a support for their practical studies. Say how you would approach the making of this film and mention the works you would select to provide a simple introduction to the basic principles of painting, sculpture and architecture.

    Preparation for this project will consider the following:

    ■ the point of the film;
    ■ the amount of money available to spend;
    ■ the length of the video required;
    ■ the preparation of the video shot by shot.

Our group has decided to ask a technician from the local film club to help with the making of this video. We made a film in transition year about the school and found we benefited from the expertise and facilities of the club in the making, editing and final presentation of the work.

We have decided to use four students from Junior Cert. art as the main subject of our film. We will concentrate on their projects and the art they studied as a support to this. The aim of the film will be to see how the older students used the work of artists as a source of inspiration for their project.

The film will begin with an *establishing shot*. This will establish where the video is concentrating. In this case it will be on the sign 'Junior Cert. Art Exhibition' which is hanging above the work in the exhibition area of the school. It will move in slowly to a close-up of the sign.

The camera will then begin with a *panning shot* of the exhibition area, then a *long shot* of the main exhibits on display, and will then move in to a *close-up* of selected pieces. Students will be asked to walk around the exhibits naturally.

We have selected a narrator, Pauline, who will then come before the camera and tell what it is we are looking at. She will outline the areas of study in Junior Cert. art and what themes this year's work was based on.

We will then move the action to a bright, evenly lit, quiet room to interview the students.

Kevin has been selected as the interviewer and talks to Deirdre first. Deirdre's project is based on horses. Kevin, on camera, will ask her why she chose horses. As she anwers, the camera will move gently away from her face to her art work on the table. Ocasionally then we will see him nod as Deirdre speaks. As she points out how Jack B. Yeats was an inspiration to her, the camera will focus on paintings of horses by the artist. She will tell a little of his life and work showing other works from a book with large illustrations. At intervals during her interview the camera will return to her own work as she speaks.

Each of the four students will be interviewed in the same manner. They have been selected to show the greatest variety. Martina has based her work on the sculpture of ancient Greece and she has also studied Oisín Kelly's dancing figures. Demons and dragons are the main subject of Colm's work and he talks about the artist Hieronymus Bosch. Emmet has constructed a large cardboard Gothic cathedral. It is based on the cathedral of Chartres. He recounts how he used his technical drawing skill to construct the roof and the spires. He points out how Brunelleschi solved his construction problems with geometry as he shows a picture of the dome of St Maria del Fiore in Florence. Gentle landscapes and crows in a field by Mildred Ann Butler are the source for Nadine's paintings of trees, fields and houses.

At the end of the interviews the four will appear together on film, each with a remark or two suggesting how much they learned from their Junior Cert. project.

The film will end as it started, focusing on visitors at the exhibition. Music will be heard as the credits roll, with one final remark from Colm before the film fades.

The film is expected to be about twenty minutes long.

1994 Higher level

12. Discuss any recent Irish feature film with reference to such visual qualities as camera work, lighting and use of colour.

Circle of Friends is Pat O'Connor's first movie for five years. It is based on the novel of the same name by Maeve Binchy. The film was quite a hit in America and has proved very popular with audiences in this country.

This romantic film concentrates on a nostalgic look back at the 1950s in Ireland. It is realistic but in an affectionate way. Some very real issues arise, like an unwanted pregnancy, but the mood remains cheerful and light hearted. Pat O'Connor has gone to some trouble to capture the mood of the times in the amazing innocence of the main characters, but it is a warm, sweet-natured film full of humour and charm. This tender mood is reflected in rustic autumnal shades which dominate the film, the subdued tones suggesting a look through rose-tinted glasses.

The story follows the fortunes of three friends who grew up together and then met again at UCD. It opens with a scene set in 1949 when the girls were making their Confirmation in the quiet rural town of Knockglen. The action swiftly moves to the scenes of excitement and incredulity when the girls realise that they will be college students. At college one of them quickly falls in love, while another unexpectedly finds herself involved with a rugby player.

The Ireland of the movie is real only in nostalgic memory, but it works because the theme is universal. Teenagers pretending to know more than they do is a feature of every age, and their fears and worries are part of living in every generation. The scenes at the dance capture the mood of excitement and the insecurity of youth, with only the music, costumes and manners of the characters making it different then to now.

Although set less than forty years ago, this was a time of sexual naivety and innocence and the film accentuates this by drawing attention to the university lecturer who tells in detail the lack of inhibitions experienced by primitive tribes, which contrasts strongly with the lives of the young girls. The excitement of the city, college life and the young and handsome Jack, the rugby player, is contrasted with the quiet country town and the local character who fancies Benny, the college student who works in her father's shop. The bustle and noise of the city end abruptly every evening when she must take the ten past six bus home. As the bus winds its way around the spectacular scenery of Ireland, we find ourselves in sympathy with her as she blows on the window of the bus and wishes herself back in Dublin.

The production is sophisticated and elegant, with a particular emphasis on period detail. Nothing is out of place, from the old-fashioned bus to the empty roads in the country. The choice of Trinity College rather than UCD was a good one, with its old-fashioned stairways and stone floors looking just the part. The street scenes in Dublin are cleverly shot from an angle that emphasises the upper older half of the buildings, and all are shot at close range to avoid any modern trappings which would spoil the illusion of this period piece.

The cast is strong and well chosen. The young actors, some in their first major role, are directed with remarkable skill. Even the hero's shaky Irish accent is acceptable. But the character who steals the show, making the audience cringe, is the slimy creature who wants to marry Benny and inherit her father's business.

The film ends where it started in Knockglen, but with an older and wiser Benny who makes her own decisions in her own way.

1995 Higher level

11. Give an account of any work of restoration or conservation of the built environment in your area. Discuss whether you agree or disagree with the work done.

Another chapter was recently added on to an 800-year-old castle in Limerick. King John's Castle today is a visitor centre in the heart of a unique heritage precinct on the King's Island where once it was a crumbling ruin.

The old castle was excavated on its eastern side revealing exciting new evidence of medieval Limerick. This work has now been preserved in the new interpretative building. A visit to the centre brings the visitor through the centuries from pre-Norman times to the present day. The walls and towers of the old building have been conserved and in some parts renovated.

The visitor enters the building over the new drawbridge and is met with replicas of old war machinery. Massive twin towers formed the original entrance to the castle and even today one can see how difficult a forced entry would have been. It is possible to walk along the walls on the original battlements between the gatehouse and the corner towers. The top of the corner towers provides a splendid view of Limerick. One can imagine how this view looked in the twelfth century. One can also imagine the bowmen defending the walls with their crossbows pointed through the narrow slit windows which were placed to give the crossbowman a perfect defensive position.

The history of King John's Castle is superbly presented throughout the building. The designers have used models, sound and colour, various artifacts and three-dimensional displays to present the visitor with many different experiences. There is a real sense of being part of history as the story of Sarsfield, Donal Mór Ó Brian and other colourful characters are brought to life.

The two floors of exhibition in the modern centre complete the history of Limerick in a colourful multimedia presentation. The ground floor concentrates on the early times from the Vikings to Elizabethan Ireland, and the upper floor tells the story of plantation and destruction. The mood of despair, misery and fear associated with siege and exile is suggested in darker colours and the dimmed lighting. A multivision show in a purpose-built auditorium completes the journey back in time before the visitor sets off from the castle on the heritage trail to the other buildings on the King's Island.

Old and new have been successfully blended in this exceptional work of conservation and restoration. The new building of glass and steel caused some initial discussion among the citizens of Limerick. It is a modern building that makes no apology for itself. It was built into the eastern wall after it was decided that any attempt to rebuild the original walls would destroy the archaeological remains. It is this very fact that makes it acceptable. It is not trying to create any illusion of being part of the original, but is very twentieth century with its own contemporary character. The old part of the castle stands, as it has survived through the centuries, battered but not crushed. It is the castle itself in the end that speaks its own story of siege and destruction. The new building with props and modern techniques provides a bridge to that past.

1992 Higher level

12. You have been chosen to organise an art exhibition of your own class's art and craftwork from last year. You have the use of your school canteen area to display the work. Using sketches and diagrams, suggest how you would display the various types of two and three-dimensional art and craft exhibits to their best advantage.

Art is a particularly strong subject for many of this year's Leaving Cert. students. Seven of my class have made portfolios and are hoping to study for various careers in art. Others in the class have produced some very fine pieces of artwork, so the teacher felt as it was such an exceptional year we should have an exhibition.

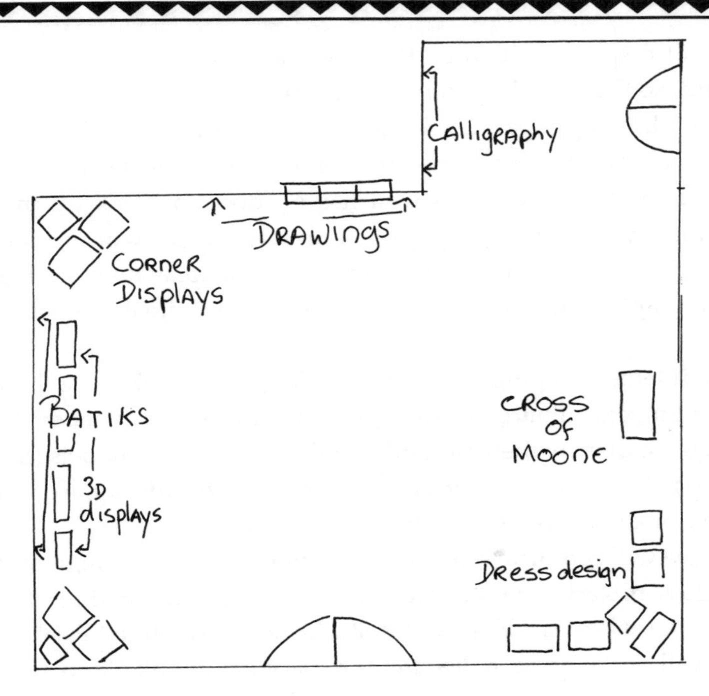

▲ *8.2 Plan of canteen area*

I myself intend to study art history and English. It is my intention, after my degree, to take a postgraduate course in Museum and Gallery studies. Because of this, the job of organising the layout of the exhibition has been given to me. During my work experience in transition year I spent some time in a large art gallery, so I feel reasonably confident.

The area we will be using has very good natural lighting from a central panel in the roof, which is a great help because we would not be able to afford the kind of spot lighting a gallery uses. However, there is one wall in an exit area that is an ideal space for a series of paintings and we have been able to rig up some strip lighting opposite which will light up the work gently.

I have decided to keep the central area of the canteen free of exhibits. This is practical for several reasons. The students will need to use the canteen and the work looks better around the walls rather than cluttered in the centre. At the gallery I learned how easy it is to make stands to display three-dimensional work. I bought some ordinary chipboard and had it cut into rectangles of various sizes. With some help from other members of the class I made closed boxes out of these, sealed the edges with masking tape and painted them white. I have been allowed to paint lengths of chipboard and attach them temporarily to the walls with the help of the caretaker. Now we have a large central area surrounded with new white boards. It looks just right for our exhibition.

Some of the students made some magnificent pottery. In both corners of the exhibition space I will place three stands together at different heights to display this work; the larger pieces will of course be behind, the smaller pieces in front, about waist high. On the wall behind this I will display the batiks. These are large, all based on the theme of early Christian Ireland, so they will look good along one wall.

I will display drawing separately on the wall opposite the batiks. Some of the large drawings from the portfolios are very rich works in charcoal. There are also some very fine mixed media and collages. This wall has no door to break up the space, so the drawings will look good there. Among the large drawings I will include some regular class life drawings. I have selected one narrow wall to display no more than six pieces of calligraphy. Calligraphy needs to be looked at closely to admire the detail, so I feel it needs a wall to itself.

One of the students is hoping to study dress design. He makes highly unusual trendy hats in velvet and mixed coloured cottons. He sells these in the street during the summer and on Saturdays. To display them properly I will borrow some models from a local shop. They have promised us four black styrofoam heads. We will add some of transition year's beaded jewellery or a scarf to these to finish off the look.

One final piece will complete our class exhibition. At the beginning of last year we all worked on a class project. The students worked in groups of three to make a four-sectioned model to scale of the High Cross of Moone. I will place this about two feet out from the third wall of the canteen, leaving the space behind blank, to show it off to best advantage.

To make our exhibition an event to remember, we will have to find someone special to open it. I suppose it would be too much to hope that the Minister for Arts, Culture and the Gaeltacht would consider it.

▲ *8.3 Drawing of a corner of the main exhibition*

AN ROINN OIDEACHAIS AGUS EOLAÍOCHTA
LEAVING CERTIFICATE EXAMINATION, 2002

ART – HISTORY AND APPRECIATION OF ART – ORDINARY LEVEL

MONDAY, 17 JUNE — AFTERNOON 2.00 TO 4.30PM

---

150 marks are assigned to this paper.

INSTRUCTIONS

(a) Write as fully as you can on **three** questions. **One** question should be selected from Section I, **one** question from Section II and **one** question from Section III.

(b) All questions carry equal marks (50).

(c) **Sketches and diagrams** must be used where possible to illustrate your points.

(d) Refer where necessary to the **illustrations on the accompanying sheet** [pages 275–279 in this book].

1. Describe and discuss the gold objects, **illustrated on the accompanying sheet**, using the following headings:
- form • function • decoration • metalworking techniques used in making the objects • historical background

Illustrate your answer.

2. Describe and discuss the Turoe Stone using the following headings:
- form • decoration • stoneworking technique • historic background
- possible function

Illustrate your answer.

3. Describe and discuss the Book of Kells using the following headings:
- function • design • calligraphy • symbols • decoration • colour

Illustrate your answer.

4. Describe and discuss any stone cross from the Early Christian Period in Ireland, using the following headings:
- form • decoration • stoneworking technique • storytelling

Name any other cross of the period.

Illustrate your answer.

5. Describe and discuss Cormac's Chapel, using the following headings:
- general information • style • structure • decoration
- stoneworking techniques

Illustrate your answer.

6. Describe and discuss the two Georgian buildings, **illustrated on the accompanying sheet**, using the following headings:
   • design/visual features • decoration • name the architect of one of these buildings

   Which building appeals to you most? Give reasons why.
   Illustrate your answer.

7. Describe and discuss the work of any ONE of the following Irish artists: Jack B. Yeats, Harry Clarke, Evie Hone, Paul Henry, Norah McGuinness, Gerard Dillon, Louis le Brocquy, Brian Bourke, Robert Ballagh, Rowan Gillespie, Kathy Prendergast, using the following headings:
   • subject matter • brushwork, if a painter • form, if a sculptor
   • composition • materials and technique • colour and/or texture

   Illustrate your answer.

Section II — European Art (1000 AD to the Present)

8. Describe and discuss the sculpture of Gislebertus on the tympanum over the doorway of Autun cathedral using the following headings:
   • style • storytelling • the human figure • faces • relationship to the architecture

   Illustrate your answer.

9. Name a painter **and** a sculptor of the Renaissance in Italy and name and describe one important work by each of them, allowing the following headings to assist you:
   • for the painting: subject matter, colour, composition, the human figure
   • for the sculpture: subject matter, medium, technique, form, texture, the human figure

   Illustrate your answer.

10. Describe and discuss the Arnolfini Wedding, **illustrated on the accompanying sheet**, by Jan van Eyck using the following headings:
    • composition • colour and light • details • medium • style • symbols

    Illustrate your answer.

11. Describe and discuss Hans Holbein's '**The Ambassadors**', **illustrated on the accompanying sheet**. Allow the following headings to assist you:
    • subject matter • composition • style of painting • clothes • objects
    • details • what do you think is the message of this painting?

    Illustrate your answer.

12. Write as fully as you can on TWO of the following paintings:
(a) 'A Country Wedding' by Pieter Bruegel the Elder
(b) 'The Village School' by Jan Steen
(c) 'The Oath of the Horatii' by Jacques-Louis David
(d) 'The Turkish Bath' by Ingres
(e) 'Le Dejeuner sur l'Herbe' by Edouard Manet
(f) 'Sunday Afternoon on the Island of La Grande Jatte' by Georges Seurat
(g) 'La Danse' by Henri Matisse

Allow the following headings to assist you:
- subject matter • the treatment of the human figure • colour
- composition • your own opinions about the painting

Illustrate your answer.

13. Describe and discuss TWO Impressionist paintings using the following headings to assist you:
- subject matter • colour and light • texture • composition
- information about the painter(s) • your own opinions about Impressionism

Illustrate your answer.

14. Describe and discuss the work of Vincent van Gogh, **illustrated on the accompanying sheet**, using the following headings:
- subject matter • composition • colour • texture
- expression of emotion

Refer to other works by the artist and/or to his life-story.
Illustrate your answer.

SECTION III — APPRECIATION

15. Describe any live-action film you have seen. Allow the following to guide you in your answer:
- camerawork • special effects • colour • storytelling

Include your opinions as to whether or not the film was VISUALLY interesting.
Illustrate your answer.

16. Describe an exhibition of art, craft or design which you have visited. Allow the following headings to guide you in your answer:
- hanging of pictures and/or placement of objects • lighting • layout of the room or spaces • labelling and/or catalogue

Then, in as much detail as possible, describe TWO of the paintings/objects which you liked best or found interesting, saying why.
Illustrate your answer.

17. Design a sculpture **or** fountain to be sited anywhere in front of the old house, **illustrated on the accompanying sheet**.

- Give reasons for the appearance, materials and placing of your sculpture or fountain.
- What must a designer take into account when planning a new structure close to an old one?

Illustrate your answer.

18. What are the visual qualities of good poster design? List and explain these in as much detail as possible. Then design a poster for a concert by Popstars group 'Six' **or** for any other musical event.
Illustrate your answer.

19. Describe the process of designing a repeat pattern, such as the one on the printed cloth used to cover the armchair, **illustrated on the accompanying sheet**.

- List and describe what makes a visually successful pattern.
- Is the pattern **illustrated** visually successful? Give reasons for your opinion.
- Name two methods of printing patterns on to cloth.

Illustrate your answer.

20. If you could have an Impressionist picture or a large, colourful abstract picture in your room, which would you choose, and why? Explain your choice as fully as possible.
Illustrate your answer.

21. Describe the decoration of the sitting-room, **illustrated on the accompanying sheet**. Allow the following headings to assist you:

- style of furniture
- the colour scheme
- the pictures and ornaments
- lighting

What changes would you make to the room to improve it visually? Give reasons for the changes you would make.
Illustrate your answer.

Acknowledgments: Q. 1 courtesy of the National Museum of Ireland. Q. 6 Custom House © Michael St. Maur Sheil/Corbis; Leinster House © Geray Sweeney/Corbis. Q. 10 © National Gallery Collection; By kind permission of the Trustees of the National Gallery, London/Corbis. Q. 11 © National Gallery Collection; By kind permission of the Trustees of the National Gallery, London/Corbis. Q. 14 Sunflowers © National Gallery Collection; By kind permission of the Trustees of the National Gallery, London/Corbis; Café Terrace At Night © Francis G. Mayer/Corbis. Q. 17 © Lucinda Lambton/Arcaid. Q. 19 courtesy Brunschwig&Fils, Inc./ Q. 21 © Jerry Tubby; Elizabeth Whiting & Associates/Corbis.

Art: History and Appreciation of Art – Ordinary Level – Illustrations 2002

Section I — Art in Ireland

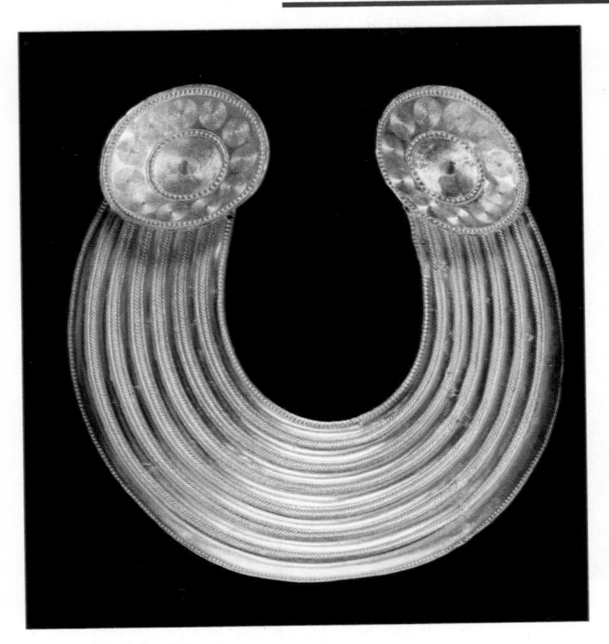

Q. 1 Gold object

Q. 1 Gold objects

Q. 1 Gold objects

Q. 6 Leinster House

Q. 6 Custom House

SECTION II — EUROPEAN ART

Q. 10 'The Arnolfini Wedding' by Jan Van Eyck

Q. 11 'The Ambassadors' by Hans Holbein

Q. 14 'Sunflowers' by Vincent van Gogh

Q. 14 'Café Terrace At Night' by Vincent van Gogh

SECTION III — GENERAL APPRECIATION

Q. 17 Old house

Q. 19 Chair

Q. 21 Sitting Room

AN ROINN OIDEACHAIS AGUS EOLAÍOCHTA

LEAVING CERTIFICATE EXAMINATION, 2002

ART – HISTORY AND APPRECIATION OF ART – HIGHER LEVEL

MONDAY, 17 JUNE — AFTERNOON 2.00 TO 4.30PM

150 marks are assigned to this paper.

INSTRUCTIONS

(a) Write as fully as you can on **three** questions. **One** question should be selected from Section I, **one** question from Section II and **one** question from Section III.

(b) All questions carry equal marks (50).

(c) **Sketches and diagrams** must be used where possible to illustrate your points.

(d) Refer where necessary to the **illustrations on the accompanying sheet** [pages 284–286 in this book].

SECTION I — ART IN IRELAND

1. The archaeological site at Newgrange may be understood both as art and architecture. Discuss this statement, referring in your answer to structure, decoration and function.

2. Describe and discuss the 'Petrie Crown', **illustrated on the accompanying sheet**, referring in your answer to form, decoration, possible function and the metalwork techniques used to produce it.

3. The Irish Romanesque style was highly decorative as evidenced by the stonecarving on the churches of the period. Discuss this statement, giving a detailed description of two examples, and referring to the imagery and decoration used.

4. Describe and discuss the development of stone crosses in Ireland. Give specific examples and refer in your answer to form, imagery, decoration, stoneworking techniques and function.

5. Describe and discuss in detail one public **and** one domestic building of the Georgian period, referring in your answer to architectural style, structural features and Classical influence.

6. Describe and discuss the use of stucco decoration during the Georgian period, referring in your answer to some important examples, the imagery/motifs used and the visual impact of the stucco decoration on the interiors.

7. Describe and discuss in detail two works by an 18th or 19th century landscape painter, referring in your answer to subject matter, painting style and technique, composition and colour.

8. Select ONE of the following artists: Walter Osborne, Albert Power, Mainie Jellett, Gerard Dillon, Camille Souter, Martin Gale, Barrie Cooke, Pauline Bewick, Dorothy Cross, Felim Egan, Kathy Prendergast. Describe and discuss his/her art, referring in your answer to subject matter, imagery, media and materials used. Integrate your own opinions into the answer.

SECTION II — EUROPEAN ART (1000 AD TO THE PRESENT)

9. Describe and discuss the major characteristics of Romanesque sculpture and architecture referring in detail in your answer to at least one major example of both.

10. Gothic sculpture is closely integrated with the architecture it decorates. Discuss this statement referring in detail in your answer to a cathedral of the period.

11. Describe and discuss the characteristics of Piero della Francesca's (c. 1410/20 – 1492) style of painting, referring in your answer to composition, the treatment of the figure, the depiction of space, and the use of colour in 'The Baptism of Christ', **illustrated on the accompanying sheet**, and in another work by him.

12. Albrecht Durer (1471 – 1528), an important artist of the Renaissance in northern Europe, was influenced by Italian art. Discuss this statement, referring in your answer to subject matter, media, and style in at least two examples of his work.

13. 'The Ecstasy of Saint Teresa' by Gianlorenzo Bernini (1598 – 1680) is characteristic of the drama of the Baroque style. Describe and discuss this sculpture and refer in your answer to one other work by Bernini.

14. Describe and discuss, in as much detail as possible, one of the following:
    (a) a painting of water and/or reflections
    (b) an Impressionist landscape painting
    (c) a painting of royalty or aristocracy or a Pope
    (d) an altarpiece

(e) a sculpture typical of the Renaissance
(f) sfumato
(g) an Expressionist artwork

You must state clearly why you consider your chosen work to be a good example of its category. You should clearly refer to the artist's style and technique and to the use of materials and colour. You should also include a brief reference to other works by the artist. Integrate your own opinions into the answer.

15. Choose ONE of the following artists:
(i) Jean-Antoine Watteau (1684 – 1721)
(ii) Jean-Baptiste-Siméon Chardin (1699 – 1779)
(iii) Joseph Mallord William Turner (1775 – 1851)
(iv) John Constable (1776 – 1837)
Describe and discuss his work, referring in your answer to typical subject matter, composition, technique, and use of colour.

16. Why was the work of the Impressionists so innovative compared with the work of the Academic painters? Make detailed reference to at least two artists and treat subject matter, technique, colour and light in your answer.

17. Describe and discuss two paintings by Paul Cézanne (1839 – 1906). Refer in your answer to his distinctive style, his use of colour and composition in the two works. Discuss briefly his influence on the development of modern art.

18. 'The Kiss' by Gustav Klimt (1862 – 1918), **illustrated on the accompanying sheet**, combines realistic and decorative elements in the one painting. Analyse this painting, referring in your answer to the above statement, the composition, treatment of the figures and the use of colour, pattern, and shape.

SECTION III — APPRECIATION

19. Describe and discuss the sitting-out area beside a college building, **illustrated on the accompanying sheet**, emphasising visual considerations. Then design a free-standing sculpture **or** relief panel(s) that would enhance the existing features. Give detailed reasons for your design decisions.

20. Describe and discuss the decoration of the room, **illustrated on the accompanying sheet**. Then suggest what additions and/or changes you would make – colour, objects, artefacts, fabrics – in order to enhance the existing décor. Give detailed reasons for these additions and changes.

21. Horror **or** fantasy **or** science-fiction live-action films portray events that cannot happen in reality. Discuss this statement referring in your answer to one such film you have seen and describing the visual means and techniques used by the film-maker in that film. Emphasise the visual aspects, not the storyline.

22. Drawing and painting are capable of a wide range of pictorial and expressive effects which are not possible in photography. Discuss this statement, saying whether or not you agree with it and supporting the reasons for your opinions by giving examples of paintings, drawings and photographs.

23. Describe and discuss Le Corbusier's church at Ronchamp **illustrated on the accompanying sheet**, referring to the sculptural form of the building. Compare and contrast it with any other church or cathedral with reference to form, materials, decoration and overall visual effect.

24. If you were to commission either a painted portrait **or** a bronze or marble portrait bust of yourself, which would you choose? Give detailed reason for your choice, comparing in your answer the visual and technical potential of the two media for portraiture. Give examples of paintings or sculptures that have influenced your choice.

25. *Answer* (i), (ii) ***and*** (iii) *below.*
    (i) Analyse the layout, lighting and general presentation of an exhibition of art, design or craft you have visited, saying whether or not these were effective, and why.
    (ii) Describe and discuss in detail TWO artefacts from the exhibition, referring in your answer to subject matter, composition, use of materials and/or colour and style.
    (iii) Because there is now such easy access to a vast range of art, design and craft images over the Internet, are traditional gallery/museum-based exhibitions any longer necessary? Give reasons for your opinions.

Acknowledgments
Q. 2 courtesy of the National Museum of Ireland. Q. 11 © National Gallery Collection; By kind permission of the Trustees of the National Gallery, London/Corbis. Q. 18 © Austrian Archives; Österreichische Galerie, Vienna/Corbis. Q. 19 © John Edward Linden/Arcaid. Q. 20 © Brownie Harris/Corbis. Q. 23 by Le Corbusier © FLC.

ART: HISTORY AND APPRECIATION OF ART – HIGHER LEVEL – ILLUSTRATIONS 2001

SECTION I — ART IN IRELAND

Q. 2 Petrie Crown

SECTION II — EUROPEAN ART

Q. 11 'The Baptism of Christ' by Piero della Francesca

Detail, 'The Kiss'

Q. 18 'The Kiss' by Gustav Klimt

SECTION III — GENERAL APPRECIATION

Q. 19 Sitting-out area

Q. 20 Room

Q. 23 Church
Notre-Dame de Haut, Ronchamp by Le Corbusier

Q16 Goya A Picnic
National Gallery London

Q16 Goya The Forcibly Bewitched
National Gallery London/The Art Archive

Q16 Goya Dona Antonia Zárate
National Gallery of Ireland

Q16 Goya Saturn Devouring his Children
National Gallery London

SECTION III
APPRECIATION

Q21
Domestic Interior *Photo Robert Harding/Designers Guild*

Q23
Pond-side location for sculpture Robert Harding

AN ROINN OIDEACHAIS AGUS EOLAÍOCHTA

LEAVING CERTIFICATE EXAMINATION, 2003

ART – HISTORY AND APPRECIATION OF ART – ORDINARY LEVEL

MONDAY, 16 JUNE — AFTERNOON 2.00 TO 4.30PM

150 marks are assigned to this paper.

INSTRUCTIONS

(a) Write as fully as you can on **three** questions. **One** question should be selected from Section I, **one** question from Section II and **one** question from Section III.

(b) All questions carry equal marks (50).

(c) **Sketches and diagrams** should be used where possible to illustrate your points.

(d) Refer where necessary to the **illustrations on the accompanying sheet** [pages xxx–xxx in this book].

SECTION I — ART IN IRELAND

1. Write as fully as you can on **Newgrange**. The following headings may help you with your answer:

- location • general description • decoration • possible function

Use sketches to illustrate your answer.

2. Look closely at the ***accompanying illustrations*** of the **Ardagh Chalice** and the **Derrynaflan Chalice**.

(a) Describe and discuss their **design** and **decoration**.

(b) Write an account of their **function** and the **materials used to make them**.

Use sketches to illustrate your answer.

3. (a) Write a description of the Irish Romanesque doorway of **Clonfert Cathedral,** ***illustrated on the accompanying sheet.***

(b) Make a sketch of the doorway and its decoration.

(c) Write a short account of Cormac's Chapel **or** of any other examples of Romanesque architecture in Ireland.

4. (a) Select your favourite building from the Georgian period and write about it in as much detail as you can, giving reasons why you like it.
The following headings may help you with your answer.

- name of the building and where it is to be found • function of the building • general description

(b) Describe three typical features of Georgian architecture that appear on your chosen building.

Use sketches to illustrate your answer.

5. The ***illustrations on the accompanying sheet*** show paintings by Jack B. Yeats and by Seán Keating.
   (a) Select the one you like best and discuss it in detail. The following headings may help you with your answer:
   - subject matter – what the painting is about • composition
   - brushwork • colour

   (b) Compare this painting with the other one.
   (c) Write what you know about one of the artists in question.

6. Describe and discuss the work of one of the following artists:
   Evie Hone, Louis le Brocquy, Brian Bourke, Kathy Prendergast, Conor Fallon, Eilis Ó Connell. Use the following headings:
   - subject matter • brushwork (if a painter) • form (if a sculptor)
   - composition • materials and techniques • colour and texture.

   Use sketches to illustrate your answer.

SECTION II — EUROPEAN ART

7. (a) Write what you know about Romanesque and Gothic sculpture.
   (b) Describe and discuss at least three similarities and three differences between the Romanesque sculpture and Gothic sculpture. The following headings may help you with your answer:
   - overall appearance • subject matter • style of carving • pattern

   Use sketches to illustrate your answer.

8. (a) Select two works that you like by **Leonardo Da Vinci (1452-1519)** and describe and discuss them under the following headings:
   - names of the chosen works • subject matter • medium used
   - composition

   (b) Give at least two reasons why you selected these works.
   Use sketches to illustrate your answer.

9. Describe and discuss *View of Toledo* by **El Greco (1541-1614)** ***illustrated on the accompanying sheet***, using the following headings:
   - subject matter • composition • colour and light • details • medium
   - style

10. Look closely at the painting of *Whistlejacket* by **George Stubbs (1724-1806)** and the painting of an *Officer of the Chasseurs Charging* by **Théodore Géricault (1719-1824)** ***illustrated on the accompanying sheet.***
    (a) Describe and discuss both paintings under the following headings:
    - subject matter • composition • use of colour • technique • overall effect

    (b) Which painting do you like best? Give reasons for your answer.

11. **Jan Vermeer (1632-1675)** painted portraits and domestic scenes with great precision. Describe any one of his paintings in such detail so that a friend can identify it from your description. Allow the following headings to help you with your answer:
    - description of the scene or portrait • composition • atmosphere • colour • texture • lighting

    Use sketches to illustrate your answer.

12. Write an account of **Impressionism**. Use the ***accompanying illustration*** of *Impression: Sunrise* by **Claude Monet (1840-1926)** and the following headings to help you with your answer:
    - methods of painting • subject matter • composition • colour • texture • lighting

    Use sketches to illustrate your answer.

13. (a) Describe and discuss one of the following:
    - a portrait • a painting or sculpture of the nude • a work of Pop Art • an abstract work of art

    You may select a work from any period you wish. You should name the artist, refer to the style and to the use of materials.

    (b) Describe another work of art by your chosen artist, allowing the following headings to help you with your answer:
    - medium • composition • colour and light • details • style

    Use sketches to illustrate your answer.

SECTION III — APPRECIATION

14. Your 6th Year class has decided to design and plant a small garden in the school grounds.

    (a) In your opinion what are the main points to consider when undertaking this project? The following headings may help you with your answer.
    - Where the garden is to be situated in relation to the school building/s
    - Shape/size • Soil • Planting • Colour • Decorative features.

    (b) Make a drawing of your proposed design and layout. Label your drawing.

15. The computer mousepad provides an opportunity to advertise products.

    (a) Describe and discuss your favourite mousepad under the following headings:
    - shape • graphic image • lettering • colour • surface and material

    (b) In your opinion is it a successful design? Give three reasons to support your answer.

    Use sketches to illustrate your answer.

16. Frames for photographs come in many materials, colours, shapes and sizes.
(a) What are the main considerations when designing a frame?
(b) Describe and discuss your favourite picture frame.
Use sketches to illustrate your answer.

17. You have been asked to write a report for your school magazine on a recent trip to an art exhibition or to a museum exhibition.
(a) Describe and discuss the exhibition under the following headings
• name and location of the exhibition • general description of the art / artefacts on display • layout • lighting • labelling of exhibits
(b) Briefly describe two exhibits that appealed to you.
Use sketches to illustrate your answer.

18. The ***accompanying illustration*** shows a space in a park where a public sculpture is to be placed.
(a) Suggest a design for a sculpture for this site.
(b) What do you think are the main considerations when designing a piece of public sculpture?
(c) Give reasons for your design.
Use sketches to illustrate your answer.

19. The bag ***illustrated on the accompanying sheet*** is familiar to most people.
(a) Describe and evaluate its design. The following headings may help you with your answer
• shape • materials used • colour • usefulness • value for money
(b) In your opinion what are the three most important features of this bag? Give your views.
Use sketches to illustrate your answer.

Acknowledgments
The publishers gratefully acknowledge the following for permission to reproduce photographic material:

Ardagh Chalice and Derrynaflan Chalice © National Museum of Ireland
Clonfert Cathedral Doorway © Dept. of the Environment, Heritage and Local Government
Men of Destiny © DACS/National Gallery of Ireland
Economic Pressure © Crawford Municipal Gallery Cork
View of Toledo © The Art Archive/Metropolitan Museum of Art New York/Album/Joseph Martin
Whistlejacket © National Gallery, London/the Bridgeman Art Library
Officer of the Chasseurs Charging © The Art Archive/Musée du Louvre Paris/Dagli Orti (A)
Impression: Sunrise © Musee Marmottan, Paris/The Bridgeman Art Library

The publishers have made every effort to trace all copyright holders, but if any have been inadvertently overlooked we would be pleased to make the necessary arrangements at the first opportunity.

ART: HISTORY AND APPRECIATION OF ART – ORDINARY LEVEL – ILLUSTRATIONS 2003

SECTION I — ART IN IRELAND

Q. 2 Ardagh Chalice

Q. 2 Derrynaflan Chalice

Q. 3 Clonfert Cathedral Doorway

Q. 5 *Men of Destiny* by Jack B. Yeats

Q. 5 *Economic Pressure* by Seán Keating

SECTION II — EUROPEAN ART

Q. 9 *View of Toledo* by El Greco

Q. 10 *Whistlejacket* by George Stubbs

Q. 10 *Officer of the Chasseurs Charging* by Théodore Géricault

Q. 12 *Impression: Sunrise* by Claude Monet

SECTION III — APPRECIATION

Q. 18 Park

Q. 19 Bag

AN ROINN OIDEACHAIS AGUS EOLAÍOCHTA

LEAVING CERTIFICATE EXAMINATION, 2003

ART – HISTORY AND APPRECIATION OF ART – HIGHER LEVEL

MONDAY, 16 JUNE — AFTERNOON 2.00 TO 4.30PM

150 marks are assigned to this paper.

INSTRUCTIONS

(a) Write as fully as you can on **three** questions. **One** question should be selected from Section I, **one** question from Section II and **one** question from Section III.

(b) All questions carry equal marks (50).

(c) **Sketches and diagrams** must be used where possible to illustrate your points.

(d) Refer where necessary to the **illustrations on the accompanying sheet** [pages xxx–xxx in this book].

SECTION I — ART IN IRELAND

1. Describe and discuss the prehistoric gold artefacts ***illustrated on the accompanying sheet*** in relation to form, function, decoration and the metalworking techniques used to produce them:

(a) *gold bulla* from **The Bog of Allen, County Kildare**

(b) *gold gorget* from **Borrisnoe, County Tipperary**

(c) *gold dress fastener* from **Clones, County Monaghan**.

2. In terms of size, proportion, decoration and figurative content how does the *North Cross of Ahenny*, County Tipperary differ from the *Cross of the Scriptures* at Clonmacnoise, County Offaly.
Both crosses are ***illustrated on the accompanying sheet.***

3. Describe and discuss an abbey, church or cathedral from the **Irish Gothic** period and compare it with a church from the **Irish Romanesque** period. Refer to plan, style, architectural features and decoration in your answer.

4. Although **William Chambers** (1726-1796) never visited Ireland he designed a gem of Irish Georgian architecture – *The Casino*, at Marino. Describe and discuss the function, design, architectural features and decoration of the Casino and compare it with another Georgian building of your choice.

5. **Roderic O'Conor** (1860-1940) and **William Orpen** (1878-1931) were contemporaries, but they painted in very different styles. Discuss this statement with detailed reference to one major work by each artist.

6. Select one of the following painters / sculptors / designers / architects: Patrick Scott, Imogen Stuart, Tony O'Malley, John Behan, Sean Scully, Ciaran Lennon, Michael Scott, Eileen Gray, Philip Treacy. Describe and discuss two specific examples of work by your chosen painter / sculptor / designer / architect. You should refer to subject matter, media, style and imagery.

SECTION II — EUROPEAN ART (1000 AD TO THE PRESENT)

7. Compare and contrast the major characteristics of Romanesque and Gothic architecture. Refer in detail to one Romanesque church and one Gothic cathedral.

8. What were the main characteristics and functions of medieval stained glass? In your answer include reference to design, colour and to the manufacturing techniques of a single window or group of windows.

9. With reference to the altarpiece, *The Annunciation* by **Simone Martini** (1284-1344), ***illustrated on the accompanying sheet,*** describe and discuss the characteristics and development of the International Gothic style of painting.

10. Select two sculptures by **Michelangelo**. Describe and discuss these in relation to the overall development of his style, their subject matter and their sculptural qualities.

11. The paintings of **Sandro Botticelli** (1455-1510) could be described as sheer visual poetry and grace. Discuss this statement with reference to *La Primavera* ***illustrated on the accompanying sheet*** and to one other work by Botticelli.

12. It was **Peter Paul Rubens'** (1577-1640) gift for arranging large colourful compositions and filling them with drama and emotion that makes his art unforgettable. Discuss this statement with reference to *Descent from the Cross,* ***illustrated on the accompanying sheet*** and to one other work by Rubens.

13. Choose a work that fits into **one** of the following categories:
    (a) a painting or graphic work featuring water
    (b) a painting depicting a battle or war
    (c) an equestrian painting or sculpture
    (d) a Baroque or Rococo palace
    (e) a painting by an Expressionist artist

(f) a nineteenth-century poster
(g) a sculpture by Auguste Rodin (1840-1917)
(h) a Modernist or post-Modernist building
(i) an installation or video-based work

Describe and discuss the work you have chosen and give your opinion on why you consider it to be a good example of its category. Refer to the artist's style and technique. You should also include a brief reference to at least one other example from the same category or at least one other work by the painter / sculptor / designer / architect you have chosen.

14. Describe and discuss the subject matter and imagery of *The Boating Party* by **Pierre-Auguste Renoir** (1841-1919) and *Sunday Afternoon at the Island of La Grande Jatte* by **Georges Seurat** (1859-1891). They are ***illustrated on the accompanying sheet***. Refer in your answer to colour, composition and to the treatment of light and the human figure.

15. Define the visual characteristics of any **one** of the following art movements. Describe and discuss the work of a painter, sculptor or architect/designer whose work was stylistically typical of the movement:
(a) Art Nouveau
(b) Cubism
(c) The Bauhaus
(d) Constructivism
(e) Surrealism
(f) Pop Art

SECTION III — APPRECIATION

16. Write a critical account of the **restoration or conservation** of a street or of a particular building with which you are familiar. Refer to its specific location, the visual qualities of the restoration or conservation and the contribution it makes to the overall environment.

17. The *Dublin Spire* in O'Connell Street commemorates the Millennium. Analyse and discuss its visual and sculptural qualities as well as the impact it has on its environment.

18. Based on a visit you made to a museum or art gallery, describe and discuss how the museum/gallery tried to inform and engage visitors with the artefacts on display. Name the museum or gallery and refer to particular displays and exhibits in your answer.

19. What are the main similarities and differences between snapshot photography and photographic work defined as art. Support your answer with reference to the elements that you consider to be important in the composition of a good photograph.

20. The Chester Beatty Library was awarded the title of European Museum of the Year in 2002. In your opinion what are the design and display considerations that might have helped the Chester Beatty Library to win this prestigious award?

21. Three-dimensional design is concerned with solving problems of function, usability and practicality. Discuss this statement with reference to the ***accompanying illustrations*** of two chairs.

22. Write a review of a fantasy/adventure film such as *Lord of the Rings: The Two Towers* or *Harry Potter: The Chamber of Secrets* to be published in an arts magazine. Refer to the technical and visual properties of your chosen film. Why, in your opinion, are these films so popular with all age groups.

Acknowledgments
The publishers gratefully acknowledge the following for permission to reproduce photographic material:

Gold bulla, gorget and dress fastener © National Museum of Ireland
North Cross and Cross of the Scriptures © Dept. of the Environment, Heritage and Local Government
The Annunciation © The Art Archive/Galleria degli Uffizi Florence/Dagli Orti
La Primavera © The Art Archive/Galleria degli Uffizi Florence/Dagli Orti (A)
Descent from the Cross © The Art Archive/Antwerp Cathedral/Album/Joseph Martin
The Boating Party © Phillips Collection, Washington/The Bridgeman Art Library
Sunday Afternoon at the Island of La Grande Jatte © The Art Archive/Chicago Art Institute/Album/Joseph Martin

The publishers have made every effort to trace all copyright holders, but if any have been inadvertently overlooked we would be pleased to make the necessary arrangements at the first opportunity.

ART: HISTORY AND APPRECIATION OF ART – HIGHER LEVEL – ILLUSTRATIONS 2003

SECTION I — ART IN IRELAND

Q. 1 *gold bulla* from The Bog of Allen, Co. Kildare

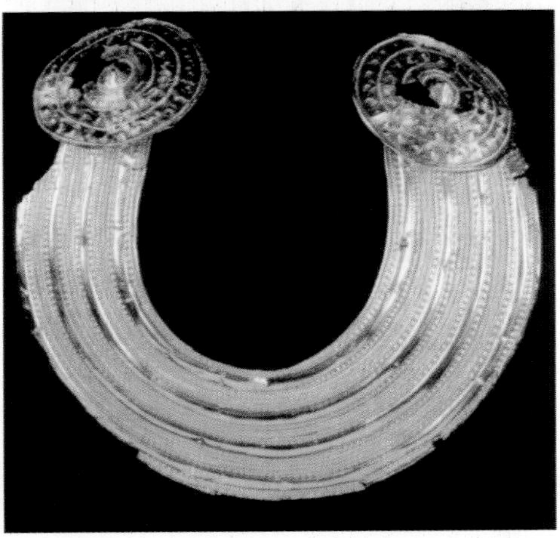

Q. 1 *gold gorget* from Borrisnoe, Co. Tipperary

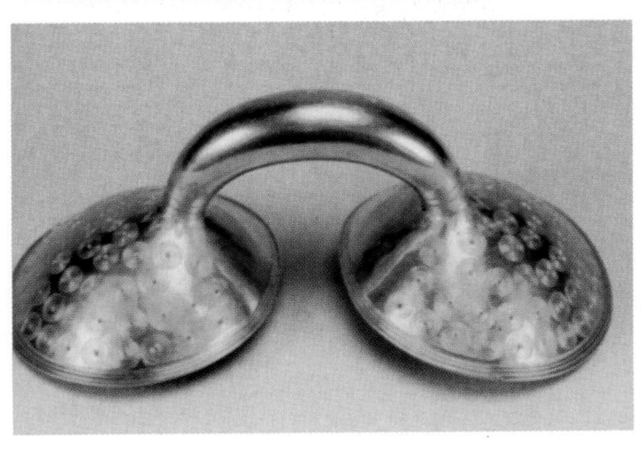

Q. 1 *gold dress fastener,* from Clones, Co. Monaghan

Q. 2 *North Cross* of Ahenny, Co. Tipperary

Q. 2 *Cross of the Scriptures*, Clonmacnoise, Co. Offaly

SECTION II — EUROPEAN ART

Q. 9 *The Annunciation* by Simone Martini

Q. 11 *La Primavera* by Sandro Botticelli

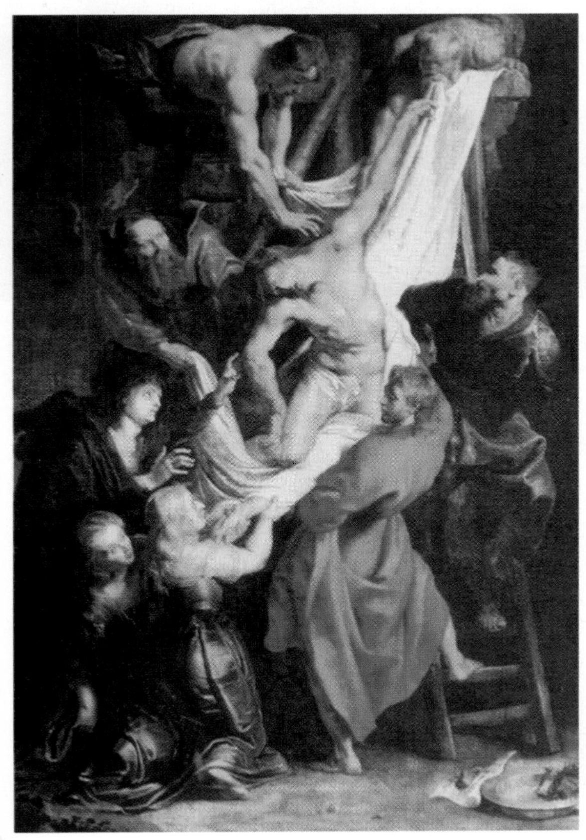

Q. 12 *Descent from the Cross* by Peter Paul Rubens

Q. 14 *The Boating Party* by Pierre Auguste Renoir

Q. 14 *Sunday Afternoon at the Island of La Grande Jatte* by Georges Seurat

SECTION III — APPRECIATION

Q. 21 Chair

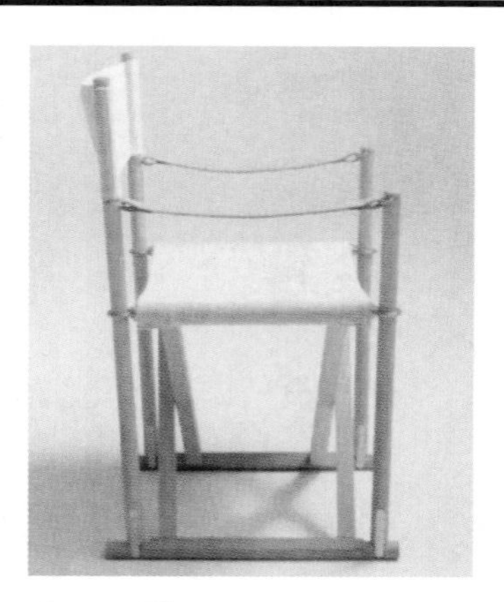

Q. 21 Chair